Sartre and Theology

Sartre and Theology

Kate Kirkpatrick

To James H. Cone

K. K.

Bloomsbury Academic
An imprint of Bloomsbury Publishing Plc

B L O O M S B U R Y
LONDON · OXFORD · NEW YORK · NEW DELHI · SYDNEY

Bloomsbury T&T Clark .

An imprint of Bloomsbury Publishing Plc

Imprint previously known as T&T Clark

50 Bedford Square	1385 Broadway
London	New York
WC1B 3DP	NY 10018
UK	USA

www.bloomsbury.com

BLOOMSBURY, T&T CLARK and the Diana logo are trademarks of Bloomsbury Publishing Plc

First published 2017

British Library Cataloguing-in-Publication Data

A catalogue record for this book is available from the British Library.

ISBN: HB: 978-0-5676-6450-1
PB: 978-0-5676-6449-5
ePDF: 978-0-5676-6451-8
ePub: 978-0-5676-6452-5

Library of Congress Cataloging-in-Publication Data

A catalog record for this book is available from the Library of Congress.

Series: Philosophy and Theology

Cover image © Nicholas Veasey/Getty

Typeset by Newgen Knowledge Works (P) Ltd., Chennai, India
Printed and bound in India

To MDK

CONTENTS

ACKNOWLEDGEMENTS

A book is a contingent thing, the existence and quality of which depend on many more people than are named on the title or acknowledgements page. The writing of this one owes much to Matthew D. Kirkpatrick (for support of too many kinds to list): thank you. I'd also like to express my gratitude to Pamela Sue Anderson and George Pattison for their encouragement and comments on drafts of this work.

Gabriel and Amelia: thank you for the joy you bring to life.

ABBREVIATIONS

Frequently cited works by Sartre appear in the text in the following abbreviations.

AR *The Age of Reason*, trans. Eric Sutton. London: Penguin, 2001.

B *Bariona*, trans. Mary Mayer and Bernard Seal, *ADAM International Review*, nos. 343–5 (1970): 37–85.

BA *Baudelaire*, trans. Martin Turnell. New York: New Directions, 1950.

BN *Being and Nothingness*, trans. Hazel Barnes. London: Routledge, 2003.

E *Emotions: The Outline of a Theory*, trans. Bernard Frechtman. New York: Open Road, 2012. Kindle Edition. References given in brackets indicate the relevant Kindle location.

EH *Existentialism Is a Humanism*, trans. Carol Macomber. London: Yale University Press, 2007.

EJ Jean-Paul Sartre and Benny Lévy, *Écrits de jeunesse* (Writings of youth). Paris: Gallimard, 1990.

EM *L'espoir maintenant: les entretiens de 1980*. Paris: Verdier, 1991.

G *Saint Genet: Actor and Martyr*, trans. Bernard Frechtman. London: Heinemann, 1963.

HN Jean-Paul Sartre and Benny Lévy, *Hope Now: The 1980 Interviews*, trans. Adrian van den Hoven. Chicago: University of Chicago Press, 1996.

I   *The Imaginary*, trans. Jonathan Webber. London: Routledge, 2004.

IF   *L'Idiot de la famille*, 2 vols. Paris: Gallimard, 1971.

M   'L'image dans la vie psychologique: rôle et nature' (The image in psychological life: role and nature), mémoire, unpublished MS held at ITEM, Paris: École Normale Supérieur.

NA   *Nausea*, trans. Robert Baldick. London: Penguin, 2000.

NE   *No Exit*, trans. Stuart Gilbert. New York: Vintage, 1989.

TE   *The Transcendence of the Ego*, trans. Andrew Brown. London: Routledge, 2011.

W   *Words*, trans. Irene Clephane. London: Penguin, 2000.

WD   *The War Diaries: November 1939–March 1940*, trans. Quintin Hoare. New York: Pantheon, 1984.

Introduction

Sartre and theology: An odd couple?

Philosophia, omnium mater artium, quid est aliud
nisi donum aut inventum Dei?
(Philosophy, mother of all the arts – what else is
it if not a gift or discovery of God?)[1]

CICERO

Jean-Paul Sartre may seem an unlikely candidate for a series on philosophy and theology. First, there is the obvious matter of his atheism. Second, Sartre's personal proclivities – for polyamory, grooming, questionable politics and so on – made him the subject of many ad hominem attacks by Christian theologians, some of whom cast him as godless immorality personified.[2] What could Sartre know about, or contribute to, theology? As one Parisian academic exclaimed when informed of the current volume, 'Sartre didn't have a theological formation!'

Unlikely or not, this book demonstrates that Sartre was influenced by and influenced theology. Many theological thinkers found him worthy of study: in addition to the theologians to be considered in Part 3 of the book, such diverse minds as Hans

---

[1]Cicero 1927: 75 (*Tusculan Disputations*, I.xxvi).
[2]Marcel, for example, described Sartre's philosophy as 'a doctrine of death on which, whatever one may say, no wisdom can be built' (Marcel 2002: 103).

Küng,[3] Jean-Luc Marion,[4] Alvin Plantinga[5] and Paul Ramsey[6] have conducted research on his work. This may be surprising to some readers today (especially those who see Sartre as Heidegger's derivative or passé cousin), but at one time Sartre was dubbed *the* philosopher of the twentieth century.[7] His output was prolific – '20 published pages a day over his working life'[8] – and diverse, including plays, short stories, novels, philosophical treatises, essays and reviews. His first novel, *Nausea* (1938), sold more than 1.6 million copies in his lifetime, and his play *Dirty Hands* (1948) nearly 2 million. Even his 700-page work of phenomenological ontology, *Being and Nothingness*, first published in 1943, went through five editions in its first three years and has never been out of print since. Although by the time of Sartre's death in 1980 his fame had faded, 50,000 mourners nevertheless followed his casket through Paris to its resting place in Montparnasse.

This book is primarily concerned with Sartre's intellectual, rather than personal, history. Although Chapter 1 contains a brief outline of Sartre's life, the aim of this chapter is to prepare the reader for the following chapters by situating them in Sartre's historical context and intellectual development. Because my argument is that there is bidirectional influence – of theology on Sartre and of Sartre on theology – it is necessary to consider the climate of Sartre's philosophical and literary formation.

Since Tertullian's famous question – 'What has Athens to do with Jerusalem?' – different generations in varied historical and geographical contexts have had to ask themselves where to draw the lines between, and how to assess the legitimacy of the claims of, philosophy and theology. And in France in the first half of the twentieth century, the lines were drawn differently than they are in the Anglo-American context of today.

Whether my reader is a philosopher of no religion or a theologian who shares Tertullian's suspicion of philosophy, therefore,

---

[3]Küng wrote his licentiate on Sartre's atheistic humanism during his studies in philosophy from 1948 to 51.
[4]Marion 1991: 36; and see explanatory note (n.19) on p. 207.
[5]See Plantinga 1958.
[6]In his discussion of Sartre, Ramsey wrote that those who take the trouble to read him 'will not doubt that he is one of the most rigorous thinkers alive today' (1962: 71).
[7]Levy 2003.
[8]*Economist* 2003.

the following shines new light on both Sartre and theology. For philosophers, understanding the pre-'phenomenological' theological influences on Sartre's thought may illuminate some of the interpretive questions concerning his much-discussed reception of 'les trois Hs' – Hegel, Husserl and Heidegger. And for theologians, this work will show the aetiology of the oft-noted religious overtones of Sartre's philosophy and demonstrate – through analyzing several twentieth-century theologians' treatments of Sartre – the fascination he held for his theological contemporaries and successors.

Before turning to Sartre's life in Chapter 1, however, it is worth laying one 'personal' matter to rest. I have said already that this book is concerned with Sartre's *ideas*, but it seems worth stating clearly at the outset what I understand to be the case about Sartre and *God* before we get to the question of Sartre and *theology*. That Sartre was an atheist is well known. But there are many varieties of atheism, and Sartre's – though perhaps one of the best documented in recent history – is nevertheless also one of the most ambiguous.

Sartre and God

Recent scholarship has seen a small flurry of interest in Sartre's atheism, with papers in both French and English treating its nature, origins and duration. But what emerges from their analyses is by no means clear cut. Although some authors are happy to assert that Sartre 'never wavered … from a complete rejection of God as both philosophically problematic and existentially irrelevant to human life',[9] Sartre's own writings suggest otherwise. As Alexis Chabot has argued, some of Sartre's words about atheism have become a little 'too famous'.[10]

Sartre's prolific output has already been mentioned, and one of the results of his creative industry is that there are many texts to which one can refer on this topic: the memoir, *Words*; other semi-autobiographical works such as his *War Diaries*; essays in *Les Temps modernes* such as 'A New Mystic'; and, of course, the controversial, late-in-life interviews with Benny Lévy published as *Espoir maintenant*. Moreover, due to Sartre's life-long relationship

---

[9]Charmé 2010: 301.
[10]Chabot 2016.

with Beauvoir, his life was doubly documented – for Beauvoir also produced three memoirs, preserved letters to (and saved letters from) Sartre and published interviews after Sartre's death, which include further sources on the question of his atheism.

In addition to work by the present author[11] there are two English-speaking scholars in particular who have recently written on Sartre and God: Gellman and Gillespie. The former has categorized Sartre's atheism as 'mystical', which is to say that Gellman takes Sartre's atheism to have originated in a mystical experience of God's non-existence rather than in any philosophically based objection. The latter, in a two-part piece in *Sartre Studies International*, discusses what he calls 'Sartre's spiritual odyssey', claiming that throughout Sartre's career, 'though his theological knowledge and his spiritual experience may have been limited, God was in his mind throughout his life'.[12] I agree with the latter claim – this book attests to the fact that Sartre's work is shot through with questions about God – but contest the first. Sartre *did* have extensive theological knowledge. In fact, I argue, that is one of the things that makes his atheism so fascinating for theologians – it is a theologically informed atheism haunted by questions of divine love, freedom and grace. Before turning to these questions, however, we consider the stories and sources of Sartre's atheism in his own words.

Gellman's argument centres around a story in Beauvoir's *Adieux* (the same story, in slightly different formulations, can also be found in *Words* and in the *War Diaries*):

> When I was about twelve … in the morning I used to take the tram with the girls next door … One day I was walking up and down outside their house for a few minutes waiting for them to get ready. I don't know where the thought came from or how it struck me, yet all at once I said to myself, 'God doesn't exist.' … As I remember very well, it was on that day and in the form of a momentary intuition that I said to myself, 'God does not exist.'[13]

But this is not the only story Sartre tells about the origins of his atheism – in *Words* alone there are three. In the first, Sartre says his

[11]Kirkpatrick 2013.
[12]Gillespie 2014: 54.
[13]Beauvoir 1984: 437.

unbelief stemmed not from 'conflicting dogma' but from his 'grand-parents' indifference' (W 64).[14] And reading a page further brings us to a famous passage in which Sartre expresses indignation about being subject to God's *gaze*:

> Once I had the feeling that he existed. I had been playing with matches and had burnt a mat; I was busy covering up my crime when suddenly God saw me. I felt His gaze inside my head and on my hands; I turned round and round in the bathroom, horribly visible, a living target. I was saved by indignation: I grew angry at such a crude lack of tact, and blasphemed, muttering like my grandfather: '*Sacré nom de Dieu de nom de Dieu de nom de Dieu*.' He never looked at me again. (W 65)

We also read other genesis myths in this and other texts, in which Sartre describes

- 'glimps[ing] evil, the absence of God' following the death of a child (W 142);
- having a 'mystic crisis' at fifteen (*BN* 520);
- having 'lost his faith at the age of twelve' (*WD* 70); and
- having 'from the outset ... had a morality without a God – without sin, but not without evil' (*WD* 70).

Considering these alongside other descriptions of Sartre's thoughts vis-à-vis atheism and God – for example that atheism is 'a cruel, long-term business' (W 157); Sartre was 'prevented' from being a Christian (W 82); and that God was an 'old flame' (W 65) – the

---

[14]He frequently describes the family with whom he grew up in terms of their religious commitments or absence thereof: for example, in *Words* he writes that his grandfather was Protestant and his grandmother was Catholic, but he writes that 'their religious feelings if decent were frigid' (*WD* 70); he also describes his mother having made him take his first communion, but not 'out of true conviction'. She is characterized as having 'no religion, but a rather vague religiosity, which consoles her a bit when necessary and leaves her strictly in peace the rest of the time' (*WD* 70). Sartre was taken to church quite often, but he presents this church-going as inspired mainly by the fine music that was to be heard there. It was an aesthetic experience – 'feelings of high spirituality were provoked' – in his mother and grand-mother, but he did not believe they had a clear idea whether 'the music thrilled them because it was religious or the religion because it was harmonious' (*WD* 71).

picture that emerges is far from clear. Defining Sartre's atheism precisely, whether one's interest is philosophical or autobiographical, looks a lot like a fool's errand.

It is no such errand, however, to note that in Sartre's context theology and atheism were differently connoted. In *Words*, for example, Sartre offers a description of 'the atheist' which is decidedly Jansenist in tone.[15] On Sartre's definition there the atheist was

> a man with a phobia about God who saw his absence everywhere and who could not open his mouth without saying his name: in short, a Gentleman with religious convictions. The believer had none: for two thousand years the Christian certainties had had time to prove themselves, they belonged to everyone, and they were required to shine in a priest's glance, in the half-light of a church, and to illumine souls, but no one needed to appropriate them to himself; they were the common patrimony. Polite society believed in God so that it need not talk of him. (*W* 62–3)

When Sartre uses the word 'atheism', therefore, it is wise not to assume his intended meaning was synonymous to that of the evidential atheism that is debated in the analytic philosophy of religion today. He is not to be classed in the same category as Russell, whose objection to God was simply 'Not enough evidence!'[16] As we will see in the next section and in Chapters 2 and 3, theological disputes shaped early modern French philosophy and literature and were part of Sartre's philosophical formation in ways that merit greater recognition.

Before concluding this section, however, it is worth citing a final passage from the *War Diaries* in which Sartre reflects on an early intuition of God's non-existence, to show how multiple and varied Sartre's own accounts of his disbelief are:

> So there you are. It's pretty thin. God existed, but I didn't concern myself with him at all. And then one day at La Rochelle, while waiting for the Machado girls, who used to keep me company every morning on my way to lycée, I grew impatient at their lateness and, to while away the time, decided to think about God.

---

[15]Sartre's exposure to Jansenism is discussed in Chapter 2.
[16]Quoted in Plantinga and Wolterstorff 1983: 17–18.

'Well,' I said, 'he doesn't exist.' It was something authentically self-evident, although I have no idea any more what it was based on. And then it was over and done with. I never thought about it again; I was no more concerned with that dead God than I had been bothered about the living God. I imagine it would be hard to find a less religious nature than mine. I settled the question once and for all at the age of twelve. Much later I studied religious proofs and atheist arguments. I appraised the fortunes of their disputes. I was fond of saying that Kant's objections did not affect Descartes' ontological proof. But all that struck me as [p. 72] hardly any more than a Quarrel of Ancients and Moderns. (*WD* 71–2)

'Once for all at the age of twelve' sounds rather final – *if* that is the only text one reads. But in the *Écrits de jeunesse* Sartre writes that he goes 'incessantly from one term to the other, from man to God, from God to man; my thinking turns in circles like a dizzy sheep' (*EJ* 327). And in *Words* he describes his Catholic upbringing as having been influenced by the 'dechristianization which was born in the Voltaire-influenced *haute bourgeoisie*' (*W* 62), and his child-hood self as 'aware of' and even hoping for 'religion' (*W* 62).

Perhaps at this point it is worth reminding the reader that Sartre was a philosopher who resisted the fixity of 'essences' and announced the anxiety that accompanies human freedom to renounce past resolutions. The Sartrean self is a self in question, so to suppose that his atheism never underwent 'dark nights' of doubt (or 'mystic crises', to use his own words) would be as inconsistent with his autobiography as it is with his philosophy.

Sartre and theology

Where Sartre's relationship to *theology* is concerned a few introductory remarks are also required. We have already made the general point that disciplinary divisions are differently drawn in different geographical and historical contexts. In France in the second quarter of the twentieth century, the term 'philosophy' encompassed a different range of preoccupations and methodologies than it does in the Anglo-American context of the first quarter of the twenty-first. This is important because the English-speaking reception of Sartre often reads him in the tradition of German phenomenology and overlooks other significant aspects of his development. When Sartre was a student, philosophy was divided into four branches – metaphysics, morals, logic and general psychology – because the emerging field of empirical psychology had not yet established itself in its own right.[17] And where the other three subdisciplines were concerned, mainstream publishers included works by Christian mystics and theologians in their series on 'philosophy'.

One French philosophical institution illustrates this disciplinary difference well: namely, the *agrégation de philosophie*. This exam is widely known within France, because for a long time every philosopher who wished to teach philosophy – whether at the *lycée* or the university level – had to pass it. Outside of France it is less well known, but as Schrift argues, attending to the *agrégation* can help explain why the French philosophical tradition differs from its counterparts in other nations, because the *agrégation* ensured that those who passed. possessed a thorough grounding in the history of philosophy, particularly in philosophy prior to 1800.

Before turning to consider the relevant syllabi for Sartre's philosophical formation, it is worth making a brief detour into the *agrégation*'s history. The exam was founded under Louis XV in 1766 and, in its first guise, was intended to be a competitive certifying exam for would-be teachers. It could be taken in one of three forms: philosophy, letters or grammar. Its founding was controversial, however, in that the certification for these subjects passed out of the hands of the Faculty of Theology at the Sorbonne and into the Faculty of Arts. Since its twelfth-century foundation the University of Paris had considered the latter faculty inferior to the other three faculties, Theology, Law and Medicine. And this shift of power is often interpreted as indicative of a shift of status. As Schrift writes, 'It would not be inappropriate to regard the withdrawal of this power in 1766 from the Theology Faculty to be in fact the first step in the secularization of French education that came to completion in the 1905 law formally separating Church and State in France.'[18]

The *agrégation* underwent several developments in the nineteenth century, including changing the required language for written

---

[17]Elkaïm-Sartre 2004: vii.
[18]Schrift 2008: 450. This assessment of the agrégation is dependent on Schrift's excellent article.

essays from Latin to French, and its structure and content were subject to rigorous debate throughout the twentieth century, too. In the early decades, the exam had two components: written and oral. The written component was composed of three essays of seven hours, with two questions dedicated to general philosophy and one to the history of philosophy. The success rate was one in four. Those who passed the written component then had to undergo several oral exams, which were intended to assess not only their philosophical knowledge and aptitude but also their ability to apply those skills pedagogically. The onerousness of each stage was in part due to state policy: they would only admit new *agrégé(e)s* in proportion to the number of teaching posts available – usually only 10 per cent of candidates were successful.

Sartre's first attempt at the *agrégation* was famously unsuccessful. He was widely regarded by his professors and peers as the top philosophy student at the École Normale Supérieure (ENS), but in 1928 Sartre received the lowest score of all fifty candidates. His friend Raymond Aron received the highest score, and suggested that Sartre's marks were so low because he included his own reflections on the philosophy of existence.[19] Sartre's own reflections on the experience support this assessment,[20] and the next year Sartre came in first place, with Beauvoir in second. The subjects given were freedom and contingency (*liberté et contingence*).[21]

Two final remarks on the *agrégation* are necessary before moving on to outline the structure of the book that follows. First, as Schrift has shown, being prepared for the written part of the exam required candidates to be familiar with everything in the assigned philosopher's corpus, and successful *agrégé(e)s* frequently, therefore, subsequently published on the topics of their exam and kept the thinkers they studied so closely as intellectual interlocutors throughout their careers.[22] Sartre's case is no exception – freedom is the subject for which he became famous, and contingency was the subject of several years of both philosophical and literary work during the 1930s, with the eventual published result being his first, and highly acclaimed, novel, *Nausea*.

---

[19]Aron 1990: 25.
[20]Sartre 1981: xlv.
[21]*Les Études philosophiques* 1929: 139.
[22]Schrift 2008: 453.

But the topics set on the *agrégation* frequently indicate the pre-occupations and interests of the older generation of philosophers, so it is worth considering the immediate context of Sartre's time at the ENS, to see what other ideas were in circulation there. In 1926 there was a change to the programme, which cannot have escaped the attention of the young Sartre: the topic for the second written competition was announced in advance (in this case, 'psychology of activity and affectivity'), and an indication of the historical composition section was also given ('Plato and Aristotle's Moral and Political Doctrines' and 'The Theory of Method in Descartes, Pascal, Malebranche and the Port-Royal Logique'). This exam's compulsory subjects in the early twentieth century – even if they were set by the Faculty of Letters rather than the Faculty of Theology – included not just the usual suspects such as Plato, Descartes, and Kant, but also Augustine, Pascal and Bergson.

The *agrégation de philosophie* may have stemmed from a historically secularizing move in what Kant called 'the conflict of the faculties', but many of the thinkers studied in the philosophy faculty were decidedly religious, and their disputes decidedly theological. For how could you understand French philosophy, historically speaking, without considering Descartes alongside Malebranche and Arnauld, or Voltaire alongside Pascal? As we shall see in Chapters 2 and 3, Sartre's own education as an *agrégé* included engagement with the philosophical *and theological* debates that shaped French philosophy prior to 1800. Clearly this is not the same sort of theological formation he might have had if he were taking orders or becoming a priest. But these theological concepts, especially the concepts of nothingness and freedom, nevertheless informed his thinking.

Chapter outlines

Before diving into this particular period of Sartre's life, however, in Chapter 1 I provide a brief biography of Sartre in order to give the reader a sense of the development of his thought. In particular, this chapter emphasizes Sartre's own description of his engagement with philosophical and theological thinkers and themes, especially in early and untranslated works. Some of these are still unpublished (in English and, in one case, even in French), and examining them sheds light on Sartre's pre-phenomenological preoccupations and influences.

Chapters 2 and 3 both treat what I have called 'Sartre's theological formation', first in philosophy and then in literature. It is an obvious point that 'philosophy' was a broader and differently inflected term in 1920s Paris than it is in 2010s Oxford. But the way twentieth-century English-speaking philosophers have received Sartre focuses so much on his indebtedness to the German phenomenological tradition that it has largely overlooked pertinent aspects of his French context. Chapter 2 therefore explores the 'theologians' Sartre encountered and wrote about in his early philosophical education.

Chapter 3 turns to consider the theological content in Sartre's literary context. Many of the philosophers Sartre studied used diverse literary genres to express their ideas – as did Sartre himself. Around 1880 French literature began to see an increase in novels experimenting with depictions of Christian lives, which trend became even stronger in the period from 1900 and reached its heyday in the decade between 1920 and 1930. The central preoccupations of these novelists reflect the debates we met in Chapter 2, concerning the nature of sin and grace, our ability to give and receive love and the extent to which the Fall affects our freedom. Of course many novels involve characters in tensive situations, in which freedom is both liberating and is a liability. But these works depict distinct theological positions with which we know Sartre was familiar.

Part 2 introduces the theological themes in *Being and Nothingness* (1943) and 'Existentialism Is a Humanism' (1945), and serves as a bridge between Parts 1 and 3, showing what theological aspects Sartre retained from his forebears and passed on to his critics.

Chapter 4 outlines a brief sketch of the phenomenological ontology for which Sartre became famous. It focuses primarily on *Being and Nothingness*, although it also makes reference to some of the early phenomenological works as well as novels and plays published up until 1952 (the point of his 'conversion' to Marxism) since Sartre's early works arguably exert the greatest influence on the theologians to be considered in Part 2. Chapter 5 is dedicated to 'Existentialism Is a Humanism', the later regretted lecture that was part of Sartre's trajectory to fame.

Part 3 moves from the influence of theology on Sartre to the legacy of Sartre for twentieth-century theologians: Protestant,

Catholic, Orthodox and liberation. Not all of the theologians in Part 3 engaged with Sartre in an equally sustained or systematic fashion, and they are not intended to provide an exhaustive account of Sartre's legacy. But taken together they show that Sartre's philosophy was considered theologically significant.

Chapter 6, on Sartre and Protestant theology, discusses the role Sartre plays in the systematic theologies of Karl Barth and Paul Tillich. The section on Barth focuses on the *Church Dogmatics*, and in particular the role Sartre plays in its doctrine of *das Nichtige*, asking whether Barth's use of Sartre sits comfortably with Barth's (stated) Christological method. The section on Tillich introduces Tillich's 'apologetic' theology. It is widely acknowledged that Tillich's theology 'answered' questions posed by many philosophers, in particular existentialist thinkers. But to date no research has explored the question of whether – or, indeed, *how* – Tillich's theology answers distinctively Sartrean questions. This section explores that question, arguing that Tillich does indeed answer Sartre in his later works, in particular, by replying to the anxiety of meaninglessness.

Chapter 7, on Sartre and Catholic theology, briefly notes the history of the Catholic Church's official reception of Sartre (including his inclusion on the *Index*) before turning to consider how Sartre was received and responded to by Gabriel Marcel and Karol Wojtyła. Marcel's response to Sartre is direct and unmediated. The situation of Wojtyła, however, resulted in a response to Sartre that was mediated by Marxism.

Chapter 8, on Sartre and Orthodox theology, opens with a brief consideration of Sartre's contemporary Vladimir Lossky before discussing the role Sartre plays in the work of Christos Yannaras and John Zizioulas. Both use Sartre in their theologies of personhood, as a foil against which to sharpen their views.

Chapter 9, on Sartre and black liberation theology, shows that Sartre's works informed Martin Luther King Jr. and James H. Cone, the latter of whose theology is examined at length in this chapter. It also explores Sartre's reception by South American and feminist liberation theologians, noting that their use of Sartre was not as extensive or favourable as the black liberationists'.

Chapter 10 draws the book to a close, asking what themes emerge from the theologians considered in Part 3, and arguing that Sartre's work is still a useful resource for the theology of the future.

These chapters are intended to serve as a guidebook – giving brief glimpses of the thinkers and traditions from which Sartre drew and to which Sartre contributed. Over the past five years my research on Sartre has shown that – far from there being a paucity of theological influences – the intersections between Sartre and theology are as rich as they are underexplored. My hope is that readers will find in this work a map to help them navigate this fascinating territory – much of which still waits to be charted.

PART 1

Sartre's theological inheritance

1

Vita brevis

Stowaway traveller, I had fallen asleep on the seat and the ticket inspector was shaking me. 'Your ticket!' I was forced to admit that I had not got one.[1]

JEAN-PAUL SARTRE

There is a story that is usually told about Sartre: that Sartre, literary genius in the making, was born on 21 June 1905, the only child of Jean-Baptiste Sartre and Anne-Marie Schweitzer, and that, a year later, his father died. The usual story tells us that Sartre started writing when he was seven years old[2] – under the illusion (which he would later renounce[3]) that he had found his 'ticket' in life, his reason to be. The usual story includes a 'Eureka!' moment, when Sartre is said to have discovered phenomenology in a conversation over cocktails. In that moment, so the story goes, Sartre the phenomenologist was born. There are a few later moments of conversion: to Marxism in 1952, and perhaps even to a mitigated position on religion near his death in 1980, though the last of these is much disputed. The astute reader will suspect, by now, that the present author does not accept the 'usual story' as the whole truth.

---

[1] W 70.
[2] EJ 11.
[3] W 157: 'I have become once again the traveller without a ticket that I was at seven.… I have renounced my vocation, but I have not unfrocked myself. I still write. What else can I do?'

This chapter certainly does not presume to offer the 'whole truth' about Sartre's life but rather to provide a brief overview with particular attention to theological aspects of Sartre's biography and bibliography. Because Part 1 of the book presents Sartre's theological inheritance, this chapter provides context for the information presented in the remainder of Part 1 and in Part 2. And because Part 3 of the book turns to considering Sartre's theological legacy, it also provides an introduction to his early philosophical and literary publications in the run-up to *Being and Nothingness* and his rise to fame.[4]

Childhood

Following the death of his father, Sartre was raised by his mother and her parents, Charles and Louise Schweitzer. Aside from one brief experience, Sartre received no public education until the age of ten. His grandfather's library contained over a thousand volumes, and *Words* is full of reminiscences on his early education at home: 'Between the first Russian Revolution and the First World War … a nineteenth-century man was imposing on his grandson ideas current under Louis-Philippe … I started off with an eighty-year handicap' (*W* 41–2). Sartre describes himself as the 'grandson of a priest', dedicated to following in Charles's footsteps as the guardian of literary culture (*W* 44). At an early age he became acquainted with many of France's greatest writers: Hugo, Voltaire, Corneille, Racine, La Fontaine.

In 1915 he began attending the Lycée Henri IV in Paris. Two years later, when Sartre was twelve, his mother married Joseph Mancy – much to the displeasure of her son. Mancy was an authoritarian figure and moved the Sartres to La Rochelle, a town known for both its Calvinism and its bourgeoisie. In school there, the young Sartre – Parisian and lazy-eyed – was frequently bullied.

Sartre's earliest writings include many religious themes. His first preserved manuscript dates from 1922, when Sartre was seventeen years old. But among those which are not preserved, we know that as a schoolboy he wrote an early composition on the passion of

---

[4]There are several lengthy biographies available. The interested reader may wish to consult those by Annie Cohen-Solal (1987 (Fr., 1985)), Thomas Flynn (2014) and (for a more popular approach) Gary Cox (2016).

Christ. In a paragraph which begins 'I hardly have any religious memories', Sartre recounts that at the age of seven or eight he 'wrote an essay on Jesus for the Abbé Dibildos's catechism class' (*WD* 70), winning a silver-paper medal for the composition. Even at the time of writing the *War Diaries* (1 December 1939) he 'was still filled with admiration and delight when I think of that essay and that medal, but there's nothing religious about this' (*WD* 70).

We have already seen in the introduction that Sartre does not seem to take pains to avoid offering contradictory stories about himself. Sartre's memoir, *Words* (published in 1964),[5] describes the period from 1907 to 1917, but as his biographer Cohen-Solal notes, he describes only those years, giving very little attention to the time when his father was alive or the time when his stepfather entered the scene.[6] Although *Words* is read as Sartre's own narrative of his childhood, it is both 'much more and much less' than an autobiography.[7] The text itself presents the reader with the question of reliability. Sartre writes, 'What I have just written is false. True. Neither true nor false, like all that is written about madmen or about men. I have set down the facts as accurately as memory permits' (*W* 45).

In 1922 Sartre moved to the Lycée Louis-le-Grand in Paris, where he studied philosophy under Colonna d'Istria. During this period he read (and found wanting) the idealist rationalism of Brunschvicg, and, on d'Istria's suggestion, began to read Bergson's *Time and Free Will* (*Essai sur les données immédiates de la conscience*, 1888). In Bergson, Sartre said, 'I immediately found a description of my own psychic life'. This proved a powerful attraction to philosophy, although Sartre later admitted that what he at the time called philosophy 'was actually psychology'.[8]

At the École Normale

Sartre entered the École Normale Supérieure (ENS) in 1924, in the company of thinkers who became so prestigious that the cohort

---

[5]It was published in 1963 in *Les Temps modernes*, issues 209 (October) and 210 (November).
[6]Cohen-Solal 1987: 28.
[7]See Schilpp 1982.
[8]See Schilpp 1982.

itself has become the stuff of lore: among the twenty-nine students admitted for Lettres, one finds not only Sartre but also Aron,
Canguilhem, Lagache and Nizan. The next year Hyppolite became
a *normalien*, and the year after that so did Merleau-Ponty.

The usual story tells us that Sartre's time at the ENS was marked
by involvement in several theatrical revues and pranks of varying
degrees of seriousness.[9] It was the birthplace of some lifelong (and
some shorter-lived) friendships. But it was also a period in which
he devoured books by the hundreds, reading Plato, Schopenhauer,
Kant, Spinoza, Mallarmé, Aristotle, Bergson, Shakespeare, Tolstoy,
Maine de Biran, Erasmus, Seneca, Lucretius, Augustine, Stendahl,
and Cicero (among many others).[10]

One of Sartre's notebooks from his first year at the ENS is extant
and has been published in French – the *Carnet Midy* is thought to
have been completed in 1924. In it he took notes on diverse subjects,
which he categorized alphabetically. In addition to entries on the
great philosophers, we find sections on the soul (*CM* 442); the relation of soul and body (*CM* 445); Bergson (*CM* 446, 7, 452; 475);
Descartes and God (*CM* 448); original sin (drawing on Pascal's and
Rousseau's accounts of childhood; *CM* 449); the human need for
a witness, which leads some to invent God (*CM* 454); a kind of
self-love that amounts to religious onanism: 'For some the love of
God is an onanism like any other' (*CM* 472); Pascal (including the
citation of several *Pensées*, *CM* 477–9); Emerson and the need of
God (*CM* 486); and so on. It does not offer us sustained discussion
or analysis, but the *Carnet Midy* offers us a glimpse into what this
curious nineteen-year-old's mind thought worthy of note.

Sartre's *mémoire* for the *diplôme d'études supérieures* (which is
often referred to in English as his master's 'dissertation', although
it ran to nearly 300 typed pages) was submitted in 1927 and
received a mark of 17/20 and a mention *très bien*. The submitted
version was never published, although heavily revised works on the
imagination eventually appeared – in two works, *L'Imagination*
(*The Imagination*, 1936) and *L'Imaginaire: psychologie phénemé-
nologique de l'imagination* (*The Imaginary: A Phenomenological
Psychology of the Imagination*, 1940). The later work, *The
Imaginary*, has been called 'the most sustained and detailed

---

[9]See Cohen-Solal 1987: 61–2.
[10]See Cohen-Solal 1987: 67, n.27, citing archives of the ENS.

account of the nature of imagination in Western literature'.[11] But the *mémoire* is often passed over in works on Sartre, partly because it is untranslated, partly because it is such an early work and partly because there is only one dactylographic copy in existence. Cohen-Solal, for example, refers to it as an 'essay', and passes over it in one sentence.[12] But as we shall see in Chapter 2, Sartre drew on Christian mystics in this work during the 1920s – and omitted them from the published works.

In 1928 he gained his certificates in psychology and in the history of philosophy. The same year he wrote an incomplete work (which has been published in French but not yet translated): *Er l'Armenien: L'Olympe chrétienne* (Er the Armenian: The Christian Olympus).[13] The project is often described as a Nietzschean commentary on Plato's Myth of Er (in *Republic*, book X),[14] but as Contat and Rybalka observe, its subtitle clearly suggests that it can be read as 'a dialogue with Greek and Christian thought, which Sartre rejects in the name of his own search for truth'.[15] In it, Sartre offers an alternative to Christian salvation and the Platonic immortality of the soul: a kind of salvation by literary works (see *EJ* 291). Contat and Rybalka suggest that the problematic of *Er the Armenian* is that of 'freedom in its nascent complexity' (*EJ* 291) and that, on the philosophical level, this work is the richest and most revealing of Sartre's writings of youth (*EJ* 291). It raises many of the recurring questions of the philosophy of religion – questions about good and evil, the Euthyphro dilemma and the role of reason in religion.[16] The novel is also full of allusions to previous thinkers on these topics – in addition to Nietzschean refrains we read about *grand déséspoir* (Pascal's despair) and *mal radical* (Kant's radical evil).[17] Insofar as it is possible to draw such conclusions from an unfinished literary work, the reasons Sartre's novel gives for rejecting Christian salvation stem from a problem that is theologically cognate to freedom: namely, the problem of evil.

[11]Webber 2004: xiii.
[12]Cohen-Solal 1987: 68.
[13]This dating is taken from *EJ* 288.
[14]See Flynn 2014: 32ff.
[15]Contat and Rybalka, *EJ* 291.
[16]See *EJ* 318–319 et passim.
[17]See *EJ* 323 and 332, respectively.

One of Sartre's characters, Ichytos, presents a thinly veiled Christian fideist point of view. We read that the concepts God, Good and Evil are all 'the fruit of Human Reason, and that they have for limits the same limits as Reason' (*EJ* 320), and that

> relationships with a God who is conceived as superior to our Reason are hopeless with concepts taken from within Reason. To say it again: you have demonstrated nothing of an ineffable God but nevertheless it is evident that the human concepts of Good and Evil, with all of their consequences, cannot be applied to him.[18]

Several of Sartre's later literary works would return to this problem. In this case, the novel's protagonist rejects fideism and Leibnizean theodicy in search of a more robust human answer. *Er the Armenian* concludes with a Nietzschean reading of St Paul's famous words that 'the Law creates sin', insisting that previous understandings of Good and Evil are to be rejected. In Apollo's words, 'A moral theory, what stupidity! But to maintain the desire to create a work of art, to search every minute, in every circumstance … Life alone will not teach you anything … Your real objective, it is the book, the painting, the statue that will emerge under your fingers' (*EJ* 330).

In 1929 Sartre received certificates in general philosophy, logic, ethics, and sociology. But before doing so, he gained one of the most significant friendships of his life. In one of Brunschvicg's classes at the Sorbonne, in 1929, Sartre met a philosophy student, Simone Lucie Ernestine Marie Bertrand de Beauvoir.

More than one account of their meeting survives, and it is worth noting that from this point onwards Sartre's public narrative was not something he produced alone. As we saw in the introduction with respect to Sartre's atheism, his autobiographical writings and the biographical writings of Beauvoir often provide us with subtly different or even rival accounts. In some cases, such as the 'mythic meeting'[19] of Sartre and Beauvoir, immortalized in an episode of

---

[18]'Les rapports d'un Dieu conçu comme supérieur à notre Raison sont nuls avec des concepts pris à l'intérieur de notre Raison. Dis alors: tu n'as rien démontre pour un Dieu ineffable mais il est évident toutefois que les concepts humains de Bien et de Mal, avec toutes leurs conséquences ne sauraient lui être appliqués' (*EJ* 320).
[19]Cohen-Solal 1987: 74.

Beauvoir's *Memoirs of a Dutiful Daughter*, a close mutual friend also published a competing account of their meeting:

> It was nothing like 'at last Sartre arrived', as she makes it sound in her *Memoirs*. There was a whole group of people, contemporaries, who knew each other fairly well and saw each other quite often. Among these were Sartre, Nizan, Maheu, Merleau-Ponty, Simone de Beauvoir, and myself. I met Simone through Merleau-Ponty, she met Maheu through me, and finally got closer to Sartre and Nizan via Maheu.[20]

They met to study the texts they needed to prepare for the oral component of the *agrégation*. Sartre had invited Beauvoir to cram in his room in the Cité Universitaire on the Boulevard Jourdan. Beauvoir said she was 'a bit scared' on entering the room:

> There were books all over the place, cigarette ends in all the corners, and the air was thick with tobacco smoke. Sartre greeted me in a worldly manner; he was smoking a pipe. Nizan, who said nothing, had a cigarette stuck in the corner of his one-sided smile and was quizzing me through his pebble lenses, with an air of thinking more than he cared to say. All day long, petrified with fear, I commented on the 'metaphysical treatise'.[21]

Beauvoir was three years his junior, and the nature of their relationship – and her subsequent estimation of Sartre as the better philosopher – has recently received a great deal of attention.[22] Beauvoir's account of their meeting and revising presents Sartre as the generous benefactor of the others in their group: 'To tell the truth, it was always he [Sartre] who knew most about all the authors and all the aspects of our syllabus … He used to do his utmost to help us benefit from his knowledge. "He is a marvellous trainer of intellects, I noted." '[23]

---

[20]Cited in Cohen-Solal 1987: 75.
[21]Beauvoir 2001: 334.
[22]See Fulbrook and Fulbrook 2008 on the Sartre–Beauvoir relationship. On this particular account of their meeting and subsequent relationship, see also Michèle Le Doeuff 2002: 119–20, and 2007: 162 ff.
[23]Beauvoir 2001: 335.

After revising together Sartre came first out of 76 candidates. Beauvoir came second. She was twenty-one: youngest in her class and the youngest ever to pass. Two members of the jury later recounted that it was difficult to decide whether she or Sartre should have received first place.

Also in 1929 Sartre participated in a survey on 'today's students' for the magazine *Les Nouvelles littéraires*. The letter he wrote to them contained the following passage:

> It is a paradox of the human mind that Man, whose business it is to create the necessary conditions, cannot raise himself above a certain level of existence .... That is why, as the root of humanity, as at the root of nature, I can see only sadness and boredom. It's not that Man does not think of himself as a *being*. On the contrary, he devotes all his energies to becoming one. Whence derive our ideas of Good and Evil, ideas of men working to improve Man. But these concepts are useless. Useless, too, is the determinism which oddly enough attempts to create a synthesis of existence and being. We are as free as you like, but helpless ... There is no such thing as the will to power. Everything is too weak: all things carry the seeds of their own death.[24]

At the age of twenty-three, three years before his 'discovery' of phenomenology and fourteen years before the publication of *Being and Nothingness*, the student Sartre already attributed human unhappiness to an impotent freedom that failed to achieve being. In Beauvoir's discussion of this letter in *Memoirs of a Dutiful Daughter*, she writes that 'the seeds of all his ideas on being, existence, necessity, and liberty' were already present. But

> he had no intention of composing a theoretical treatise on conventional lines. He loved Stendhal as much as Spinoza and refused to separate philosophy from literature. In his view, Contingency was no abstract notion, but an actual dimension of real life: it would be necessary to make use of all the resources of

---

[24]'Enquête auprès des étudiants d'aujourd'hui', by Roland Alix, *Les nouvelles littéraires*, 2 Feb. 1929. Parts of the letter are also reprinted in Beauvoir 2001: 342–3, from which this is taken; emphasis in original.

art to make the human heart aware of that secret 'failing' which he perceived in Man and the world around him.[25]

The same year, Sartre was drafted into the French army, and served as a meteorologist from 1929 to 1931. With one gap during the Second World War, from 1931 to 1945, Sartre taught philosophy at various lycées: first at Le Havre (1931–36), then Laon (1936–37) and, finally, Paris (at the Lycées Pasteur, 1937–39, and Condorcet, 1941–44). During Sartre's years as a teacher he wrote and published his phenomenological works, which leads us to the Bec De Gaz, on the rue Montparnasse, Paris, at the turn of 1932–33.

Accounts of Sartre's philosophical formation usually include the story of his discovery of phenomenology – indeed, if there were a mythological canon in continental philosophy, this legend would surely be one of its most frequently recounted. As Beauvoir tells it in *The Prime of Life*, Aron had returned to Paris from Berlin and, over apricot cocktails,[26] told Sartre about phenomenology, saying, 'You see, my dear fellow, if you are a phenomenologist you can talk about this cocktail and make philosophy out of it!'[27] Sartre was so excited by the discovery that he immediately set off to search the bookshops of Paris, with Beauvoir in tow, for a book on Husserl's phenomenology. They found Levinas's *Theory of Intuition in Husserl's Phenomenology* (*La Théorie de l'intuition dans la phénoménologie de Husserl*, 1930) and Sartre was so impatient with expectation that 'he leafed through the volume as we walked along, without even having cut the pages'.[28] Later the same year, Sartre travelled to Berlin to study Husserl and Heidegger during a nine-month sabbatical at the French Institute (taking up the position Aron had held the previous year), and thus Sartre the phenomenologist was born.[29]

[25]Beauvoir 2001: 343.
[26]In a later interview with Sartre (in 1972), Sartre recalls a different beverage: beer (Sartre 1978: 26).
[27]Beauvoir 1965: 135.
[28]Beauvoir 1989: 157.
[29]In the *War Diaries* Sartre describes reading Heidegger's *What Is Metaphysics?* in 1930 in the journal *Bifur*. He bought a copy of *Being and Time* in December 1933, but was too 'saturated in Husserl' and befuddled by the German vocabulary, and gave up reading after fifty pages. He returned to read it in full during Easter 1939 (*WD* 183). In a later interview published in 2009 Sartre is dismissive of Aron's influence, calling him a 'con man' and stating that Fernando Gerassi had been talking to him about Husserl for two years before Aron went to Germany. 'I had even read a

Admittedly, Sartre's cocktail moment with Aron was to prove very influential in the development of his life and thought. However, the weight it is given in intellectual biographies (and Sartre scholarship more widely) seems disproportionate to this author. Sartre was twenty-eight years old at the time of this conversation, and he had already undergone substantial philosophical training and written several stories, notebooks, and his *mémoire* on the image for his *diplôme d'études supérieure*. And as we shall see in Chapters 2 and 3, the pre-cocktail influences on Sartre's thought are not only literary and philosophical but also theological.

Also in 1932, Sartre began a work on a treatise on contingency, one of the topics set in his *agrégation*. It underwent several drafts before publication, morphing from a philosophical treatise into a novel. In the meantime, in 1936, Sartre published two phenomenological works – *Imagination: A Psychological Critique* and *The Transcendence of the Ego*. The former essay defined the imagination as 'an act by which consciousness poses its object as absent'. Sartre developed this further in his 1940 work, *The Imaginary*, offering the conclusion that 'the imagination is not an empirical power added to consciousness' but rather 'the whole of consciousness as it realizes freedom' (I 86). In these works we can see both Sartre's debt to and departure from Bergson, who also held that mental images are not weakened perceptions. Whereas perception involves taking objects to be real and present, Sartre argues that imagination 'posits its object as a nothingness'. As Howells notes, Sartre's 'attitude towards the imagination is from the outset ambivalent: both the essence of freedom and yet a permanent temptation to escape from the real and contingent into a fantasy world which would temporarily allay desire without satisfying it'.[30] Despite its dangers the imaginary is valuable, for without 'imaging consciousness' there could be no 'realizing consciousness' that brings imagined things into existence (I 188).

The second work that appeared in 1936, *The Transcendence of the Ego*, set out to correct a problem Sartre detected in Husserl's interpretation of Kant's transcendental unity of apperception. First, Sartre disagrees with his predecessors, denying that there is a

---

book by Levinas about it. No, what Aron made me want to do is go to Germany, all expenses paid, to have a good time' (Gerassi 2009: 253).
[30]Howells 1988: 10.

'transcendental ego', or an a priori structure of consciousness that unifies beliefs and perceptions. Second, in rejecting the transcendental ego, Sartre introduces a different form of consciousness: *reflective consciousness*. In Sartre's own words, 'the consciousness which says "I think" is precisely not the consciousness which thinks' (*TE* 45). The 'I' of Descartes's famous 'I think therefore I am' is not discovered but rather created.

To give a concrete example, when I am engaged in my habitual life there is no ego involved. As I write this chapter, I am aware of the words I combine and the sound of the keyboard as I type them, but no 'I' inhabits this consciousness. The 'I' only comes into being with reflection. Then I see the action as 'mine', for example, by thinking, 'I wrote this chapter today', thinking about the book being finished or desiring to be the self that has finished it. With such steps, the 'ego' comes into existence as the intentional object of consciousness, as an object which is constituted by me. Sartre's point is that this ego (as self-known) presupposes consciousness (as self-knowing).

Out of obscurity

His first novel, *Nausea*, was published in 1938 and brought him a great deal of literary acclaim: its reception gave him a reputation as an up-and-coming novelist. It has been called 'a seamless marriage of fiction and philosophy',[31] in which Sartre used literature's scope for description and irony, its capacity to express through atmosphere rather than argument, to communicate a philosophical problem in an extremely effective, indirect manner.

The problem is this: the novel's protagonist, Roquentin, has discovered that he cannot justify his existence. It is not that he objects to the quality of his life, nor that he wonders whether life is worth living – this is no contemplation of suicide. His discovery is simply that there is not a reason to exist at all. He is superfluous, contingent and reminded of this fact by 'nausea', which haunts every dimension of his experience. We read that he arrived at this conclusion – that is, that there is no reason to exist – during his travels,

[31]Cox 2009: 80.

after which he was prompted to return to France. But in France, he finds no solace in others – unlike the other customers in the cafés he frequents. For a while he finds some justification for his existence in his research on Adhémar, the Marquis de Rollebon, an aristocrat who lived around the time of the French Revolution. However, soon even this distraction loses its grip on him, and he comes to the conclusion that the tasks one sets oneself only serve to veil what he calls the absurdity of existence.

Once unveiled, absurdity is ubiquitous. In the scenes that follow, Roquentin visits the town's museum and, looking at the portraits of its leading citizens, he feels his own right to exist is challenged by them – challenged by men who never questioned their own lives and privilege, pompous civilians (or 'bastards' (*salauds*), as he calls them) who went through the motions and acquired the trappings of justification: status, family, learning, money etc. He observes families walking on fashionable streets on Sunday afternoon – everyone *comme il faut*, but no one knowing why.

The novel concludes with an unexpected glimmer of hope. Sitting in a café at which Roquentin was a regular before catching a train from Bouville to start life over in Paris, the waitress asks if he would like to hear his favourite song, 'Some of These Days', for one last time. He says yes, before embarking on a disdainful train of thought about the bourgeois idiocy that accompanies many appreciators of Chopin or Wagner – the idea that music offers 'consolation' or 'refreshment', that 'beauty is compassionate towards them' (*N* 246). Wordsworth's 'sense sublime of something far more deeply interfused',[32] for Roquentin, is nothing short of ridiculous. All alluring and all-too-respectable beauties are nothing but empty, temporary respites. But Roquentin's song is sung by a black woman and written by a Jew.[33] And as he listens to it, he realizes that though the author and articulator will pass away, the melody stays the same. It comes from 'beyond' – it is not, like himself, superfluous. More importantly, his thoughts start to wander in the direction of redemption: the man who wrote this tune and the woman who sings it – they who give birth to something beyond themselves – have 'cleansed themselves of the sin of existing' (*N* 251).

[32]Wordsworth, *Tintern Abbey*, July 1798.
[33]Adumbrating the themes of freedom and oppression which would be considered further in 'Black Orpheus' (1948) and *The Anti-Semite and the Jew* (1946).

Roquentin is bowled over. He had lost hope, and dares not move for fear that the feeling will go away. He feels joy, an emotion we have not encountered anywhere else in the novel. But then joy turns to intimidation. If one can justify one's existence, be cleansed of sin, the question then becomes, how? The answer is in writing a book. A novel. Something which would enable him 'to recall [his] life without repugnance' (*N* 252). Although Sartre would later renounce it, at this time he believed in a 'morality of salvation through art' (*WD* 78).

In the late 1930s Sartre eventually began to distance himself from phenomenology, which Beata Stawarska attributes to a 'crisis of faith in a philosophy that was too attached to ideas and representations in its doctrine, but also, and more importantly, too attached to the comfortable refuge of the academia in its practice and way of life'.[34] However 1939 nonetheless saw the publication of the *Sketch for a Theory of the Emotions*: 'an experiment in phenomenological psychology' in which Sartre sought to 'study emotion as a pure transcendental phenomenon'. His interest was not in particular emotions but rather in attempting 'to attain and elucidate the transcendental essence of emotion as an organized type of consciousness' (*E* 104). Sartre was critical of psychological accounts of emotion for failing to recognize the proximity of the investigator to the thing investigated, and for seeing emotions as 'facts' that are insignificant (in the sense of not conveying meaning). On Sartre's view, 'facts' will never add up to a satisfying picture of human nature. Phenomenology 'is the study of phenomena – not facts' (*E* 122), making it a preferable methodology for investigating the human condition.

In September 1939 Sartre was again drafted into the French army and again he served as a meteorologist. His duties were light: he was required to make observations in the morning and evening, and therefore he found himself with seven hours a day to read and write, much more time than he had had in civilian life. He kept a diary – parts of which survived to be published as *War Diaries* – and wrote to Beauvoir regularly, requesting books and taking down notes and reflections in his diaries and letters. In the *War Diaries* we see the development of several Sartrean

---

[34]Stawarska 2013: 13.

concepts – anxiety, freedom, being – alongside the thoughts pro-voked by his reading.

He read Kierkegaard's *The Concept of Anxiety* during this period,[35] which prompted pages of reflection on the relationship of freedom and nothingness.[36] In 1940 he was captured by German troops in Padoux.[37] He spent nine months as a prisoner of war, in Nancy and finally in Stalag XII-D, near Trèves, where he read Heidegger's *Being and Time* and wrote his first theatrical piece: a Christmas play, *Bariona*.[38] Sartre described the experience of stag-ing and performing it as a profound discovery. 'As I addressed my comrades across the footlights, speaking to them of their state as prisoners, when I suddenly saw them so remarkably silent and attentive, I realised what theatre ought to be: a great, collective, religious phenomenon … a theatre of myths.'[39]

Bariona is intriguing not only because of its origins but also because Sartre suppressed it, refusing to allow subsequent perfor-mances or professional publication.[40] And it is intriguing because, as one of Sartre's closest companions in the Stalag remarked, even if the play is not 'Christian properly so called, it unfolds in the con-text of Christmas'.[41] It stands in the tradition of medieval mystery plays, complete with angels, shepherds and wise men. Why would one of the twentieth century's most prominent atheists write a Christmas play?

Sartre's use of the Christmas story fulfilled two important cri-teria: one aesthetic and one practical. Aesthetically, it gave him a powerful myth to rework for his own purposes (he set several of his plays in classical or significant historical settings). Practically,

---

[35] *WD* 131–2.

[36] For example, we read that 'if Nothingness is introduced into the world through man, anguish at Nothingness is simply anguish at freedom, or, if you prefer, free-dom's anguish at itself' (*WD* 132); 'Freedom is Nothingness, once again, because it aims to suppress itself by nihilating the Nothingness it contains' (*WD* 134).

[37] Boulé 2005: 114.

[38] See Vincent de Coorebyter (2005) 'Bariona, ou la Nativité d'un athée', *Revue internationale de philosophie* 1 (231): 15–49.

[39] Sartre describes the play in *Théâtre des Situations*; *Sartre on Theatre*, p. 39.

[40] He claimed it was because it is a bad play. See Contat and Rybalka, vol. 2, p. 411.

[41] Perrin 1980: 65. Sartre allowed the printing of the 1962 edition dacty-lographiée in response to the requests of his fellow prisoners and scholars. See also Esslin 1970.

it furnished a built-in distance, which meant that, in a Nazi prison camp where an outright denunciation of fascism would not have escaped the censors, a message of resistance and hope could nonetheless be conveyed to the audience. Several scholars take the character of Balthazar (the role played by Sartre in the 1940 production) to express Sartre's view. His counsel to Bariona is that '*It is you who give it its meaning and make it what it is*' (*B* 80; emphasis in original).

At Stalag XII D, Sartre was on friendly terms with many priests, especially the abbé, who, we hear, won him over by both charm and 'the rigorous way in which he made his conduct match his beliefs'. Beauvoir described the abbé as having

> a keen sense of what freedom meant; in his eyes Fascism, by reducing men to bondage, was defying God's will: 'God,' he said, 'has so great a respect for liberty that He willed His creatures to be free rather than incapable of sin.' This conviction, coupled with his deep-seated humanism, endeared him to Sartre. During endless discussions, which Sartre became passionately interested in, he argued against the Jesuits in the camp that Christ had become fully man. Jesus had been born, like every child, in filth and suffering; the Virgin had not been granted a miraculous delivery. Sartre backed him up: the myth of the Incarnation lost its beauty if Christ did not take all the ills of our human condition upon him.[42]

In *Bariona* there are monologues dedicated to the incarnation. Bariona scoffs at the idea:

> A God, to be changed into a man? What a fairy tale! I don't see what could possibly tempt him into our human condition.... A God change himself into a man? The all-powerful in the heart of his glory contemplating the lice who swarm on the old crust of the earth and pollute it with their excrement! Can you imagine him saying 'I want to be one of those vermin'? That makes me laugh. (*B* 66)

[42]Cited in Contat and Rybalka 1974, vol. 1: 411.

And yet, Bariona confides, if God were to become human for his sake,

> I should love him to the exclusion of all the others, it would be as if there were a blood bond between him and me, and I would not find it too much to give my life out of gratitude. Bariona is not ungrateful. But what God would be foolish enough to do that? Not ours, certainly. He has always shown himself to be proud. (B 67)

After *Bariona*, Sartre wrote ten plays that were professionally produced. Although there is not space to discuss them here, it is worth noting that several of the plays exhibit theological preoccupations, whether drawing on explicitly Christian themes (for example, *The Devil and the Good Lord*, *No Exit*) or an anachronistic (Christianized) representation of ancient Greece (as in *The Flies* and *Trojan Women*).

Sartre was released from Stalag XII-D in April 1941, on the grounds of poor health (he claimed that his poor vision and exotropia affected his balance). He was given civilian status and returned to Paris, briefly resuming his teaching position at the Lycée Pasteur before, in October of 1941, moving to the Lycée Condorcet to replace a Jewish teacher. Sartre would later call his wartime experiences 'the real turning-point' of his life. Up to that point, he later recalled:

> I believed myself sovereign; I had to encounter the negation of my own freedom – through being mobilized – in order to become aware of the weight of the world and my links with all those other fellows and their links with me.... You might say that in it I passed from the individualism, the pure individual, of before the war to the social and to socialism.[43]

After this 'turning-point' Sartre contributed to founding an underground group, Socialisme et Liberté (Socialism and Liberty), but it dissolved and Sartre decided to write rather than involve himself in active resistance. That decision resulted in the production of some

---

[43]Sartre 1976: 180.

of his best-known works: *Being and Nothingness* was published in 1943, the same year *The Flies* was staged, and *No Exit* followed on swiftly in 1944. In 1945 he co-founded the quarterly political and literary review *Les Temps modernes*.[44] He stopped teaching and dedicated his time to writing and political activism.

Out of the war

After the war Parisian existentialism reached its popularity zenith. Sartre gave the famous lecture 'Existentialism Is a Humanism' at Club Maintenant on 29 October 1945. By the following year Sartre's popularity had crossed the Atlantic, the evidence of which appears in some surprising places: Sartre was published in the pages of *Atlantic Monthly* and *Vogue* (twice) in 1944–46, and Beauvoir (writing on Sartre) was published in *Harper's Bazaar*. As Jean Wahl wrote in his 'Existentialism: A Preface' – an essay in the *New Republic* which was intended to distinguish Sartre's ideas from those of other existential philosophies – 'There is much talk in Paris, in Greenwich Village, even in the center of Manhattan, about existence and existentialism.'[45] When Sartre visited New York in 1946, *TIME* magazine wrote that 'the literary lion of Paris bounced into Manhattan last week'.[46] And when *No Exit* premiered in America in Manhattan in 1946, reviewers recommended it as 'a phenomenon' that 'should be seen whether you like it or not'.[47] In 1947 the existentialist craze was the subject of Boris Vian's spoof novel *L'Écume des jours*. Its protagonist, Jean-Sol Partre, travels to his lectures by elephant and addresses his adoring audiences from a throne.

Sartre's rise to fame brought more serious reactions from other quarters. The French communists, for example, criticized existentialism's insistence on personal freedom. Sartre's 1948 political play, *Dirty Hands*, did little to garner their favour. In addition to publishing his trilogy of novels, *The Roads to Freedom*, between

[44]Fulton 1999: 12.
[45]Wahl 1945: 442.
[46]Sartre 1944, 1945 and 1946; *TIME* 1946. See Cotkin: chapter 5 for more on 'The Vogue of French Existentialism'.
[47]Young 1946.

1945 and 1949, in the late 1940s Sartre drafted some notes for the
work on ethics which he' had promised in *Being and Nothingness*.
It was never completed, although it was published posthumously
as the *Notebooks for an Ethics*. In that text he shows some movement in his thought. In particular, whereas *Being and Nothingness*
claimed that the essence of being with others was 'conflict', in these
notebooks Sartre introduces the word 'reciprocity' as a possible
descriptor of ethical human relationships.

After Sartre's 1946 visit to America he began to turn his pen to
one particularly nonreciprocal relationship: the relationship between
blacks and whites. Sartre's one American play, *The Respectful
Prostitute*, was written soon after his visit in 1946. And the years that
followed brought several other writings on race: 'The Oppression
of the Blacks in the United States' (in the *Notebooks for an Ethics*),
'Black Presence' (1947) and then *Black Orpheus* (1948), in which
he describes 'Negritude' as a poetic avenue of rebirth for the black
man. Along with *Anti-Semite and Jew*, Andrew Leak has called *Black
Orpheus* an exercise in 'applied Sartreanism'.[48] The year 1948 also
saw the publication of *What Is Literature?*, in which Sartre developed
his notion of 'commitment' and defined the goal of literature as 'to
reveal the world and particularly to reveal man to other men so that
the latter may assume full responsibility before the object which has
been thus laid bare' (*WL* 15).

In 1952, following a long period of indecision about his political allegiances – in his own words, 'after ten years of ruminating' –
Sartre experienced a political 'conversion'. He decided that he must
be committed to communism and *engaged* as an intellectual. He
wrote a long essay entitled 'The Communists and Peace', a justification of the Soviet state, which he published in *Les Temps modernes*. The essay proposed that political situations should be decided
by asking how they look 'to the eyes of the least favoured', but its
publication had several unintended consequences – increasing the
distance between Sartre and Albert Camus and between Sartre and
Merleau-Ponty (his co-editor who, among other things, was under-
standably upset that Sartre printed the essay without showing it to
him).[49]

[48]Leak 2006: 79.
[49]They also disagreed politically, for reasons that can be seen in Merleau-Ponty's
Adventures of the Dialectic, in the chapter entitled 'Sartre and Ultrabolshevism'.

There followed a highly politicized period of political involve-ment. It was detrimental to his health and reputation – the for-mer because he overstretched himself out of fear of not producing enough, and the latter because he supported causes (such as Soviet Communism) that hindsight revealed to be less than worthy. After the Hungarian uprising in 1956 Sartre began work on a philosoph-ical treatise that corrected the errors of his early existentialism with a Marxist emphasis on concrete situations and action. In 1957, in the essay 'Existentialism and Marxism,' Sartre declared that Marxism was 'the one philosophy of our times which we cannot go beyond', and in 1960 he published the theoretical product of this period of rumination: *The Critique of Dialectical Reason.*[50] In that work he denounced colonialism and defended anticolonial coun-terviolence, continuing his public opposition to political oppres-sion in various ways, including the one he knew best: writing. He wrote the introduction to Albert Memmi's *The Colonizer and the Colonized* (1957) and the preface to Frantz Fanon's *The Wretched of the Earth* (1961), and several other essays on colonialism which were published as *Situations V: Colonialism and Neocolonialism* (1964).

In the *Critique of Dialectical Reason* Sartre made it very clear that he no longer endorsed the ontology of *Being and Nothingness.* While he still saw a distinction between human and non-human beings, in the later work he discusses the role of praxis in struc-turing our engagement with the world, expressing agreement with Marx that human beings relate to others and the world in a dia-lectical way, with mutual interaction and causation, and that this relationality can restrict individual freedoms.

Because we have already passed out of the period of Sartre's works that proved most influential for the theologians to be consid-ered in Part 2, however, the remainder of this chapter moves quickly through Sartre's later life. In 1964 his memoir, *Words* was published, and Sartre publicly renounced literature as a means of salvation. In October of the same year Sartre was awarded the Nobel Prize for literature. The Swedish Academy's announcement described his work as 'rich in ideas and filled with the spirit of freedom and the

---

[50]The first volume was published in 1960; the second volume was published posthumously.

quest for truth', and as having 'exerted a far-reaching influence on our age'.[51]

But Sartre declined it – and declining a Nobel Prize proved a rather scandalous thing to do. On 23 October he published an announcement in *Le Figaro* expressing regret that his refusal had resulted in scandal. He explained that, not realizing that the Academy's choice was irreversible, he had attempted to prevent their choice of him by sending a letter specifying his reasons for refusal, that no slight was intended to the Swedish Academy, but that personal and objective reasons prevented his acceptance.

For his own part (the personal reasons), Sartre wrote that his understanding of the writer's task precluded the acceptance of such honours (he had refused other honours in the past, such as membership of the Legion of Honour and the Collège de France): 'the writer must refuse to let himself be transformed by institutions'.[52] And on behalf of others (the objective reasons), Sartre expressed concern that institutional intervention was not the best way to encourage exchange between cultures. Since the past prizes had not been conferred equally on writers of all ideologies and nations, he was concerned that accepting such a prize might give rise to misinterpretation. Sartre concluded with an expression of affection for the Swedish public. As his biographer Cohen-Solal put it, he did not want to be 'embalmed alive, to be made into a living statue and prematurely canonized'.[53]

But whether he wanted to be canonized or not, he already was a French institution: during the May 1968 strikes in Paris, Sartre was arrested for civil disobedience, but President Charles de Gaulle reputedly intervened and pardoned him, saying, 'You don't imprison Voltaire.'

Hope Now

In the 1970s Sartre's health declined, partly because of compulsive overwork fuelled by amphetamines, partly because of hypertension[54]

---

[51]Nobelprize.org, http://www.nobelprize.org/nobel_prizes/literature/laureates/1964/press.html.
[52]Press statement taken by Carl-Gustav Bjurström, 22 October 1964.
[53]Cohen-Solal 1987: 449; see pp. 444–51 for a discussion of his rejection of the prize.
[54]Hayman 1992: 464.

and partly because of his relentless chain-smoking. Sartre died on 15 April 1980, in Paris, from pulmonary edema. He did not wish to be buried with his mother and stepfather at Père-Lachaise Cemetery, so he was buried instead in Montparnasse.

Three times in *Being and Nothingness* Sartre cites a line from Malraux: 'The terrible thing about Death is that it transforms life into Destiny.'[55] Once dead, according to the Sartre of *Being and Nothingness*, we are defined by the gazes of those who outlast or come after us. No longer present to resist the meanings others give us, our being takes on the fixity of a thing.

Just before Sartre's death, in March 1980, the French paper *Le Nouvel observateur* published a series of interviews between Sartre and his young assistant, Benny Lévy, which led to a controversy that shows just how much conflicting 'gazes' on the meaning of a life can vary.

Lévy (also referred to as Pierre Victor at some stages of his life) had been part of Sartre's life since May 1968, but during the period of their acquaintance he had turned from Maoism to the Talmud. He had worked closely with Sartre over several years, and the *Hope Now* interviews were published (with Sartre's consent) on the 10th, 17th and 24th of March 1980. Their title indicates one of their themes: hope. But they also discuss failure, politics, religion, violence and, of course, Sartre's philosophy. The problem was that the Sartre who appeared on these pages was not the Sartre others expected to see.

In these interviews Sartre distances himself from several of his earlier positions: in particular, concerning being-for-others. The Sartre of *Hope Now* admits 'the dependence of each individual on all other individuals' (*HN* 72), which Lévy immediately remarks will come as a surprise his readers. But Sartre clarifies that he has realized that dependence need not imply slavery. In the interview Sartre describes being treated like an old man – an experience Beauvoir described as being like 'a corpse under suspended sentence' in her book on old age – and his experience of needing to rely on another (Lévy) since due to his physical decline he could no longer write for himself. He describes this fact as having 'completely changed [his] mode of inquiry' (*HN* 73).

[55]*BN* 135, 138 and 563.

He discusses his inheritance of Christianity and its impossible ideals – the desire to be God, to be *ens causa sui* – and attributes his use of these conceptual apparati to his historicity (*HN* 60). But Sartre he does not think the goals we should look for in ethics can be found in Christianity (*BN* 61). He is more open to – although does not explicitly adopt – Judaism, and praises Jewish messianism as something that could be used 'by non-Jews for other purposes', as a means of gaining hope for the world (*HN* 107ff). It is on the basis of this passage that some claim Sartre underwent a deathbed conversion, although Sartre is quite clear that the 'use' he envisages for messianism is a political, revolutionary one.

After Sartre's death the combination of his age, blindness, and ill-health, on the one hand, and his radically changed views, on the other, led many of those closest to Sartre to question the reliability of the interviews. As Cohen-Solal writes, in the months and years after Sartre's death, Lévy, Beauvoir and several of Sartre's longer-standing friends published contradictory accounts in order to defend and preserve what she calls the 'Sartrean Truth'.[56]

Many scholars express reservations about taking the *Hope Now* interviews as indicative of a genuine change of heart on Sartre's part.[57] Whether or not Beauvoir's vitriolic depiction of Lévy as a 'petty boss' who 'extorted' statements from Sartre is fair, or whether or not it constitutes ageism, plain and simple, to think Sartre was not in *enough* control of his 74-year-old faculties, are difficult questions to answer in hindsight. But on Beauvoir's account in *Adieux*, Lévy pressured Sartre for days in conversation, and then Sartre eventually just gave in and gave his consent to publish.

Beauvoir attributed Sartre's consent to his stubbornness: she advised against it, so he did it. Beauvoir did not accuse Lévy of falsifying the text. But her allegations about bullying Sartre into agreement provoked a series of public responses – from Aron, and, eventually, Sartre's adopted daughter, Arlette Elkaïm-Sartre. In 1981, the latter published an open letter to Beauvoir:

When Sartre and I were alone together, I tried to be his eyes as much as possible. As I did with the other interviews of the same period, I therefore read and reread their [Sartre's and Lévy's]

---

[56]See Cohen Solal 1987: 510ff. for an account of the controversy.
[57]For example, Aronson 1996: 5.

dialogue to him, repeating word after word as well as the whole text several times, to the point of irritating him, aware that certain phrases of his would be surprising. Sartre added and corrected as he wished. He thought that he would explain himself in greater depth in their future book. I grant that my rereadings didn't achieve the intimacy that one has with one's own text when one reads it oneself, but how could that be helped? (Aronson 1996:8)

In the words of Aronson, the text was 'damned for all time by Beauvoir', who dismissed the interviews as 'the abduction of an old man'.[58] But, as Aronson also states, time has revealed just how constructed the Sartre–Beauvoir image was. In her own interviews with Sartre, conducted in 1974 and published in *Adieux* after Sartre's death as a corrective to the 'false' picture portrayed by Lévy, Beauvoir frequently insists on points that Sartre resists, shaping the conversation in order to dictate the tone of Sartre's remarks.

It is famously difficult to assess just how true the 'Sartrean Truth' Beauvoir and others fought to preserve really was. After all, lengthy though Beauvoir's rejoinder was, it was based on seven-year-old interviews and accompanied by a low estimation of Sartre's capacities – for change, and for a man of his age. Elkaïm-Sartre's reply defended Sartre on both counts:

Before his death, Sartre was quite alive: he virtually no longer saw anything, his organism was deteriorating, but he heard [*entendait*] in both senses [understood and heard] of the word, and you treated him as a dead man who, inconveniently enough, appeared in public – this last comparison is not mine but his. Neither my indignation nor the odious character that you assign to Benny Lévy explains it. Perhaps your way of perceiving his old age … Otherwise, how can one understand that you were able to say to him, *to him*, that you were thinking of having a 'Sartrean tribunal' to meet to judge these interviews. (Aronson 1996: 11)

Perhaps, if Malraux were to rewrite his line for this story, he might choose the plural noun: 'death transforms life into destin*ies*'.

---

[58]Aronson 1996: 8.

2

Sartre's theological formation: In philosophy

'You see, my dear fellow, if you are a phenomenologist you can talk about this cocktail and make philosophy out of it!'[1] As genesis myths go, Beauvoir's is a good one: Sartre the phenomenologist was born over a philosophical cocktail. But some scholars have expressed doubts about its accuracy, raising questions about the reliability of autobiography in general and the Sartre–Beauvoir public relations machine in particular.

For one thing, some have argued that Beauvoir played a more active role in introducing Sartre to phenomenology. Margaret Simons has shown that Beauvoir had already encountered phenomenology during her studies at the Sorbonne. Beauvoir studied with Jean Baruzi, who was a student of Husserl's phenomenology and whose lectures on Leibniz in 1926 referred to Husserl's method of reduction. In 1924 Baruzi published a work entitled *Saint Jean de la Croix et le problème de l'éxperience mystique*, which describes religious anguish in existential terms, drawing particularly on the lived experience of the mystic. Simons notes that although Beauvoir gives Sartre the glory for introducing her to phenomenology in the 1930s, 'given her close work with Baruzi in 1927, it is possible that she misrepresented the date of her introduction to phenomenology just as she did her early interest in philosophy'.[2] Given that Beauvoir used the category of lived experience in her own work, it seems

---

[1] Beauvoir 1965: 135.
[2] Beauvoir 2006: 49n.

likely that she would already have been familiar with Husserl's phenomenology by the time she met Sartre in 1929.

On Sartre's side, too, there have been suggestions that he encountered phenomenology before the iconic incident with Aron and even before meeting Beauvoir. Light has drawn attention to an earlier brush with German phenomenology in 1928, when Sartre had regular conversations with the Japanese philosopher Shuzo Kuki (who had studied with Husserl and Heidegger in Germany).[3]

But the pre-1928 Sartre has received very little scholarly attention.[4] Who did this Sartre read? Who were his intellectual interlocutors, living or dead? This chapter considers several sources in order to answer these questions: (1) Sartre's later assessment of his influences in the manuscripts preserved at the John Gerassi collection at Yale University; (2) Sartre's *mémoire* for the *diplome d'études supérieure*; and (3) the philosophers and theologians with whom Sartre would have had to be familiar as an *agregé* in philosophy in the 1920s. Naturally, we cannot explore all of these in great depth, but the cumulative picture they present nevertheless demonstrates that Sartre's early philosophical formation included *theology*, and moreover that he, like Beauvoir, had also encountered phenomenology before the legendary meeting with Aron.

Sartre's readings from youth

In a folder in the John Gerassi collection of manuscripts at Yale University, there are four handwritten pages of notes Sartre made (at Gerassi's request) on the subject of the early reading which Sartre considered to be intellectually formative. Here Sartre describes his reading prior to the age of sixteen as 'littérature populaire', and lists several Western novels like *Texas Jack* and *Sitting Bull* as well as detective fiction. At the sixteen-year mark we see some heavier fare: first, Hugo's *Les Misérables* and *La Légende des siècles*, then Stendhal, Dostoevsky, and Proust.[5] At eighteen years Sartre

---

[3]Light 1987: 4.
[4]Exceptions tend to treat Sartre and Bergson: see Richmond 2007 (in English) and studies by Cormann and Englebert (in French).
[5]In *EJ*, Sartre mentions discussing Dostoevsky and Tolstoy with his grandmother (*EJ* 55).

remembered reading Bergson, Descartes, and Pascal. And then, around eighteen to nineteen years, we find a list including Alain, Valéry, 'the stoics', 'epicureans', Plato, Kant, and Spinoza. On the second page of this manuscript Sartre's dating system changes from his age to the calendar year or span of years under consideration. Here, for the period 1930–35, he lists Husserl, Heidegger, Scheler; and for 1939–45 Heidegger (underlined twice) and Kierkegaard (with Abraham in parentheses, and the *Concept of Anxiety* mentioned by name).

Those who know Sartre well will not find any of this particularly surprising. Clearly, many of these authors fit neatly into the categories 'philosophy' and 'literature': in the former, we have the usual suspects, Plato, Descartes, Spinoza, Kant. And in the latter: Hugo, Stendhal, Proust. But what about Bergson, Alain and Pascal? They were philosophers by the reckoning of their contemporaries. But they also treated religious themes, and those themes were explored at great depth by their advocates in 1920s France, in particular by Bergson's student Delacroix (under whose supervision Sartre wrote his *diplôme d'études supérieures*), and by Baruzi, Brunschvicg, and Wahl, all of whom Sartre demonstrably engaged with, whether by reading or in person.

Sartre's *mémoire*

We have already seen in Chapter 1 that once Sartre received his *licence*, he spent the 1926–27 academic year writing his *mémoire* for the DES. To supervise his *mémoire* he chose Delacroix, teacher of psychology at the Sorbonne and assessor at the Faculty of Letters in Paris. Delacroix's first master was Bergson, and Sartre drew on this work as well as Delacroix's study of Christian mysticism, *Étude d'histoire et de psychologie du mysticisme*, in his *mémoire*.[6] The subject of Sartre's study was the image (that is, the kinds of mental images that occur in memory or imagination). Entitled *L'Image dans la vie psychologique: rôle et nature*, the original manuscript for this work has disappeared, but there

---

[6] Although it is clear that Sartre disagrees with Delacroix on several points (see, e.g., M 164).

is a dactylographic copy at the Institut des Textes et Manuscrits Modernes (ITEM) in Paris.

Because the work is not published or translated it has not been widely consulted or indeed discussed in the secondary literature. There is a brief mention of it in an online catalogue of an exhibition at the ENS, which describes its five-chapter structure and praises Sartre's erudite treatment of 'the physiological theory, Gestalt theory, Würzburg-school psychologists, American psychologists, Théodule Ribot, Henri Bergson'.[7] However this description omits an important component: that Sartre also drew on Christian *mystics* in his work on the image.

The section of the third chapter that treats these mystics is missing from the electronic version of the manuscript I consulted; I have not been able to ascertain whether it is also missing from the original. However, his endnotes and list of references show that Sartre, too, was reading not only secondary sources about mysticism – including Baruzi's book on John of the Cross, Delacroix's works (*Le Mysticisme en Allemagne au XIVe siècle* and *Étude de psychologie et d'histoire du mysticisme*) and Gilson on Bonaventure – but also mystics themselves, in particular Tauler and Teresa of Ávila.

In the *mémoire* Sartre argues that the image 'has a different logic to that of thought: left to itself it has a mode of development [128] analogous to that of things perceived. Like a plant grows or a stone falls, thus the image falls or grows' (*M* 127–8). Much of Sartre's thesis concerns what is at stake in having what Sartre calls (following Rignano) *mental experiences*. He describes these in various ways – for example, Sartre claims that Brunschvicg made Sartre see 'with the eyes of the soul' that there was a 'nature and spirit' that comes from an 'élan' that is primitive, spiritual and creative (*M* 133).

This work provides insight into Sartre's early development, both in terms of the ideas that preoccupied him and the thinkers he found worthy of engagement. With respect to the former, the relation of inner and outer experience, or with the 'internal' and 'external' worlds, is a guiding question. What reality should be assigned to perception as opposed to imagination? Sartre argues

---

[7]http://www.bib.ens.fr/A-l-Ecole-normale-su.707.0.html; see also the introduction of the *Écrits de jeunesse*, for example, which describes this manuscript simply as 'an important manuscript of 272 dactylographic pages'.

that psychology's role, as a philosophical discipline, is to study internal processes – what Sartre calls 'spiritual facts' (*faits*) – and as such its domain is the same as that of the image (*M* 136):

> In effect it offers us a spatial world which borrows its laws from those of perception and which is given to us as being the spiritual world. Psychology is an effort to constitute a spatial image of the unextended. And, without a doubt, the most profound psychologists observe it. Bergson, for example, writes 'We necessarily express ourselves in words and we think most often in space. In other words, language demands that we establish between our ideas the same neat and precise distinctions, the same discontinuity that there is between material objects. This assimilation is useful in practical life and necessary in most of the sciences. But one could ask whether the insurmountable difficulties raised by certain philosophical problems do not come from juxtaposing in space phenomena that do not occupy space'.[8]

Bergson's work on consciousness and intuition is discussed at several points. For example, Sartre considers a 'spiritual reality that introspection cannot touch directly'. Bergson's suggestion is that another means of investigation is required to reach it: intuition (*M* 144). Bergson's 'intuition' was intended to overcome the epistemological blows of Kant's critical project by re-establishing the possibility of knowledge. 'Intuition' is a kind of experience that Bergson calls 'the true empiricism',[9] a way of knowing through 'sympathy',[10] namely, putting ourselves in others' places. Rather than approaching things from the outside, we 'enter into' things, and by doing so we gain absolute knowledge. But the knowledge we gain is always 'a component part',[11] which is to say a part of the duration of myself rather than the whole. But Sartre dismisses intuition, claiming that it is impossible 'to say that the intuition is not an image'. On Sartre's definition,

[8]Sartre is quoting Bergson, *Données immédiates*, avant propos; *M* 136–7.
[9]Bergson 1992: 175.
[10]Bergson 1992: 159.
[11]Bergson 1992: 170–2.

philosophical intuition is the consideration of a certain image, spontaneously arising, and which is the substitute for that which the philosopher will never see: his spiritual essence or the order of the universe. The effort of the philosopher is therefore to reattach to each other the fundamental images that reappear without order in his spirit. (*M* 145).[12]

Sartre's exploration with the inner/outer distinction is also couched in terms of the nature of consciousness. He disagrees with Spinoza, saying that consciousness is not 'the idea of an idea but the image of an image; there is an infinite reaction to a first image posed and these reactions are again images' (*M* 157).[13] This is why we are so complex psychologically, and these questions led Sartre to ask 'why the notion of the image is linked to that of consciousness and by what law' (*M* 152).

The answer Sartre would later give in the so-called phenomeno-logical works on the imagination (published in 1936 and 1940) is *nothingness*. 'Where perception involves taking an object to be real and present, he claims, imagination "posits its object as a noth-ingness".'[14] As Richmond notes, Sartre's interest in phenomenology 'co-existed with and was an instrument for his wish to demonstrate the existence of human freedom, and his sense that the way to do this was by establishing an essential connection of consciousness with nothingness'.[15]

For consciousness to be able to imagine it must be free, 'able to escape from the world by its very nature' (*I* 184). In these early works Sartre follows Bergson in claiming that

there cannot be an intuition of nothingness, precisely because nothingness is nothing and because all consciousness – intuitive or not – is consciousness of something. Nothingness can be given only as an infrastructure of something. The experience of nothingness is not, strictly speaking, an indirect experience, but is an experience that is, on principle, given 'with' and 'in'. Bergson's analyses remain valid here: an attempt to conceive

[12]The discussion of Bergson's *Matière et mémoire* begins on *M* 140.
[13]Discusses the 'psychological simplicity' of the heros of the Bible (*M* 154).
[14]Webber 2004: xxiv.
[15]Richmond 2013: 94.

death or the nothingness of existence directly is by nature doomed to fail. (*I* 187)

The imagination, whatever degree of reality one assigns to it, is powerful: 'the image is an invisible persuasion' (*M* 150). It can be used creatively and in order to understand, but Sartre finds a parallel structure in the creative effort and that of a reader, for example: 'it is always a matter of isolating oneself from perceptible reality and building another in our 'interior space' (*espace intérieur*) (*M* 150).

One of the examples he gives of this process concerns belief in God. He discusses the effectiveness of proofs for God's existence, such as the teleological argument, writing that 'Pascal, well before Kant, had denounced its poverty' (*M* 53). An argument like this, however sound, will not persuade unless it is accompanied by an imaginative transformation. 'Even for the Christian', Sartre writes, 'the existence of the world cannot directly suffice to prove God … It must therefore take *experience* (in the sense of *Erlebniss*) … it takes a revelation to make God descend to earth' (*M* 54; emphasis in original).

Drawing on William James's notion of subuniverses Sartre writes that 'All philosophical theory is an arbitrary limitation of the exterior world, and the production of a sub-universe (*sous-univers*) in the medium of images' (*M* 146).[16] But it is not just philosophers who exercise this creative imagination: all human beings have a fundamental tendency 'to the Demiurge', Sartre writes – 'all men want to create their world' (*M* 152). As an example of the 'interior space' (*éspace intérieur*) (see *M* 150) he uses Teresa of Ávila's image of the 'interior castle' (*M* 182).

In fact, even in this manuscript Sartre mentions 'the logician', 'Hüsserl' [sic] (*M* 72–3), demonstrating that Sartre encountered 'phenomenology' (in both the method and movement senses of the term) much earlier than the cocktail story suggests. As Simons argues with respect to Beauvoir, so we can argue with respect to Sartre that having read Baruzi's work on mysticism – which concerns the interior life of *individuals*[17] and the 'rhythm of lived experience'[18] – and

---

[16]See also *M* 96 and *M* 138 for further references to James.
[17]Baruzi 1924: ii; Delacroix 1938: iv.
[18]Baruzi 1924: iv.

worked with Delacroix, he had certainly already encountered the tradition before the 'revelatory' conversation with Aron.

We will look at the philosophers and mystics who shaped this tradition in greater depth in the next section, but before doing so we must mention another pertinent feature of Sartre's student context. The late 1920s and early 1930s saw the emergence of a high-profile and systematic debate on the question of whether there is any such thing as 'Christian philosophy'. The question raised perennial problems such as the relationship between the nature of faith and reason, and indeed theology and philosophy. Its participants, some religious and some not, included many of the most prestigious philosophical minds in France: Étienne Gilson, Léon Brunschvicg, Jacques Maritain, Maurice Blondel, Émile Bréhier, Gabriel Marcel.

In particular, it is worth elaborating on the involvement of Brunschvicg in this discussion. Among other things Brunschvicg was responsible for the edition of Pascal's *Pensées* which was current in the 1920s, when the tercentenary of Pascal's birth was celebrated (in 1923, three years before Pascal appeared on the *agrégation de philosophie*). Against Bréhier (a historian of philosophy who completely rejected the historical influence of Christianity on philosophy and the possibility of a 'Christian philosophy'), Brunschvicg acknowledged that 'I would not recognize myself in what I think and what I feel if the entire movement of Christianity had not existed.'[19]

But could there be a '*specifically* Christian philosophy'? Brunschvicg, like many evolutionist thinkers of the early twentieth century, thought philosophy was constantly developing, emerging originally from religion and progressively being liberated from the immaturity of its protophilosophical forbears (much like Tylor's and Frazer's theories of 'primitive religion'). Religion and religious thought provide *symbols* of true spirituality, on Brunschvicg's view: but only philosophy can deliver the real deal.

> We come back to the position that I have called, granted very naively, that of the Western consciousness, which is prior by five centuries to the blossoming of Christianity. From that point of view, faith, insofar as faith, is only the prefiguration, the sensible

[19]Brunschvicg 1931: 73.

symbol, the approximation of what properly human effort will be able to set in full light. We understand then how one can recognize that philosophy exists, and Christianity exists, without having the right to conclude that a Christian philosophy would exist.[20]

On Brunschvicg's view, revelation is not really revelation. Philosophy's gradual ascent to truth has shown that there is, in fact, no supernatural, be it Christian or otherwise. He argues that all forms of rationality prior to the seventeenth century were immature – and insufficiently 'philosophical' to be considered 'Christian philosophy'.

Brunschvicg outlines three relations a thinker may occupy with respect to her Christianity and philosophy: (1) being a philosopher first and a Christian second (in which case, one is doing *philosophy* and there is nothing intrinsically Christian about it); (2) being a Christian first and a philosopher secondarily (in which case, he thinks, what such a person is doing is not really philosophy). Brunschvicg appeals to Pascal as an exemplum, writing that 'his Christianity … uncover[ed] for him a way of philosophizing that is not that of the philosophers'.[21] And finally, in cases of type (3)

we would have to recognize that there is something it would be appropriate to call, without equivocation and without compromise, a Christian philosophy. This is the case where a metaphysician, reflecting in a manner deep and 'naïve' at the same time, would arrive at that conviction that philosophy ends up only posing problems, entangling itself in difficulties. The clearer a consciousness it will have of these problems, the deeper it will sound the abyss into which these difficulties throw philosophy, the more it will be persuaded that only Christianity's own solutions will satisfy philosophical problems.[22]

This type is not only possible, according to Brunschvicg, but also actual – in Malebranche.

[20]Brunschvicg 1931: 74–5.
[21]Brunschvicg 1931: 76.
[22]Brunschvicg 1931: 76.

Although the extent to which Sartre followed these debates is difficult to determine, in 1926 he presented an 'Exposé' on Descartes during the *décade de Pontigny* (an international conference of intellectuals hosted at the property of Desjardins) on the theme of *l'empreinte chrétienne* (the Christian imprint, or legacy), which took place from 15–25 August of that year.[23] The same year, 'the high dignitary of university philosophy'[24] – Brunschvicg – also presented.

When Sartre was a student at the ENS the idealism of Brunschvicg dominated the philosophical climate.[25] Sartre attended and, indeed, presented at Brunschvicg's seminars in Paris – on the topic of what counts as philosophy. Again underscoring the different disciplinary boundaries of the period, in 1927 Sartre presented a paper at Brunschvicg's seminar at the Sorbonne entitled 'Nietzsche: Is He a Philosopher?' Sartre's answer was no. (He had come to that conclusion a few years earlier, writing in the *Carnet Midy* that Nietzsche was 'a poet who had the misfortune of having been taken for a philosopher'.[26])

Philosophers and mystics

Whether we call them 'philosophy', 'theology', or 'mysticism', the sources Sartre read during his time at the ENS introduced him to an ontological vision of the human being as between 'being and nothingness'. Moreover, these writers anticipate many Sartrean themes, such as the irreducibility of individual experience, the importance of the imagination, the perdurance of the self in time (or lack thereof) and the paradoxical power of nothingness. Baruzi's book argued that the classification of mystical states is vain because attending to lived experience is an individual matter. And Sartre's supervisor Delacroix's 1908 study of mysticism

[23]See Chaubet 1998 for the history of these colloquia.
[24]Chaubet 1998: 38.
[25]Stawarska 2013: 13.
[26]Nietzsche was not widely regarded as a philosopher by the French philosophical scene until after the publication of Deleuze's *Neitzsche et la philosophie* in 1962. He appeared on the *agrégation* programme for the first time in 1929, when *The Genealogy of Morals* appeared as an option for German.

describes the subject of his enquiry as a mysticism '*vécu et pratique*' (lived and practical).[27]

The mystics Delacroix and Baruzi read, described their lived experience in ontological terms. Baruzi associates *lived* mysticism – and indeed, theology – with the early modern theologian Bérulle above all.[28] The founder of what Brémond dubbed 'the French school of spirituality', Bérulle has been called one of the 'masters of the masters' of French mysticism.[29] Bérulle was personally acquainted with the French translators of John of the Cross and Teresa of Ávila, and indeed was present at meetings in 1601 and 1602 that were intended to assure the foundation of the French Carmelite order.[30] But prior to these translations Bérulle's own publications outline a mystical theology in which nothingness (*le néant*) plays a profound role.[31]

This is worth considering at length for two reasons: first, because Bérulle's exposition of Saint Augustine would exert a powerful influence on the seventeenth-century French philosophy, theology and literature we know Sartre read. The pre-1800s philosophy with which *agrégé(e)s* in philosophy were required to be familiar involved many conversations between philosophers and theologians, and Bérulle was both the founder of a flourishing mystical school and the spiritual director of Descartes. The remainder of this chapter therefore outlines (in brief) some of the pertinent developments in seventeenth-century philosophy which later came to be known as the 'quarrel of Augustinianisms'.

Divided followers of Augustine

The thinkers we are about to consider owed a considerable debt to Saint Augustine, who famously replied to the question 'whence

---

[27]Delacroix 1938: iv.

[28]Baruzi mentions Bérulle's theology as 'une théologie subtilement vécue'<AQ: Should there be a word connecting these two quoted phrases, like "and"?> 'tel avant tout' (Baruzi 1924: 390).

[29]Daniel Rops 1941: 37 quotes Brémond referring to Sales and Bérulle as 'les maîtres des maîtres'.

[30]Baruzi 1924: 784.

[31]The French reception of the Spanish mystics Sartre studied in his *mémoire* was shaped by Bérulle's 'École Française', such that scholars such as Baruzi could apply the label 'mystique térésienne et bérullienne' (Baruzi 1924: 736).

evil?' with a confusing set of answers. Intent on exculpating God of any responsibility for the presence of the evil in the world, Augustine defines evil as a *privation* of good, and sin as a lack of being (or tending toward nothingness) which results from humans having been created *ex nihilo*. Many of Augustine's writings were polemical, raising the question of what weight we should assign to rhetorical emphasis when he discusses things like grace or depravity. In his debate with Pelagians especially, as the controversy progressed he articulated his views with increasing extremity, leaving later generations of readers to wonder just how free or determined Augustine thought human beings were – whether by sin or grace. This question resurfaced in Reformation and counterreformation theology, but the aspect of its history that is particularly relevant to this work is Augustine's reception in seventeenth-century France, starting with the Cardinal Pierre de Bérulle.

Bérulle

In circles where Bérulle is renowned, he is known for rejecting the abstract mysticism of his predecessors for having 'Christological gaps', that is to say, for ignoring the humanity of Jesus. For Bérulle, theology and spirituality are inseparable. In his own words, 'Some distinguish between a mystical and a practical theology, but this is a distinction which I do not wish to employ'. 'All God's graces distributed upon earth are to enable us to act better.'[32]

We need such grace because, on Bérulle's anthropology, nothingness (*le néant*) plays a central role in human experience.[33] Indeed, Thompson describes the French School Bérulle is thought to have founded as 'rigorous in its phenomenology of human depravity', noting that 'it moves beyond the surface to the *fond*, from a symptomatology of evil and sin to its roots'.[34] Two centuries before Hegel published the *Phenomenology* and its famous master–slave dialectic, Bérulle wrote that the first quality of being human is to be

---

[32]Quoted in Thompson 1989: 32.

[33]See, e.g., Bellemare 1959: 19; Cognet 1949: 66. Problematically, some render the French *néant* as 'nougt' in English, which loses the ontological and cosmological connotations of the original (see, e.g., Dupré and Saliers 1989: 51).

[34]Thompson 1989: 86. Thompson also notes here that this accent in Bérulle became even more pronounced in the thought of his successor Olier.

in a relation of inferiority or superiority with the world, in a rela-tionship of dependence.[35] In his own words,

> There is nothing better known in the world, by the senses or by reason, than the difference between and condition of being master and servant. It is the most general and applicable quality in the world. It applies to all men: it enters into their sentiments and affections; it enters into or even invades every state and condition … and if they are masters of some, they are servants in the eyes of others.[36]

This condition of dependence and servitude is inseparable from being human, on Bérulle's view: we are creatures, and our crea-turely origin is such that, though made *by* God, we were made *from* nothing.[37]

The human being, on this mystical anthropology, is 'a nothing-ness that tends to nothingness':

> We are a nothingness which tends to nothingness, who seek nothingness, who occupy ourselves with nothingness, who content ourselves with nothingness, who fill ourselves with nothingness, and who finally ruin and destroy ourselves for a nothingness. It is true that we must be a nothingness – to this we are suited by nature – but a nothingness in the hand of God, a nothingness destined for God, a nothingness consecrated to God; a nothingness full of God, a finally a nothingness possessed by and possessing God, and to this we are suited by grace.[38]

Bérulle writes that 'our being is full of nothingness; our understand-ing is full of ignorance, our power is full of weakness and impo-tence; because there is more nothingness than being in our being.'[39]

---

[35]Bachmann 1964: 1. See also Cognet 1949: 58 on this theme, which Cognet attrib-utes to Bérulle's Augustinianism.
[36]Bérulle 1944: 1145.
[37]Bérulle 1859: 219.
[38]Bérulle 1944: 1129.
[39]'notre être est rempli de néant; notre lumière est remplie d'ignorance, notre puis-sance est remplie de faiblesse et impuissance; car il y a plus du nu néant que de l'être dans notre être' (Bérulle 1944: 1014).

Bérulle understood human beings under sin to have been corrupted by self-love.[40] For Bérulle as for Augustine sin is the absence (or *privation*) of good and of being. The nothingness of sin reveals creaturely weakness – the creature cannot stand out of nothingness by itself, and it is only by grace that our being is continuously created in God. If humanity seeks itself outside of God, there is nothing to find but the nothingness from which we issue.[41]

This anthropology of nothingness, Augustinian in origin and Bérullian in articulation, was to have a profound influence on French philosophy and literature in the seventeenth century and beyond. It has already been mentioned that Bérulle was the spiritual director of Descartes – but it is worth emphasizing that this relationship was a deep and formative one: Gilson described Bérulle as one of the most important factors acting on Descartes's philosophical activity, and other commentators describe Bérulle's influence as 'the greatest influence on the spirit of Descartes [after God]'.[42]

Descartes

Descartes's Augustinianism has recently received substantial scholarly treatment in the works of Friedman and Menn, so I will not rehearse their findings here.[43] But it is worth noting that the phrase from which Sartre is thought to have taken the title of *Being and Nothingness* is found in the Fourth Meditation, in the context of Descartes's ontological, Bérullian-Augustinian account of human error:

> I am, as it were, an intermediary between God and nothingness, or between supreme being and non-being[44]: my nature is such that

[40]He was also first to use the French term *amour-propre* to translate Augustine's *amor sui* (Thweatt 1980: 79).

[41]'[J]e vous [dis] que le fonds de votre esprit est à Dieu ... Si vous contemplez votre origine sans regarder Dieu, vous ne trouverez que le néant, duquel nous sommes tous issus, et qui est notre unique et premier état hors la main de Dieu, et ainsi le néant nous appartient par le fond de la nature; le néant, dis-je, absolu, néant d'être' (Bérulle 1944: 1237).

[42]Gilson 1913: 161; Baillet, *Vie de Descartes*, p. 163, cited in Lavelle 1948: 4.

[43]See Friedman 2010 and Menn 2002.

[44]In French, 'entre le Dieu et le néant, c'est-à-dire placé de telle sorte entre le souverain être et le non-être' (Descartes 1981: 70; méditation quatrième).

insofar as I was created by the supreme being, there is nothing in me to enable me to go wrong or lead me astray; but insofar as I participate in nothingness or non-being, that is, in so far as I am not myself the supreme being and am lacking in countless respects, it is no wonder that I make mistakes. I understand, then, that error as such is not something real which depends on God, but merely a defect.[45]

For just as in Bérulle an Augustinian notion of nothingness is employed to explain our moral failings and experience of lack, in Descartes it is employed to epistemological ends.

In 1946 Sartre edited and wrote an introduction to a short selection of texts by Descartes. In the introduction, entitled 'Cartesian Freedom', Sartre notes that Descartes's philosophy attempted to reconcile a rationalist metaphysics with Christian theology: 'it translated, into the vocabulary of the time, this consciousness which had always known itself to be a pure nothingness'.[46] But Sartre thinks that Descartes misunderstood freedom: Descartes 'perpetually oscillates between identifying freedom with negativity or the negation of being … and the conception of free will as the simple negation of negation. In a word, he failed to conceive of negativity as productive.'[47] Cartesian freedom (as well as the *ego* of the *cogito*) is also discussed at length in *Being and Nothingness*.[48]

Jansenism

Bérulle's ontological anthropology also provided fertile soil for another work that was to shape French intellectual life and culture: Jansenism. Indeed, Bérulle's circle has been described as 'a first generation of Jansenists',[49] as Jansenists before Jansenism.

In 1640, Cornelius Jansen published a 1,300-page treatise in Latin entitled *Augustinus*. It was published very soon thereafter

[45]Descartes 1988: 99–100 (fourth meditation, 'On Truth and Falsity'). The *Meditations* were first published, in Latin, in 1641.
[46]Sartre 1946: 30.
[47]Sartre 1946: 38–9, translation mine. Descartes also figures heavily in *Being and Nothingness*.
[48]Sartre's references to Descartes in *BN* are too numerous to list in full: see, e.g., *BN* 48–9, 103–9, 275–6, 460–3, 602–3.
[49]Foreaux 2010: 225.

in French as *l'Augustin*. The work and the controversy which followed it left few cultural domains unaffected, but despite its political aspect the focus of what follows is on the content of Jansenist ideas and their legacy in the history of French philosophy.

Jansen's aim in writing *l'Augustin* was to defend the 'doctor of grace' (Augustine) against the 'Pelagianism' he perceived in the Jesuits of his day. Jansen argued that salvation could not be achieved without God's grace, and that such grace was irresistible. After the Fall, all good, all being was completely effaced from the human creature, and it is only by divine grace that we can desire or will the good. On Jansenism – sometimes referred to as the 'Catholic Calvinism' – humans are determined by the forces of sin and grace, with some consigned to the nothingness from which they were created and others to flourishing participation in God.

The Council of Trent (1545–63), by contrast, had affirmed the reality of free will alongside the necessity of divine grace. But on this subject Jansen was adamant, writing that 'after the Fall, man *lost his free will*; any good works are the gratuitous gift of God, and the predestination of the elect is an effect, not of the foreknowledge He has of our works, but of His pure will'.[50]

The people referred to as 'Jansenists' usually denied the existence of such an 'ism' – on their own view they were true Christians, the true interpreters of Saint Augustine. But despite their protests, Jansenism was to become a persistent problem for the Catholic Church. The Jansenist controversy spanned several decades in the seventeenth century, and by the eighteenth century, precisely what had happened in the seventeenth century was the subject of further disagreement. Whether or not it is always deserved, Jansenism gained a reputation for a pessimistic emphasis on human depravity and determinism. This pessimism was accompanied by an austere ethics, and a fear that divine grace – even once given – could be withdrawn.

We shall see in Chapter 3 that the extreme self-abnegation of Jansenism lent itself well to literary representations in both tragic and comic keys, with which Sartre was familiar.[51] But before leaving 'philosophy' for 'literature', however, it is worth noting some of

---

[50]Jansen, *l'Augustin*, cited in Louandre 1847: 714; emphasis added.
[51]See, e.g., *WL* 171.

the ways in which Jansenism's legacy shaped further philosophical developments in the seventeenth and eighteenth centuries.

Port-Royal

The generation after Descartes's *Meditations* (1641) and Jansen's *Augustinus* (1640) saw several influential developments in the history of philosophy with which we know Sartre was familiar. In 1662, for example, the first edition of Antoine Arnauld and Pierre Nicole's *Port-Royal Logique* was published.[52] The Abbey of Port-Royal was a centre of the Jansenist movement, and Arnauld and Nicole two of its leading lights. But they disagreed with the view of some Jansenists that reason was not efficacious, embracing Cartesian rationalism alongside the theology of Saint Augustine. However far we have fallen, they thought, reason was not entirely corrupt and could lead us closer to God. The nothingness of sin, on their view, had not entirely effaced the human ability to recognize truth.

Malebranche

In 1660 we find Malebranche – whom his contemporary Pierre Bayle called 'the premier philosopher of our age' – leaving the study of theology at the Sorbonne to enter the Oratory of France, the religious congregation founded by Bérulle. At the Oratory, he continued his theological studies and, in particular, dedicated himself to a thorough study of Augustine.

Malebranche, like Sartre, had his own cocktail moment of sorts, recorded by an early biographer – in a Paris bookstall in 1664 he is said to have found a copy of Descartes's *Treatise on Man*. As the biographer Father André put it, when Malebranche read the volume he became so 'ecstatic' that he had 'violent palpitations' and 'was obliged to leave his book at frequent intervals, and to interrupt his reading of it in order to breathe more easily'.[53]

The combined study of Descartes and Augustine resulted in a synthesis of their ideas, including Malebranche's view that we only see bodies through ideas in God and his occasionalist conclusion

---

[52]The Port-Royal ethics are mentioned by name in *WL* 116.
[53]André 1970: 11–12.

that God is the only causal agent. The resulting work, *The Search after Truth* (1674–75), focused on the source of human error and the method for avoiding it. It was this work which earned Malebranche his reputation among contemporaries. It also brought him criticism, however, and resulted in a dispute that was to become one of the major intellectual disagreements of the time. Arnauld (of the *Port-Royal Logique*) criticized Malebranche for denying central tenets of Scripture and tradition with respect to the doctrine of grace. Malebranche offered a reply in 1680 entitled *Treatise on Nature and Grace*, and Arnauld's riposte followed in 1683. *On True and False Ideas* did not attack *Nature and Grace* but rather Malebranche's earlier work on truth, for if his philosophical foundations could be undermined then the edifice he built on them would fall easily.[54]

What we find in the doctrines and disputes of seventeenth-century French philosophy, therefore, goes well beyond the textbook stories about Cartesian dualism, Malebranche's occasionalism or Port-Royal's semantic theory. The major contributions of these thinkers to questions of epistemology, metaphysics and ethics were accompanied by works treating *theological* questions about the doctrines of creation and Fall, nothingness and being, sin and grace, and the nature of the God who damns some and saves others.

Pascal

Sartre's early works demonstrate that he encountered these themes in another seventeenth-century 'inheritor of Augustine', Pascal. In Chapter 1 it was noted that Sartre's *Carnet Midy*, a notebook thought to have been compiled in 1924, includes eighteen aphorisms from the *Pensées* and the *Discours sur les passions de l'amour*.[55] In 1926 (that is to say, two years before Sartre's first, failed, attempt), Pascal appeared on the programme for the *agrégation de philosophie*, where the scope of the historical composition section was 'The Theory of Method in Descartes, Pascal, Malebranche, and the

---

[54]Sartre refers to Malebranche's *On True and False Ideas* in his *mémoire* (M 22ff.) and to Malebranche's 'vision in God' in *Being and Nothingness* (BN 273).

[55]Sartre filled this notebook (largely with notes and quotes) in the early 1920s. The Pléiade edition places the date around 1922–23, but Sicard, relying on Sartre's correspondence, suggests that it was completed in the early months of 1924 (see Sicard 1990: 439).

Port-Royal *Logique*'.[56] The edition of the *Pensées* current in Sartre's time was edited by the Sorbonne's Brunschvicg, under whose supervision Beauvoir wrote her *diplôme* on Leibniz in 1928.[57] In his 1924 book *La Génie de Pascal*, Brunschvicg interpreted Pascal as a practical rather than a rational genius, as a thinker interested in the particular and concrete.

Pascal's anthropology is clearly on the Jansenist end of the Augustinian spectrum. In fact, his view of the corruption of the human being after the Fall is so thoroughgoing that he has been called 'more Jansenist than the Jansenists themselves'.[58] As Thweatt writes, 'Among the Augustinian writers, whether clerical or lay, whether Jansenist or not, it is the Pascal of the *Pensées* who dominates his century.'[59]

The Pensées

Human beings, in nature, are '*un néant*' (a nothingness), alienated from understanding both the nothingness from which we issued or the infinite that engulfs us (L199/B72).[60] For Pascal original sin

---

[56]Schrift 2008: 457.

[57]Moriarty 2006: 127ff. includes a useful examination of Pascal's editors' views of the role played by the Fall in the *Pensées* (unfortunately Brunschvicg is not among those considered). It is also worth noting that Beauvoir's diaries from this period also include reflections on Pascal. In the entry dated 21 May 1927, in which Beauvoir writes that 'there is only one problem and one that has no solution … It is the one formulated by Pascal … I would want to believe in something – to meet with total exigency – to justify my life. In short, I would want God' (Beauvoir 2006: 262).

[58]Geberon (quoted by Goldmann 1964: 54). See Blondel's 1923 'Le jansénisme et l'anti-jansénisme de Pascal', in the *Revue métaphysique et de morale*, for a contemporary treatment of the question.

[59]Thweatt 1980: 88. Because the *Pensées* were left unfinished and published posthumously, different editions of the *Pensées* have proliferated, as have debates concerning the best way to interpret it. Lafuma respects the provisional classification suggested by the order of MS copies, whereas Brunschvicg rearranged the fragments thematically, rejecting the possibility of any 'true' ordering (see Van Den Abbeele 1994). In the following references to the *Pensées* I have provided the Lafuma/Brunschvicg fragment numbers; the former because Lafuma's edition is still widely respected, and the latter because it was the edition prevalent in Sartre's time (and, indeed, cited in the *Carnet Midy*).

[60]The *Pensées* include 32 uses of *néant* or *anéantir* in total, and we will see the psychological importance of nothingness for 'diversion' in what follows. See L199/B72: 'Toutes choses sont sorties du néant, et portées jusqu'à l'infini.'

is folly in human eyes, but 'though its transmission is the mystery furthest from our understanding' it is something 'without which we can have no understanding of ourselves' (L131/B434).

This is because, on Pascal's view, the post-lapsarian person is subject to a three-fold concupiscence: *volupté*, *curiosité* and *autorité*. These three fallen desires – to satisfy the desires of the flesh, to know (in order to differentiate oneself from and dominate others), and to have authority (or power) over others – guide our action, but we hide them from our conscious attention by self-deception and *divertissement*, diversions that distract us from the pain of our lonely condition.

> All men naturally hate each other. We have used concupiscence as best we can to make it serve the common good, but this is only pretence and a false image of true charity, because at bottom it is only hate. We have created and drawn from concupiscence admirable rules of government, morality, and justice, but, at root, this evil root of man, this *figmentum malum*, is only covered up; not pulled up.[61]

Sartre cites Pascal on diversion – the 'covering up' of our condition – in several of his works.[62] But Pascal's pessimism was not restricted to ethics, however: epistemologically, too, he had little faith in what mere reason could accomplish. Goldmann argues that Pascal's 'most urgent and essential task lay in proving against the Cartesians that human reason was limited and inadequate',[63] that there are limitations which mathematics and science 'cannot escape when they try to deal with man'.[64] It is in this way that Sartre seems to have read him (at the stage of the *mémoire*) as an expositor of the 'interior spaces' of the human person. On Pascal's view, knowledge (*savoir*) of ourselves and God is impossible: one can only see these things for what they are with the eyes of faith. On Pascal's view it is not *reason* that 'senses' God but rather the heart.[65] This is the essence of faith: 'one can recognize that there is a God without

---

[61]L210–211/B451.
[62]See, e.g., *NM* 258, *BN* 583, *WD* 250–1 and *WL* 139 et passim.
[63]See Goldmann 1964: 221.
[64]Goldmann 1964: 242.
[65]L424/B278.

knowing that there is' ('on peut bien connaître qu'il y a un Dieu sans savoir ce qu'il est').[66]

As we have seen already, this Pascalian scepticism about reason informed Sartre's discussion of the imagination in the *mémoire*. To repeat a phrase already discussed above, Sartre wrote that 'Pascal, well before Kant, had denounced' the 'poverty' of proofs such as the teleological argument because arguments alone do not transform the imagination. 'Even for the Christian', Sartre writes, 'the existence of the world cannot directly suffice to prove God' (*M* 53).

How pessimistically to read Pascal – whose God hides himself from searching human eyes and whose reason has little confidence in its own deliverances – was a question much debated by subsequent interpreters. In one of Pascal's last surviving works, the *Ecrit sur la signature du Formulaire* (1661), he went so far as to say that to condemn Jansen was to condemn Augustine. But the fragmentary form and posthumous publication of the *Pensées* left a variety of interpretations open. We consider Pascal further in the next chapter, but before concluding the philosophical side of our seventeenth-century tour there is one further stop.

Quietism

In the strict sense of the term quietism was developed in the writings of Molinos, whose sixty-eight propositions were condemned by Pope Innocent XI in 1687. The French quietist controversy with which we know Sartre was familiar,[67] however, involved Madame Guyon and Fénelon – and Fénelon's subsequent debate with Bossuet. Both men held positions of power in Louis XIV's court, where theological disagreements could have grave professional repercussions. Fénelon advanced a mystical theology, a love-mysticism on which the soul can be unified to God, such that it no longer has any voluntary desire on its own behalf *except* in cases where it does not faithfully communicate with grace. The publication in which he advanced these views, the *Explication de Maximes des Saints*, contained doctrines suggested by Molinos, but it was decidedly less extreme (and for that reason is sometimes called semiquietism).

The controversy between Fénelon and Bossuet arose from a difference opinion as to the orthodoxy of Madame Guyon's ideas.

---

[66]L418/B233.
[67]From discussions in *WL* (75 et passim).

When Madame de Maintenon (the second wife of Louis XIV) questioned the orthodoxy of Madame Guyon's opinions, an ecclesiastical commission was appointed to assess the matter. One of the assessors was Bossuet, who concluded that Madame Guyon's ideas were too close to the condemned views of Molinos. The commission published thirty-four articles (the *Articles d'Issy*) in which Madame Guyon's ideas were condemned with an official statement on the Catholic view of prayer. Bossuet himself then proceeded to publish another work in which he expanded on his explanation of the articles at greater length. Fénelon disagreed with him, and published his own interpretation of the *Articles d'Issy* in the *Explication des Maximes des Saints*. This attracted the attention of the Sun King, who reproached Bossuet for not warning him that his grandsons' tutor (Fénelon) had such unorthodox views. Throughout 1697–99 Bossuet and Fénelon argued – in personal letters and public pamphlets – until the Inquisition condemned Fénelon's *Maximes* on 12 March 1699.

We know Sartre was familiar with this dispute because Delacroix's book on mysticism (which he cites in his *mémoire*) dedicates several chapters to Madame Guyon and Fénelon and because he writes about it in *What Is Literature?*

> In the seventeenth century convictions were unshakeable; the religious ideology went hand in hand with a political ideology which the temporal itself secreted: no one publicly questioned the existence of God or the divine right of kings.... As the two historical facts which it constantly pondered – original sin and redemption – belonged to a remote past.... God was too perfect to change. (*WL* 67)

Like many of his seventeenth-century fellows, Fénelon was indebted to the conceptual scheme of Bérullian Augustinianism. In particular, Leduc-Lafayette highlights that Fénelon inherited the conceptual scheme of 'creaturely dependence'; the 'first nothingness', which is creation; and also 'le néant où Adam nous met par le péché' ('the nothingness where Adam placed us by his sin').[68] His 'philosophical' works also engage in the theological questions that preoccupied

---

[68]Leduc-Lafayette 1996b: 98 (citing Bérulle, *Opuscules de Piété*, Paris: Aubier, 1944, CXXXVI).

his day. Fénelon's *Treatise on the Existence of God*, for example, is a work framed in – and questioning – Cartesian doubt. Fénelon's scepticism goes even further than Descartes's, however: the *ego cogito* cannot, of its own power, pull itself out of nothingness. Only the Plenitude of Being can call something out of nothing.[69] On Fénelon's anthropology, though we have 'come out of' (*sorti du*) nothingness, we are always on the verge of falling back into it (*prêt à y retomber*).[70]

As created beings, humans are entirely dependent on their Creator, for 'that which has no being except by another cannot keep it by itself'.[71] Human existence is accidental, contingent.[72] Moreover, the notion of time plays an important role, with Fénelon calling it 'the change of created being'; 'the negation of a very real and supremely positive thing that is the permanence of being'. Unlike God, human beings' temporal existence is constantly subject to change and what Fénelon calls *la défaillance de l'être*.[73] Thus we read,

> I am not, O my God, what is; alas, I am almost what is not. I see myself as an incomprehensible intermediate between nothingness and being. I am the one who has been; I am the one who will be; I am the one who is no longer what he has been; I am the one who is not yet what he will be; and, in this in-between that I am, something unknowable that cannot be held in itself, that has no consistency, that flows away like water; something unknowable that I cannot seize, that flees from my hands, that is no longer as soon as I wish to grasp or perceive it; something unknowable that finishes at the very instant in which it begins; so that I can never at any moment find myself stable and present to myself, so as to say simply that I am. Thus my duration is nothing but a perpetual failure/lack [défaillance] of being.[74]

[69]Fénelon 1880: 112. For the Plenitude of Being, see also p. 174. Fénelon is self-avowedly Augustinian, as can be seen here and in his use of privation theory (1880: 120).
[70]1880: 121.
[71]1880: 123. ('ce qui n'a l'être que par autrui ne peut le garder par soi-même')
[72]1880: 132.
[73]1880: 176.
[74]1880: 180.

For Fénelon, 'everything which is not truly being is nothingness',[75] and it is only by the gift of God that we are kept in being.[76] This gift is described by Fénelon (following earlier French mystics) as a *rapport*, a link or relationship – between the Creator and the created.[77]

It is hardly surprising that Sartre read and cited Fénelon given his historical and literary significance.[78] Donneau writes that, by the time of the recently published 'Liberté – Égalité' (a manuscript from 1951), Sartre was intimately familiar with seventeenth-century theological debates, citing Molinos, Jansen and others directly: 'He had to familiarize himself with their polemical exchanges, which were so closely linked to the development of the classical literature he studied.'[79] But even in earlier works such as *What Is Literature?* (1948) Sartre explicitly mentions 'Jansenist ideology' (*WL* 115).

By now it should be clear to the reader that these debates about freedom and sin were not constrained to the halls of the theological academy. They were to have far-reaching implications for French politics and literature, shaping the cultural life of the nation in significant ways over subsequent centuries. In de Maistre's *Considerations on France*, for example, a famous royalist work published in the half-century after the French Revolution, we read that human beings 'act at the same time voluntarily and necessarily', simultaneously acting as they will and enacting divine providence.[80] This position was invoked in order to draw out some convenient entailments: for example, that through the will of the revolutionaries, the Revolution was God's means of punishing sin: 'Never had the divinity shown itself so clearly in any human event. If it employs the vilest instruments, it is a case of punishing in order to regenerate.'[81]

---

[75]1880: 140. (Tout ce qui n'est point réellement l'être est le néant.)

[76]1880: 76. Fénelon, too, invokes an idea of continual creation (un don perpétuel) to solve the problem of *durée*, invoking the imagery of manna from heaven to illustrate the way in which future needs will be met: 'Le jour de demain aura soin de lui-même. Celui qui nourrit aujourd'hui est le même qui nourrira demain. On reverra la manne tomber du ciel dans le désert, plutôt que de laisser les enfants de Dieu sans nourriture.' (Fénelon: Correspondance, 11 vols. Paris 1827/1829, vol. 6, p. 329.)

[77]1880: 183.

[78]See *WL* 75.

[79]Donneau 2010: 62.

[80]de Maistre 1838: 2.

[81]de Maistre 1838: 21.

Conclusion

We have seen now that during Sartre's studies in the 1920s, with Baruzi and Delacroix, Sartre was exposed to philosophies of lived experience that were *theological* in their commitments and articulation. These philosophies (largely inspired by Augustine) often assigned nothingness a prominent explanatory role in their epistemologies and anthropologies. In the theological debates of seventeenth-century France, the question of the extent to which we are free was closely related to the question of whether, and how far, we tend to nothingness. And the question about the extent to which we tend to nothingness raises further questions about creation, the goodness of God and the possibility of being held responsible for worlds and selves which are not of our choosing.

This chapter's aim was to set out some of the ways in which Sartre encountered *theology* in his early philosophical formation. It drew on textual and historical evidence from Sartre's readings of youth and the *mémoire* in order to show that Sartre's exposure to methodological attention to lived experience – and to Husserl – predates the famous conversation with Aron, and that Sartre's early work drew on publications by and about mystical theologians in ways that have not been adequately acknowledged or investigated. The religious infighting brought about by the seventeenth-century debates concerning the correct interpretation of Augustine did not escape Sartre's attention. Nor did he think it interesting merely as a piece of intellectual history.

Several years later, in the *War Diaries*, there is a passage in which Sartre assigns Christianity a singular place in the understanding of nothingness:

> It is perhaps Christianity which has come closest to this necessary recognition, by showing the human soul as 'animated' by lack of God; and the writings of the mystics abound in striking descriptions of this inner nothingness there is within the heart of man. Yet it must be noted that most Christian thinkers, led astray by their monist conception of being as an *in-itself*, have confused – like Heidegger, moreover – the existential nothingness of human consciousness with its finitude. Now finitude, being an external limit of being, cannot be at the root of lack, which is found at the very heart of consciousness.... what is quite apparent is that

desire will never be explained without one having recourse to an existential lack. (*WD* 230)

The cocktail story – if not a cock-and-bull story – is not the whole truth.

3

Sartre's theological formation: In literature

We have seen in Chapters 1 and 2 that Sartre's biographical and philosophical formation included theological elements. In this final 'formation' chapter, we consider the literary fate of the 'quarrel of Augustinianisms' and, in particular, the way literary representations of sin and grace, and damnation and salvation, feature in the literary works Sartre studied – classical and contemporary.

Variations on these themes flowed from many French pens in the period of French classicism, whether the ink was coloured with Jansenist piety (in the case of Pascal, Corneille or Racine), or laced with sarcasm (in the case of Voltaire). But their legacy was not confined to the century that French literary scholars have dubbed 'the century of Augustine'. As Sartre himself wrote in *What Is Literature?*, 'The casuistry of the Jesuits, the etiquette of the Précieuses, the portrait game, the ethics of Nicole, and the religious conception of the passions are at the origin of a hundred other works' (*WL* 71). In addition to what Sellier has called the 'diffuse Augustinianism' of French literature after the seventeenth century,[1] Sartre's more immediate context – the 1920s – saw a flurry of publications of novels treating explicitly theological themes.

Given the likelihood that readers may approach this book with expertise in philosophy and/or theology rather than French literature, this chapter is therefore composed of two parts: the first introduces some of the seventeenth-century French writers who gave literary expression to the Augustinian preoccupations we met in

[1]Sellier 2000, v. 2: 74.

Chapter 2. The second looks at Sartre's more immediate literary context, the 1920s, in which we find a resurgence of Catholic novels treating similar preoccupations concerning freedom and sin, love and grace. This period saw the publication of 'a cluster of aesthetic masterpieces' that sought to redress 'the great sin of the modern world',[2] namely, not believing in sin.

The century of Augustine

In an essay on Jansenism and literature, Mesnard suggests that the magnitude of Jansenism's contribution to French literature was so great that 'one can even wonder if its destiny wasn't literary, above all'.[3] Sellier, similarly, writes that literature and theology have 'never known a similar osmosis'.[4] Jansenism's 'literary destiny' took shape in several genres. In this section we explore some of the literary expressions the 'century of Augustine' offered:[5] in the works of the *moralistes* Pascal and La Rochefoucauld, and the playwrights Racine, Corneille and Molière.

Les moralistes

We know Sartre was familiar with *les moralistes*.[6] The French *'moraliste'* is not to be confused with the English 'moralist'. The former is often used to describe religious writers, 'bad' philosophers or a particular group of seventeenth-century authors (and the extent to which these categories include or exclude each other is contested). Scholars dispute which literary works can rightly be

---

[2]O'Connell 1994: 855.

[3]Mesnard 1992: 'On peut se même demander si sa destinée n'a pas été surtout littéraire.'

[4]Sellier 2000, v. 2: 30. NB Sellier prefers 'Port-Royal' or 'le groupe de Port Royal' over Jansenisme (2000: 72).

[5]Those wishing for a book-length treatment on Jansenism and literature should see Sellier 2002.

[6]Sartre refers to *les moralistes* as a group and by name in many of his works: In *TE* 17, for example, he refers to La Rochefoucauld and *les moralistes* because he is not content to have a 'purely psychological theory' that rids the presence of the *me* from consciousness. In the *WD*, Sartre describes himself as 'affected by moralism, and … moralism often has its source in religion' (*WD* 72).

called 'moralist': 'By some accounts, every French classical author is a moralist.'[7] But for our purposes 'moralism' will be defined as a seventeenth-century French literary trend which articulated a critique of humanity rooted in Montaigne's humanism, the Jansenist revival of Augustine and the legacy of Descartes.

Chapter 2 introduced themes from Pascal's *Pensées* (published posthumously in 1670 and compiled before his death in 1662), which, due to its anthropological pessimism as well as its aphoristic form, is often classified in this genre. In France he is equally famous for his *Lettres provinciales* (*Provincial Letters*), which were published pseudonymously during 1656 and 1657 in the midst of the formulary controversy between the Jansenists and the Jesuits. This controversy concerned the extent to which we are free or determined by sin or grace – and Pascal wrote to defend Arnauld against charges of heresy.

The letters employ wry wit to undermine the Jesuits' authority, in particular, on account of their casuistry (a rhetorical method often used by Jesuit theologians) and moral laxity. The letters were written as reports from a Parisian to a friend in the country, which kept the provincial reader informed of the moral and theological issues that were being debated in the capital. Their satirical style was such that, quite apart from its religious content, it was a popular literary work – in its own day and for subsequent generations. What, Sartre asks in *What Is Literature?*, could be more boring 'than the idea of attacking the Jesuits? Yet out of this Pascal made his *Provincial Letters*' (WL 16).

The *Provinciales* were also subsumed into the French literary canon, and above all, as Kolakowski notes, 'a part of the libertine-liberal-anti-clerical-Voltairian canon. It functioned as a pamphlet that unmasked "Jesuit hypocrisy" and, by extension, the hypocrisy of the Catholic clergy and, by a further extension, the hypocrisy of the Christian religion.'[8] Pascal's literary influence was widespread: Nietzsche wrote that 'Pascal's blood flows in my veins',[9] and Stendhal once confided that 'when I read Pascal, I feel that I reread myself'.[10]

---

[7]Van Den Abbeele 1994: 327.
[8]Kolakowski 1998: 63.
[9]Friedrich Nietzsche, *Gesammelte Werke* (Munich: Musarion Verlag, 1922–29), 21:89, cited in Melzer 1986: 1.
[10]'Quand je lis Pascal, il semble que je me relis. Je crois que c'est celui de tous les écrivains à qui je ressemble le plus par l'âme.' (Stendhal, *Pensées*, cited in Victor Del

The next decade saw the publication of a *locus classicus* of French moralism: la Rochefoucauld's *Réflexions ou sentences et maximes morales* (1665), usually referred to by its short title, *Maximes*. The *Maximes* contain several numbered reflections on human nature, covering a broad range of topics including pride and self-love, the passions, emotions, sincerity, love and politics. For example, we read that

> Self-Love is the love of a man's own self, and of everything else, for his own sake. It makes people idolaters to themselves, and tyrants to all the world besides.[11]

Both Pascal and La Rochefoucauld are sceptical about the human person's ability to know him or herself. Self-love – the *moraliste* rendering of Augustine's concupiscence, which Bérulle first translated as *amour-propre*, is 'the most celebrated moralist concept'.[12] Self-love distorts the human person's view of the world and his or her place in it. As Van Den Abbeele writes, in La Rochefoucauld's hands 'it becomes, more than the sin of denying God the love owed him, the autonomy of a fundamental narcissism underlying and motivating the near totality of human behavior'.[13] It is 'more ingenious than the most ingenious man in the world', 'the greatest flatterer',[14] making us so accustomed to wearing disguises 'before others that we finally appear disguised before ourselves'.[15] La Rochefoucauld was steeped in Augustine, and indeed has been described as 'more truly Augustinian than Pascal'.[16] We have already seen that Sartre was familiar with Pascal's writings. He also engaged directly with La Rochefoucauld, discussing the latter's treatment of *amour-propre* in *The Transcendence of the Ego* (*TE* 17), and referring to him in *What Is Literature?*, where we read that

Litto, *La vie intellectuelle de Stendhal: genèse et évolution de ses idées (1802–1821)*, Geneva: Slatkine, 1997, p. 177).
[11]La Rochefoucauld 1664: p. 83 (this maxim was cut after the first edition).
[12]Van Den Abbeele 1994: 331.
[13]Van Den Abbeele 1994: 332.
[14]La Rochefoucauld 1664: maxims IV and II (p. 7).
[15]La Rochefoucauld 1664: maxim CXXIII (p. 193).
[16]Thweatt 1980: 99. Sellier (2000, v.2: 74) notes that La Rochefoucauld was 'nourished on *The City of God*' and took for his themes 'the corruption of fallen man and *amour de soi*, the principle of the earthly city'.

La Rochefoucauld borrows the form and the content of his maxims from the diversions of the salons … Society is thoroughly delighted at seeing itself mirrored in them because it recognizes the notions it has about itself; it does not ask to be shown what it is, but it asks rather for a reflection of what it thinks it is (*WL* 71).

Theatre

Theological dramas between Jesuits and Jansenists were also to be played out on stage (despite the Jansenists' disdain for worldly diversions). As we saw in Chapter 2, the Abbey of Port-Royal was the centre of Jansenist thought in the seventeenth century. Arnauld was there, and two of his sisters were nuns at the convent. The abbey had several projects, one of which was the foundation of the Little Schools of Port-Royal, which had a very famous literary pupil: Jean Racine.

Goldmann has argued that all of Racine's plays are Jansenist tragedies.[17] They are certainly replete with divided selves, forbidden loves and despair. On Goldmann's reading, Racine's theatre offers a 'tragic vision' of God, the world and man. Jansenist readings of *Phèdre* (first staged in 1677) have a long provenance – and present the play's protagonist as someone from whom grace has been withdrawn. In her own words,

> The gods are witness, they who in my breast
> Have lit the fire fatal to all my line
> Those gods whose cruel glory it has been
> To lead astray a feeble mortal's heart. (II.5.679–82)

Sartre himself makes asides that support the tragic reading of Racine, demonstrating his knowledge of both this literature and the theological debates of its context. In *Saint Genet* Sartre writes that 'Racine was not wrong when he said that "the passions are presented before your eyes only to show all the disorder of which they are the cause"' (*G* 73).

---

[17]Goldmann 1964: 317, 376 ff.

In the same work Sartre explicitly discusses questions of election and grace in a work of Racine's contemporary and rival, Corneille. Grace is here described by Sartre as 'a kind of luck' by which 'one recognizes merit and predestination'. For (in Corneille's words)

> Heaven, which knows better than we what we are,
> Measures its favours by men's merit
> And you would have had the benefit of such aid
> Had it been able to find in you the virtues it found in him.
> These are graces from on high, rare and singular,
> Which do not descend for vulgar souls.[18]

Again questions of sin and grace recur, as does the helplessness of humanity in the face of a Jansenist God. The Jansenist subject is radically unfree – and Racine's art, Sartre wrote, had to be invented on this basis (*WL* 115). The psychology of Corneille and Pascal, on Sartre's reading, is 'a cathartic appeal to freedom' (*WL* 89).

The third great playwright of the seventeenth-century French triumvirate, Molière, also satirized the religious men of his day. Although opinion diverges as to whether the target of his famous *La Tartuffe* was the Jesuits (or at least, the Jesuits of polemical caricature), Jansenists or the lesser-known Compagnie du Saint-Sacrament, each reading has been made.[19] Molière provides an interesting case study in 'diffuse Augustinianism'. Although he was not devout himself, and most scholars resist reading a Jansenist motif in his work,[20] he nevertheless seems to have borrowed extensively from Pascal, including direct phrases from the *Lettres Provinciales*.[21]

Le siècle des lumières

The French appetite for religious satire did not wane with the close of the seventeenth century. In the eighteenth Voltaire turned his pen

---

[18]Cited in *G* 90.
[19]See Calder 2002: 154 ff.
[20]Though such a reading has been made by Jasinski (see *Molière et le Misanthrope*, Paris: Nizet, 1951).
[21]See Gaines 2002: 359.

to it, making Jansenists in general and Pascal in particular the subject of his mockery. His father and brother were both Jansenist, but he certainly held no punches on their accounts. Jansenists appear in prose and verse, in 'Le Mondain' (or 'Apologie du luxe' (1736)), *Candide* and other works.

Perhaps most famously, Voltaire's 25th *Lettre philosophique* (also known by the name 'l'Anti-Pascal') offers to take 'the part of humanity against this sublime misanthrope'. This is hardly the best of all possible worlds, Voltaire admits, but neither is it as bad as M. Pascal would have us believe. In the letter he offers a selection from Pascal's *Pensées*, with commentary. The emphasis on sin is scorned, and the reasoning of the wager waved aside as 'good for nothing but making atheists'. Voltaire admits to the misanthrope that 'I have an interest, without a doubt, in there being a God; but in your system God has only come for a few people; if the small number of the elect is so frightful; if I can never do anything at all by myself, tell me, I beg you, what interest do I have in believing you?'[22]

Alongside the emergence of deism, Augustinian threads in French literature can be traced throughout the eighteenth and nineteenth centuries, where the question of human freedom and theological determinism is explored in particular lives. From the pen of Voltaire, whom Sartre regarded as 'the symbol of the engaged intellectual',[23] the absurdity of such determinism is displayed not only by abstract argument but by concrete example.

The theological 'return' in early twentieth-century literature

Around 1880 several spheres of French public life – literary, political and economic – underwent a change. Into an intellectual climate dominated by naturalism and positivism, the works of writers like Paul Verlaine, J. K. Huysmans, Léon Bloy, Paul Claudel and André Gide (among others) began to present Christian visions of life. One may dispute how orthodox the Christianity or how successful

[22]Voltaire 1819: 276.
[23]Noudelmann and Philippe 2013: 517.

the literature, but novelistic depictions of Christian points of view saw a resurgence this period, both by native French authors and in works newly translated from Russian. One theme they shared in common was interiority: an emphasis on the inner life and inner conflicts lived in concrete human experience.

For example, Huysmans's 1884 novel *À rebours* is widely noted literarily for its stylistic departure from naturalism to symbolism, but its focus on the inner life of its principal character, Des Esseintes, led Bloy to describe its author as capable of the most 'exalted mysticism'.[24] Interest in religious experience pervades several of Huysmans's novels, in which we find Kabbalists and Rosicrucians, black masses and Satanism alongside priests who profess a desperate desire for belief. In the last line of *À rebours* the protagonist likens his return to society to the return of a doubter to belief: 'O Lord, pity the Christian who doubts, the sceptic who would believe, the convict of life embarking alone in the night, under a sky no longer illumined by the consoling beacons of ancient faith.'[25]

In the late 1880s the translated works of Tolstoy and Dostoevsky also began to appear in French. The Russian novelists' religious dimensions and their rich depictions of interiority were widely noted. Sartre certainly read Dostoevsky and made reference to him in works as early as the *Écrits de Jeunesse*, where he mentions discussing Dostoevsky with his grandmother (*EJ* 55). In the *War Diaries* there is a discussion of Dostoevsky in which Sartre questions the God's right to 'poke his nose in' to the question of morality (*WD* 108), citing the line 'If God does not exist, all is permitted'. In the same work we also find references to Dostoevsky's *The House of the Dead* (*WD* 161), and in *Being and Nothingness* Sartre makes further references to Dostoevsky vis-à-vis death (*BN* 590ff) and freedom (*BN* 498 and 497).

As Simon writes, the close of the nineteenth century saw a rupture with the 'primacy of positivity'. Philosophers and novelists contended that there was a domain that escaped the grasp of rational analysis and logical expression. In philosophy, Bergson's *Time and Free Will* (*Essai sur les donées immédiates de la conscience*) (1889) furnished an example of a rigorous analysis in which the reader is

---

[24]Cited in Baldick 2006: 135.
[25]Huysmans 2004. Five paragraphs earlier the protagonist considers an aphorism of Pascal.

logically guided to recognize that there is an 'au-dela de la logique' (a *beyond* logic), an explanatory or experiential fissure in the dominant methodology.

'By natural consequence', Simon writes, in this fissure themes that were 'colored by Christianity' appeared.[26] Untempered rationalism was no longer the only viable intellectual option, and in the first twenty years of the twentieth century there was a resurgence of traditionalism in literature. As Simon writes, 'a psychology of sin and grace' formed the heart of many novels. Some authors expressed explicitly religious intent. Paul Bourget, for example, described his novels as 'experimental apologetics'. His method was to show that 'one converts out of a negation, not purely out of a purely expectant attitude ... It would be easy for me to show that, if there is a development of thought, there is not a contradiction'.[27] Charles Péguy, writing a few years later, would also explain his own religious evolution as a similar process.

Many of Bourget's prominent novels of this period, *L'Etape* (1903), *Un Divorce* (1904), *L'Émigré* (1907) and *Le Démon de midi* (1914), accentuate the lived experience of their characters' moral development. As such, they have sometimes been classified as *romans à thèse* – novels intended to communicate moral messages. The genre has been called a descendant of the ancient apologia. Bourget's experimental apologetics were explicitly intended to establish a series of observations on human life – but with everything 'as if' Christianity were true – in order to provoke thought on behalf of the reader. We can see similar provocations in Péguy's poem *d'Eve*, for example, which provokes its reader to ask whether the worlds of grace and nature are far apart after all:

Car le surnaturel est lui-même charnel
Et l'arbre de la grâce est raciné profond
Et plonge dans le sol et cherche jusqu'au fond
Et l'arbre de la race est lui-même éternel.

Et l'éternité même est dans le temporel
Et l'arbre de la grâce est raciné profond
Et plonge dans le sol et touche jusqu'au fond
Et le temps est lui-même un temps intemporel.

[26]Simon 1957: 15.
[27]Cited in Simon 1957: 44; from a preface published in 1899.

Et l'arbre de la grâce et l'arbre de nature
Ont lié leurs deux troncs de nœuds si solennels,
Ils ont tant confondu leurs destins fraternels
Que c'est la même essence et la même stature.[28]

Naturally, novels, plays and poems may not instruct their readers in the manner the authors intended. Doctrines are not always graceful skeletons on which to flesh out a good story, and the religious conscience can seem moralizing and off-putting rather than loving and winsome. But the themes such novels treated raised different answers from both literary critical and theological points of view.

Philosophical questions about the role of reason in faith also appear in works of this period. Barrès defines the Intellectual as the Devil (*l'Adversaire*), who attempts to persuade others that 'society must be founded on logic, who ignores that it rests in fact on necessities anterior and maybe even superior to individual reason'.[29] He is anti-Cartesian, anti-Kantian and anti-humanist – which he shares in common with the 'Catholic writers' (as Sartre called them) of the 1920s and 1930s: François Mauriac, Georges Bernanos and Paul Claudel. Barrès was influential in Mauriac's earliest successes – he praised Mauriac's early collection of poetry, *Les Mains jointes* (1909), as the work of an up-and-coming talent. Mauriac did not disappoint Barrès's predictions: he won a Nobel Prize for literature in 1952. But he is best known for several novels published within the decade from 1922 to 1932. Taken together with the works of Bernanos and Claudel, I shall give this period a mnemonic title: the decade of sin.

The decade of sin

In 1920 Joan of Arc was canonized. But was she a sinner? She was burned at the stake as a heretic in 1431, though rehabilitated in 1456 and beatified in 1909. As O'Connell has written, in the period

---

[28]Péguy, *Eve*, C 1041.
[29]Barrès 1902: 44. In *Plaidoyer pour les intellectuels* Sartre traces the origins of the term 'intellectual' to the Dreyfus affair (and, implicitly, Barrès).

from the interwar years through the German Occupation, Joan of Arc was a national 'emblem of [a] recurring sense of sin':

> The Vichy regime, seeking a symbol to concretize France's guilt and shame for its abysmal defeat in 1940, attempted to substitute her feast day (11 May) for 14 July and 11 November as the official holiday. Joan's self-sacrifice for the welfare of the collectivity was presented as a necessary corrective to what was officially held to be France's pre-war decadence exemplified in an exaggerated importance accorded to the individual over the group. The fact that Joan was burned on French soil under the English occupation played into the hands of those who saw in Albion the most perfidious of false friends.[30]

National sin was not the only kind that preoccupied the French public, however. As has already been mentioned, diverse sins (and more or less explicit hamartiologies) also appeared on the pages of their novels.

Mauriac

Mauriac was raised a Jansenist and saw sin in everything, explicitly seeking to give artistic expression to the lived tensions of the Jansenist point of view.[31] Like Pascal and Racine, who thought that individuals must attempt to earn grace even though their efforts had no effect on their damnation or salvation, Mauriac's works offer characters tormented by sinful temptations and uncertainty about love:

> Am I loved? Do I love?
> Did I love? I don't know.
> I know that I am never weary
> Of feeling tenderness for myself.[32]

---

[30]O'Connell 1994: 856.
[31]In addition to novels and poetry he wrote biographies of both Racine (1927) Pascal (1931).
[32]These lines, from Mauriac's 'L'étudiant–Départ II' (from *Les mains jointes*) are cited in Beauvoir's student journals from 6 August 1926 (see Beauvoir 2006: 54).

Consequently, Mauriac repeatedly received criticism from other Catholics for depicting lives in which God seemed cruelly absent.[33]

In *Le Baiser au lépreux* (1922) Jean Péloueyre is the eponymous 'leper', a man who reads Nietzsche and concludes that he is a slave rather than a master. He follows along with his family's wishes for him to marry a woman who will bring them financial gain. The marriage coincides with the discovery that he feels revulsion toward his own body. Péloueyre attempts to escape this feeling by leaving his wife, Noémi, in order to go to Paris to work on research. Shortly after he returns he dies of tuberculosis, after which Noémi plays the dutiful spouse. Mauriac's epilogue presents her, dressed in black, several years later. Is she a saint? The answer to the question depends on whether one considers sainthood to be a matter of form or of substance.

The psychological dramas Mauriac's characters undergo are explicitly theological – they concern the interior duel between grace and sin. But it must be understood here that 'sin' does not signify the transgression of a divine law but rather a refusal of the creative and redemptive God. Mauriac's sin is that of the moralists and mystics; sin is a failure (*defaillance*) of love. But this raises a theological problem: for if sin is a failure of love, those furthest from God are not necessarily those most *guilty*. This type of Christian novel depicts a God whose justice is questionable: it can portray the damnation of the sinner whose condition is inescapable and whose thirst for love is never gratified.

The theme of failure to communicate between spouses also appears in *Thèrese Desqueyroux* (1927) and *Le Noeud de vipères* (1932). In the former, Thèrese seems determined to do evil, although she cannot explain why: her motives only make sense on a determinist anthropology. And in *Le Noeud de vipères* we read about grace breaking into the hardened soul of its protagonist, Louis. The novel takes the form of a letter written by an elderly man after a lifetime of hatred for his family. His adult children are waiting for him to die so they can receive their inheritance, and initially the letter is intended as a spiteful evening of the score. However, in the process of his writing the letter, grace breaks in. After his death, his

---

[33]Sartre himself defined Mauriac's sin as 'the place from which God is absent' (*WL* 138).

children and grandchildren find the letter and disagree about how to interpret it, but in Mauriac's Jansenist worldview, what matters is not such external effects but rather that grace transformed Louis's inner reality. But whether damned like Thèrese or graced like Louis, these characters are not *free* to choose their destinies: that pleasure is God's.

Bernanos

Bernanos (1888–1948) was married to a direct descendant of Joan of Arc's brother, and held to a medieval view of chivalry – to a life dedicated to others. In 1934 he published a biography of Joan (*Jeanne, relapse et sainte*) in which he defended this view. Unlike Mauriac, Bernanos's novels portray the devil as an active agent in human life.

Bernanos's protagonists are often priests – the battleground of their souls made a good setting for exploring the boundaries of good and evil. In his early novels – *Under the Star of Satan* (1927), *Joy* (1927), *A Crime* (1935) – he attempted to show that evil is not just a psychological phenomenon. *The Diary of a Country Priest* (1936) has been ranked among the 'half-dozen most powerful French novels of the twentieth century'.[34] The unnamed young *curé*, recently ordained, finds himself in a flock that care only for the typical currencies of status and propriety: money, power and pleasure. The tale that unfolds involves death, guilt and terminal illness, but the message that Bernanos sought to convey (through the words of the dying *curé*) is that all is grace ('Tout est grâce') if one converts to hope. But if one does not, the consequences of the Fall are such that we can no longer perceive anything in us or outside of us except under the form of boredom, anguish and despair. The novel is replete with Pascalian and Kierkegaardian themes: the young *curé* considers his parish to be suffering from 'the fermentation of a Christianity in decay'.[35] (And lest Bernanos's description should sound too optimistic, it should be noted that the composition of his Christianity has been described as 99 per cent doubt at 1 per cent hope.[36])

[34]See O'Connell 1994: 858.
[35]Bernanos 1937: 11.
[36]Vuilleumier 2005: 69.

Claudel

To Bernanos's 'tout est grâce', Claudel's reply would be *etiam pec-cata* – 'even our sins!', in the words of Saint Augustine, can be worked for the good by God. Claudel (1868–1955) already had a reputation as a poet before the First World War. After abandoning the Catholicism of his childhood he had a religious experience in Christmas of 1886 that led to his reconversion. This experience lies behind the optimism of his writings, for however far we have fallen, on his view, God's love will make things right.

Claudel's theology was intensely mystical: like Augustine, he had known the love of a God more intimate to him than his own self ('quelqu'un qui soit en moi plus moi-même que moi').[37] The proper vocation of humanity in the claudélien world is the adoration of God. When human beings accomplish this adoration, there is order and fullness. When there is not, and human beings turn to them-selves or give to things a love that only their Creator is due, there is disorder, sin and sadness. Against philosophies that placed human beings at the centre of the world – whether Voltaire's, Marx's, or Gide's, Claudel's novels answer: no.

Two of Claudel's works – one play and one libretto – include Joan of Arc. In the former, *L'annonce faite à Marie* (written between 1892 and 1911), the character of Joan is invoked to imply that with the end of the Middle Ages human beings can no longer see mean-ingful correspondences between the visible and the invisible world (or at least not with certainty). But this is not a foregone conclusion. In Claudel's own words, 'the happiness of being Catholic is above all, for me, that of communing with the universe, of being sold with those first and fundamental things that are the sea, the earth, the sky, and the word of God'.[38] Like Bergson, Claudel rejected the view that discursive reason is the only means of knowing about the world.

This 'decade of sin' saw the publication of the most famous works of Mauriac and Bernanos, and confirmed Claudel's place

---

[37]Claudel 1967: 18.
[38]'Le Bonheur d'être catholique, c'etait d'abord, pour moi, celui de communier avec l'univers, d'être solide avec ces choses premieres et fondamentales qui sont la mer, la terre, le ciel et la parole de Dieu.'

in literature. These writers engaged with each other, sometimes even discussing each other's works in their characters' dialogue.[39] Readers were presented with a tapestry of theological options, ranging from Jansenist pessimism to mystical optimism. It also discovered the work and personality of Péguy, and saw the popularity of Gide, Henry de Montherlant and Marcel Jouhandeau – on whose pages God and the devil played subtle games.[40]

The young Sartre's appetite for literature was as voracious as his pen was prodigious. He not only read Mauriac but published a reproach of his literary characters. In a 1939 article entitled 'Monsieur François Mauriac et la liberté' (Mr François Mauriac and freedom) he charged that Mauriac's characters lacked freedom.[41] Some have argued that this article was an opportunistic attempt on Sartre's part – a young novelist attempting to gain notice by criticizing an established one – or that Mauriac represented the archetype of everything Sartre rejected: the bourgeois Catholic writer.[42] But it seems at least as plausible that Sartre objected to Mauriac's *Jansenist* universe – that already Sartre's account of freedom was being honed in response to theological forms of determinism. Discussing *Thérèse Desqueyroux*, Sartre writes to Mauriac, 'Would you like your characters to be alive? Then make them free. It is not a case of defining them, even less of explaining them, but only of presenting their passions and actions unforeseeably.'[43]

---

[39]E.g. Bernanos, in *The Diary of the Country Priest*: the protagonist and his friend the Curé de Torcy discuss Claudel's *The Hostage* (see Bernanos 1937: 218ff.).

[40]All three were celebrated writers, though the latter two are not as well known to English-speaking audiences as Gide: Montherlant was a novelist, essayist and playwright whose works include a play on Port-Royal; Jouhandeau was a mystical Catholic whose homosexuality provoked great guilt and sexual mortification. He published several novels in the 1920s. *De l'abjection* (1939) was published after he married Élisabeth Toulemont, who hoped to cure him of his homosexuality. But her efforts were unsuccessful (and documented in his later works *Chronique d'une passion* and *Eloge de la volupté*).

[41]Sartre 1939.

[42]See Casseville 1993.

[43]Sartre 1939: 215. The next year Sartre writes a letter to Beauvoir asking what his friend means by saying that he is being published in tandem with Mauriac (Beauvoir 1993: 14), and describes one of Mauriac's poems as long and insipid (Beauvoir 1993: 21).

Sartre read Bernanos's *Diary of a Country Priest*, and both he and Beauvoir wrote about it.[44] In *The Family Idiot* Sartre presents the humble priest as inspiring an emotion so sincere that even unbelievers wish to raise God from the tomb in order to save him.[45] And we know he read Claudel, too[46] – their literary paths crossed at least from the Occupation onwards, when Barrault (the director originally set to produce Sartre's first Parisian play, *The Flies*) decided to produce Claudel's *Le Soulier de satin* with the Comédie Française. The next year, when *No Exit* appeared, Claudel anticipated many later theologians' reactions to Sartre's philosophy of self-other relations, writing, 'Sartre says: Hell is other people. And I say: Our paradise is our neighbour, because it is he who holds for us the keys to paradise.'[47] In June 1951 Claudel wrote in his *Journal* that 'Jean-Paul Sartre gives us a play entitled *The Devil and the Good Lord*', which claims to be a humanist counterpart to *Le Soulier de satin*. All the usual banalities.'[48] The critics sided with Claudel, saying that Sartre's play lacked 'flesh' – it was an intellectual play, condemned by its too-evident 'wish to prove the nonexistence of God'.[49]

There are several other authors who exhibit similar preoccupations with sin or with the absence of God, and whose works we know Sartre read carefully (for example Gide, in whose journals one can read: 'Le péché, c'est ce qu'on ne fait librement. Délivrez moi de cette captivité, Seigneur!' ('Sin is what one does not do freely. Deliver me from this captivity, Lord!')). This selection of authors does not claim to be exhaustive, but rather indicative of the types of theological themes we know Sartre read in literature: namely, themes concerning human freedom and its limits. These themes are evident not only in the literary authors Sartre read, however, but also in those he wrote about.

---

[44]Beauvoir writes that 'though we were far from sharing his outlook, his *Journal d'un curé de compagne* compelled our admiration' (1965: 286). Sartre's letters to Beauvoir also mention Bernanos, recommending one of his articles to her because it contained 'excellent things' (Beauvoir 1993: 227).

[45]See *IF* 2124.

[46]Sartre cites a characteristically optimistic claudélien phrase ('the worst is not always certain') on *B* 73.

[47]See Louette 1998 on theological reactions to Sartre's early theatre.

[48]Claudel 1969: 772. See also Contat and Rybalka 1974, v. 1: 178,

[49]See Contat and Rybalka 1974, v. 1: 249.

Sartre's biographies

We have now seen that, whether it came from the seventeenth century or the twentieth, Sartre read literature that intentionally treated theological questions. Sartre was well enough versed in the debates between Molinists and Jesuits, or between Jansenists and mystics of divine love, to read Racine and Corneille, Mauriac and Claudel, without missing the changes in theological key and affective register.

A final point is worth making before concluding this chapter, namely, that the subjects Sartre chose for his existential biographies – Baudelaire, Genet and Flaubert (published in 1947, 1952 and 1971–72, respectively) – were authors with tormented religious consciousnesses (at least, Sartre presents them as such). They were also authors whose works got them into trouble. In the same year Baudelaire and Flaubert were indicted for 'offense to public and religious morality and to good morals' on grounds of both sexual and religious indecency.[50] When Sartre's biography of Genet was published, Claudel wrote to Gallimard in indignation: how he could face his children and justify publishing such unseemly stuff?

Sellier cites Baudelaire's *Les Fleurs du mal* as a paramount example of the 'diffuse Augustinianism' of French literature – and Sartre's existential biography of Baudelaire is plagued by questions of salvation and judgement.[51] Sartre highlights passages in Baudelaire's works that show the ambiguous flux of his thinking about God, for example, that 'Even if God did not exist, Religion would still be holy and *Divine*' (cited in *B* 58), or that 'God is the only being who in order to reign does not even need to exist' (cited in *B* 59). But ambiguous though Baudelaire may be, on Sartre's reading he is not the kind of atheist who just 'doesn't bother about God because … God doesn't exist' (*B* 71). Baudelaire's perverse pleasures would be less pleasurable if they were not forbidden. It is not by chance, Sartre writes, 'that Baudelaire saw in Satan the perfect type of suffering beauty':

Satan, who was vanquished, fallen, guilty, denounced by the whole of Nature, banned from the universe, crushed beneath the

[50]In 1857, for *Les Fleurs du mal* and *Madame Bovary* respectively. The problem with the latter was not only its objectionable depiction of marriage but its satire of religion.
[51]Sellier 2000, v. 2: 74.

memory of an unforgivable sin, devoured by insatiable ambition, transfixed by the eye of God, which froze him in his diabolical essence, and compelled to accept tho the bottom of his heart the supremacy of Good – Satan, nevertheless, prevailed against God, his master and conqueror, by his suffering, but that flame of non-satisfaction which, at the very moment when divine omnipotence crushed him, at the very moment when he acquiesced in being crushed, shone like an unquenchable reproach. (B 99)

Genet, too – *Saint* Genet, in Sartre's title – is described as attempting to live the inverse of a saintly life, according to which Genet chooses Evil because he wants to disappear 'into a darkness which God's gaze cannot pierce' (G 214). Genet cannot blame God for his crisis. He cannot say,

'since it's you who made me, *you're* the guilty one,' for in this magical concept nature and freedom are one and the same: although the thief is enchained since he is unable to change, he is free since he is condemned. This is reminiscent of Calvinistic predestination which leaves the evildoer full responsibility for Evil while taking from him the possibility of doing Good. (G 19)

To blame God for his destiny is merely to exchange one set of chains for another.

Questions of determinism (or as Mueller has shown, *destiny*) recur on several levels in *The Family Idiot*.[52] Sartre's Flaubert is portrayed as making a wager similar to the one for which Pascal is famous. But while Pascal bet his life on the existence of God – arguing that if wrong his loss would only be finite and temporal, but if he won infinite and eternal – Flaubert wants to bargain with God in order to become an artist. Sartre's Flaubert, like Sartre's Baudelaire, is not an atheist who is indifferent to God's nonexistence: he *suffers* the absence of God. He beseeches God:

Hidden God, in whom I must not believe and whom, if I had the permission, I would love with all my soul, behold: I am defeated in all that men have given me, look at me naked and alone, virgin

[52]See Mueller 2014.

wax as on the day of my birth, for I wish to count on none but You. (*IF* 2,077)

Conclusion

Mauriac, Bernanos and Claudel, as O'Connell writes, 'took up the challenge to concretize sin and expose it beneath the surface of modern materialism and scepticism'.[53] This trend in literature unfolded in the same decade as the debate about Christian philosophy: novelists offered competing Christian visions of life; philosophers offered a variety of Christian philosophies intended to suit the needs of the modern world.

During the same period Bergson published *Les Deux sources de la morale et de la religion* (1932), in which he discussed the vocation of the saint, the essence and necessity of mysticism and religious perfection. And between 1916 and 1936 Brémond's monumental *Histoire du sentiment religieux en France* was being published with the intention of valourizing mystics – of showing how their pursuit of truth was also a pursuit of love (*charité*). Brémond argued that all writers, whether sinners or devout, were thirsty for love – and that they had the power, with or without consciously willing it, to serve the God who is Love. For Brémond, the boundaries between poetry and prayer are porous; both can lift the soul in ascent to God.[54]

If, for the Sartre of the 1920s, poetry was not quite powerful enough to lift the soul to God, he still thought literature was enough to save it. These debates between competing Catholicisms – and the competing ends of philosophy and literature – did not escape his notice. In *Being and Nothingness* he cites the 'Catholic novelists' in his discussion of the human impulse toward being (noting that they see erotic love as pointing beyond its earthly satisfaction to God).[55]

These influences have been overlooked in part because the English-speaking canon of philosophy assigns greater weight to Husserl and Heidegger than it does to Bergson and Delacroix or

---

[53]O'Connell 1994: 856.
[54]Bremond published several works in the 1920s on the subjects of poetry and prayer: in 1926 alone appeared *La Poésie pure*, *Un débat sur la poésie* and *Prière et Poésie*.
[55]*BN* 583–4.

Bernanos and Claudel, and in part because many of Sartre's early works have still not been translated into English. Clearly, literary texts are polyphonous and polyvalent, and therefore cannot be taken as authoritative sources of knowledge about Sartre's philosophical or theological positions. But they can be taken to indicate his philosophical and theological preoccupations.

In *What Is Literature?*, Sartre frames his concept of 'commitment' with a discussion of Pascal's statement that 'We are embarked'. Every human being, Sartre says, is embarked. But that does not mean he is aware of it:

> Most men pass their time in hiding their commitment from themselves. That does not necessarily mean that they attempt evasions by lying, by artificial paradises, or by a life of make-believe. It is enough for them to dim their lanterns, to see the foreground without the background and, vice versa, to see the ends while passing over the means in silence ... Writers can have recourse to all this just like anyone else. There are some, and they are the majority, who furnish a whole arsenal of tricks to the reader who wants to go on sleeping quietly. (*WL* 57)

The writer's task, on Sartre's definition, is therefore to 'achieve the most lucid and the most complete consciousness of being embarked' in order to help himself and others wake up. In the next two chapters, we shall meet Sartre's vision of what 'waking up' entails.

PART 2

Sartre's theological themes

4

Being and Nothingness

We have already seen in Chapter 1 that Sartre's life was dedicated to exploring philosophical questions, especially questions concerning the nature and meaning of human existence. Distilling his 'theological themes' from the thousands of published pages he wrote – of philosophy, literature, plays, essays, reviews etc. – is necessarily a selective task. This section therefore highlights some of the most pertinent aspects of Sartrean existentialism, which is to say, it focuses on the early Sartre of the phenomenological and existentialist periods of the 1930s and early 1940s. There will be some reference to the later works where they can offer illumination of this earlier period. However, because Sartre's reception by the theologians discussed in Part 3 of this book primarily concerns the phenomenological and post-war Sartre, that period receives the bulk of the attention in this section.

Sartre's theological language

Sartre's language reveals his embeddedness in French theological traditions. Some commentators have noticed the theological connotations of the terms us uses, even comparing Sartre's ontology in *Being and Nothingness* to the ontologies of theologians such as Augustine or Aquinas,[1] or to various forms of mysticism.[2]

---

[1]On language, see Howells 1981; Hopkins 1994; Richmond 2004; and Marion 1991: 36; for comparative work on ontology, see Kirkpatrick 2015 on Augustine and Wang 2009 on Aquinas.
[2]Salvan 1967: chapter 6.

It is hard *not* to notice how theological the vocabulary of Sartre's anthropology is: the reason human beings suffer, on Sartre's view, is that they misguidedly 'desire to be God'. This desire takes many shapes in *Being and Nothingness*: to be *ens causa sui*, to be self-caused and self-coincident, to say, like God, 'I am that I am'. Sartre presents human beings as plagued by 'unrealizable ideals', many of which are ideals the Christian tradition ascribes only to God. In addition to the unrealizable unity of being ('unity of the for-itself') (*BN* 102), we also find 'the beautiful' (*BN* 218); 'unity with the other' (*BN* 388); God (BN 473, 'as in-itself-for-itself' and 'unrealizable Third'); and love (*BN* 388). On Sartre's account, we experience these 'unrealizables' 'as irritating absences' (*BN* 548).

A chapter such as this cannot offer a fully developed theological reading of *Being and Nothingness*. The aim of this chapter is to highlight some of the pertinent concepts and themes which demonstrate the bidirectional influence this book outlines.[3] For ease of discussion in Part 3, I have divided the following discussion of *Being and Nothingness* into two parts: the 'pessimistic' Sartre and the 'optimistic' Sartre. As we shall see in Chapter 5, *Being and Nothingness* immediately encountered criticism on account of its pessimism (and Sartre responded soon afterwards in 'Existentialism Is a Humanism'). Although European theologians usually engaged with the pessimistic Sartre in their writings, Cone drew on the optimistic Sartre in developing his theology of liberation. In characterizing Sartre as 'optimistic' and 'pessimistic' in this way I recognize that there is a danger of caricature – indeed, in places some of the theologians who are considered in Part 3 arguably succumbed to it. But as long as we bear in mind Catalano's reminder that the parts of *Being and Nothingness* should be read as 'progression(s) in a reflection',[4] this distinction may provide a useful mnemonic tool.

The pessimistic Sartre: Anxiety, bad faith, being-with-others

We saw in Chapter 1 that Sartre's *Transcendence of the Ego* introduced the notion of reflective consciousness and the idea that the

---

[3]See Kirkpatrick forthcoming for a fuller reading of the theological themes in *Being and Nothingness*.
[4]Catalano 1998: 158.

self is an intentional object of such consciousness. To put it another way, there is an ontological distinction between the self-knowing (consciousness) and self-known (intentional object of consciousness). This distinction is very important for Sartre's philosophical anthropology because it leads to the 'pessimistic' consequence that human beings are always and unavoidably alienated from knowledge of themselves.

Sartre's understanding of human persons radically controverts earlier notions of personal identity. Aristotle, for example, claimed that identity is 'the fact that a thing is itself'.[5] But what does it mean for you to be yourself? Human beings are free to do many different things, and throughout the history philosophers have asked *why*? Are you who you are through the free exercise of your will? Or is your freedom mitigated by determinisms, whether biological, theological, or psychological? Many answers to such why-questions invoke 'motives' or 'reasons' or 'causes' as the explanatory antecedents of action, admitting varying degrees of freedom of the will or constraints by external influence.

Whether situational or personal, Sartre finds such explanations of human identity dissatisfying. On his view, it is only *by acting* that we establish an identity and allow our action to be shaped by external demands. Consider a trustworthy man, for example. Why would we call him trustworthy unless his *action* indicated that he is worthy of trust? In slogan form, as we shall see in Chapter 5, Sartre famously wrote that 'existence precedes essence'. But the kind of 'essence' (or 'identity') that follows existence is insecure and ambiguous. For the trustworthy man is free to be otherwise; his subsequent action may reveal him to be entirely unworthy of trust.

In the Introduction to *Being and Nothingness* Sartre revisits much of the material he covered in *The Transcendence of the Ego*, in particular the relationship between consciousness and the ego. In the later work, Sartre defines consciousness as 'the knowing being in so far as he is, not in so far as he is known' (*BN* 7) and reiterates that the pre-reflective cogito (what I have called the self-knowing) is the condition of the Cartesian cogito (the self-as-object, or self-known). This latter ego is 'a perpetually deceptive mirage' (*TE* 38–9); it constantly eludes us, 'offer[ing] itself only in fleeting and successive profiles' (*BN* 17).

---

[5]Aristotle 1979: VII.17.

Being and Nothingness clearly has among its interlocutors
Descartes and 'les trois H' – Hegel, Husserl and Heidegger. After
referring to the groundwork covered in *The Transcendence of
the Ego*, Sartre defines his phenomenological subject (adapting
Heidegger) as '*a being such that in its being, its being is in question in so far as this being implies a being other than itself*' (*BN* 18;
emphasis in original). Unlike being, which is entirely self-coincident,
the being of human subjects 'is what it is not and is not what it is'.[6]
For Sartre, the Socratic injunction to 'know yourself' is impossible –
an unrealizable ideal.

In *Being and Nothingness*, on the basis of phenomenological
analysis (he claims), Sartre divides reality into two: *being-for-itself*
(consciousness) and *being-in-itself*. On Sartre's view, consciousness
is aware of its lack of being, and simultaneously aware that it is
'uncreated' and 'without reason for being' (*BN* 22). The root of this
sense of superfluity (of being *de trop*) is *nothingness* (*le néant*).

> We set upon our pursuit of being, and it seemed to us that the
> series of our questions had led us to the heart of being. But
> behold, at the moment when we thought we were arriving at
> the goal, a glance cast on the question itself has revealed to
> us suddenly that we are encompassed with nothingness. The
> permanent possibility of non-being, outside us and within us,
> conditions our questions about being. (*BN* 29)

For Sartre, *negation* is the 'original basis of a relation of man to
the world' (*BN* 31); it is distinctive of human beings that they can
negate and destroy – to *refuse* existence (*BN* 35). The capacity to
negate separates humanity from the unthinking world – being-
for-itself (*pour soi*) from being-in-itself (*en soi*). He characterizes
humanity as 'the Being by which Nothingness arrives in the world'
(*BN* 47 and 48), writing that 'the necessary condition for our saying not is that non-being be a perpetual presence in us and outside
of us, that nothingness *haunt* being' (*BN* 35; emphasis in original).

Sartre provides a detailed historical narrative in *Being and
Nothingness*, restating the conclusions of *The Transcendence of the
Ego* and then turning to Hegel and Heidegger.

---

[6]Cf. *BN* 79–82 and 124.

But where the concept of nothingness is concerned these two are also found wanting. When Hegel writes '(Being and nothingness) are empty abstractions, and the one is as empty as the other,' he forgets that emptiness is emptiness of something. Being is empty *of* all other determination than identity with itself, but that non-being is empty *of being*. In a word, we must recall here against Hegel that being *is* and that nothingness *is not*. (*BN* 39; emphasis in original)

Heidegger's view is more accurate than Hegel's (on Sartre's view), since it allows for the possibility of finding oneself 'face to face' with nothingness in anxiety (*BN* 41), but his concept of nothingness still does not go far enough. As Howells notes, 'neither Hegel nor Heidegger carries his study of negation through to its source in *le néant* of human consciousness'.[7]

I have argued elsewhere that Sartre's rejection of the nonsubjectivist accounts of Hegel and Heidegger reflects the influence of the *néant* of French Augustinian debates, and this is one of the reasons why: Sartre thinks that human existence includes several 'realities' such as 'absence, change, otherness, repulsion, regret, distraction', and distance, which are not just objects of judgement but also are 'experienced, opposed, feared, etc., by the human being and which in their inner structure are inhabited by negation' (*BN* 45).[8]

For Sartre, absences are not present; possibilities are not actualities; and values are not facts. Rather, 'For Pierre to be absent in relation to Thérèse is a particular way of his being present' (*BN* 302). As Morris writes, there is 'a widespread intellectual prejudice against the non-existent, the non-actual, and the absent, as well as the non-quantifiable and the non-measurable', which she entitles 'the prejudice for the existent'.[9] This prejudice takes it to be the case that only the existent is real. But Sartre's point is that there are many ways of being absent – if my friend Pierre fails to arrive at the café because he is dead, his absence will be experienced differently

---

[7] Howells 1988: 15.
[8] This is why Sartre was charged with reifying nothingness in early analytic receptions of his work, for if, as Sartre says it does, nothingness *conditions* reality, must it not be something after all? See, for example, Ayer's reading of the 'novelist-philosopher' (Ayer 1945).
[9] Morris 2008: 47.

than if he fails to arrive because his train has been delayed, and different again if he carelessly stood me up. Sartre's existential biographies could be argued to demonstrate this point with respect to God. For a God whose absence I grieve is experienced differently from one whose nonexistence I consider a matter of indifference.

Sartre's concept of nothingness is slippery and at times looks contradictory. Nothingness 'is not', he writes, and yet it is also 'made-to-be' (*BN* 46). What he means by the latter, rather perplexing statement is that some *négatités* (though nothing) are experienced by human beings – if you are waiting for a friend or mourning a lost one, then you *make nothingness* (as absence) *be*. That is why he takes human beings to be nihilating beings, nothingness-makers, beings '*by which nothingness comes to things*' (*BN* 46; emphasis in original).

Sartre identifies *freedom* as the condition for the possibility of nihilation, claiming that Descartes recognized and named 'this possibility which human reality has to secrete a nothingness which isolates it – it is *freedom*' (*BN* 48; emphasis in original). Sartre develops his philosophical concept of freedom in part 4 of *Being and Nothingness*, but at this point he emphasizes – repeatedly – that it is through the human that nothingness enters the world. Indeed, Sebastian Gardner writes that if the philosophy of *Being and Nothingness* were to be reduced to a single principle, 'that principle would be the identification of the human being with nothingness'.[10]

Like many of his French Augustinian predecessors, Sartre offers an anthropology of *néant*. After introducing his ontology in the Introduction, he goes on to describe the *effects* of this ontology in lived experience. This chapter has a selective focus on a few of these effects – because of their legacy in Sartre studies and the theological reception of Sartre, because of their applicability to everyday experience, and because I take them to be demonstrative of the 'theological' formation Sartre had, as outlined in Chapters 2 and 3.

For Sartre (as for previous generations of theologians) nothingness gives rise to problems that are *suffered* in experience. They fall into two categories: problems of the self (anxiety and bad faith) and problems of the other (shame and objectification).

---

[10]Gardner 2009: 71.

Anxiety

We have already seen that for Sartre the ego (as self-known) is indeterminate. It is only by existing, by *action*, that I gain an essence, but as long as I still have the capacity to act I have the capacity to rescript my part, to reject any previous 'essence' my actions have accrued in pursuit of another me. This indeterminacy of the self, *our freedom* to become other than we are, gives rise to anxiety. Anxiety (*angoisse*) reveals freedom as the 'possible destroyer in the present and in the future of what I am' (*BN* 61). Sartre acknowledges the accounts of both Kierkegaard's and Heidegger's notions of anxiety in presenting his own, but before moving past this point it is worth noting that both Kierkegaard and Heidegger had Augustinian influences,[11] and reminding the reader that Sartre also encountered literary depictions of postlapsarian (that is, post-Fall) anxiety in the works of, for example, Bernanos.

In *Being and Nothingness* Sartre reads Kierkegaard's anxiety (vis-à-vis sin) and Heidegger's notion of anxiety (vis-à-vis nothingness) as complementary (*BN* 53). In his *War Diaries* he writes that they are 'one and the same':

> [Anxiety] at Nothingness, with Heidegger? Dread of freedom with Kierkegaard? In my view it's one and the same thing, for freedom is the apparition of Nothingness in the world . . .
>
> So [Anxiety] is indeed the experience of Nothingness, hence it isn't a psychological phenomenon. It's an existential structure of human reality, it's simply freedom becoming conscious of itself as its own nothingness ... Thus the existential grasping of our facticity is Nausea, and the existential apprehension of our freedom is [Anxiety]. (*WD* 132–33)[12]

In *Being and Nothingness*, Sartre restates several of Kierkegaard's observations, writing that anxiety is distinctively human, that it is not to be confused with fear, that it has no object (or the object of anxiety is nothing) and that anxiety reveals 'freedom's possibility'.

---

[11]Indeed, Barrett goes so far as to say that theologically, Kierkegaard was 'closer to Augustine than he was to Luther' (Barrett 2013: 3).

[12]We will turn to consider 'nausea' at greater length in Chapter 5, alongside Sartre's phenomenology of the body.

Anxiety, Sartre writes is a 'reflective apprehension of the self' (*BN* 54) because it reveals the relation of the self to its possibilities. However,

> a nothingness has slipped into the heart of this relation; I *am* not the self which I will be. First I am not that self because time separates me from it. Secondly, I am not that self because what I am is not the foundation of what I will be. Finally I am not that self because no actual existent can determine strictly what I am going to be. Yet as I am already what I will be (otherwise I would not be interested in any one being more than another), *I am the self which I will be, in the mode of not being it.* (*BN* 56; emphasis in original)

For Sartrean consciousness – unlike the Cartesian *ego*, for which anxiety is impossible – the past and future must be confronted as 'a self which it is in the mode of not-being' (*BN* 58). We are estranged from ourselves by time, which implies 'a constantly renewed obligation to remake the self' (*BN* 58), because 'man is always separated by a nothingness from his essence' (*BN* 59): 'Nothing can ensure me against myself, cut off from the world and from my essence by this nothingness which I *am*' (*BN* 63).

It is not just Kierkegaard and Heidegger who can be heard here, but echoes of the first half of a Pascalian–Fénelonian refrain: Who am I? And what will keep me from the nothingness that I am? The idea that the human person is haunted by nothingness recurs throughout Sartre's work.[13] But the second half of the refrain is distinctly lacking in Sartre. Where the seventeenth-century *mystiques du néant* could seek refuge from nothingness in *grace*, Sartre offers his reader no such concept, writing simply that 'it is certain that we cannot overcome [anxiety], for we *are* '[anxiety]' (*BN* 67; emphasis in original).

But anxiety is uncomfortable. And so, Sartre says, we attempt to avoid it – 'our essential and immediate behaviour with respect to [anxiety] is flight' (*BN* 64). There are several ways to flee. Psychological determinism, for example, provides one means by which we may excuse ourselves from the recognition of freedom

---

[13]See, e.g., *BN* 113 and 390.

and all that it entails. If we accept that there are 'antagonistic forces within us' whose existence is 'comparable to things', then how could it be otherwise? Determinism offers a seductive solace, attempting to 'fill the void which encircles us, to re-establish the links between past and present, between present and future' (*BN* 64). If I am determined to be an alcoholic, my essence is fixed and resistance is futile.

Sartre thinks human beings prefer not to be free – to the extent that we would deny our transcendence in order to inhabit the order of things. We need not accept determinism to do this, however. There are other strategies to adopt. In particular, Sartre names 'distraction' a 'more complete activity of flight' which conceals our anxiety (*BN* 65). Distraction involves considering my possibilities abstractly – as things that sometimes happen to people rather than a life I fully inhabit. It is one thing to admit that 'sometimes people neglect their loved ones' and quite another to admit that my neglect is letting love die. It is easier to consider myself determined or to distract myself from such thoughts.

The ubiquity of these patterns of flight explains why anxiety is so rare. The importance of freedom in Sartre's philosophy has often – and rightly – been emphasized. But at least as important is the wish to flee it – and by it my incompleteness. As Warnock observed, 'Sartre, who thinks we are responsible for everything, also thinks that the burden of responsibility is more than we can bear; and so we develop tricks and devices for evading it'.[14]

In this Sartre follows Pascal, although the latter invoked diversions (*divertissement*) in support of his view of humans as fallen. If our condition were truly happy, Pascal wrote, 'we should not have to divert ourselves from thinking about it'.[15] But human beings are capable of 'feeling' (*sentir*) their nothingness without knowing it (*le connaître*).[16] In a fragment on boredom, Pascal writes that

> nothing is so intolerable for man as to be in a state of complete tranquility, without passions, without business, without diversion, without effort. Then he feels his nothingness, his abandonment, his inadequacy, his dependence, his helplessness, his emptiness.

[14]Warnock 1965: 52–3.
[15]See Pascal, *Pensées* L132/B170; L136/B139.
[16]Pascal, *Pensées* L36/B164.

At once from the depths of his soul arises boredom, gloom, sadness, grief, vexation, despair.[17]

For Sartre, consciousness is defined as 'a being, the nature of which is to be conscious of the nothingness of its being' (*BN* 70). There are many human practices of self-negation, Sartre writes, too many to include in his study. So he restricts his scope to one that he takes to be 'essential to human reality': bad faith (*BN* 71).

Bad faith

At the start of his chapter on bad faith Sartre begins by reviewing the conditions that render it possible. In short, Sartre writes, 'For man to be able to question, he must be capable of being his own nothingness.' Anxiety acquaints us with our freedom – 'the aspect [of my being] which I do not wish to see' – and confronts us with the fact that 'I must of necessity perpetually carry within me what I wish to flee' (*BN* 43).

Bad faith is frequently but mistakenly identified with lying. Bad faith has a different structure; lying implies that the liar is in possession of the truth. The liar *intends* to deceive. As such, the lie is 'a normal phenomenon of what Heidegger calls the *Mitsein* [of being with others]. It presupposes my existence, the existence of the *Other*, my existence *for* the Other, and the existence of the Other *for* me' (*BN* 72; emphasis in original). The same cannot be said for bad faith, which is a lie to oneself. For though 'the one who practises bad faith is hiding a displeasing truth or presenting as truth a pleasing untruth', the appearance of lying is changed by the fact that it is from myself that I hide the truth: 'the duality of the deceiver and the deceived does not exist here' (*BN* 72).

Sartre is aware of the paradox of self-deception: 'if I deliberately and cynically attempt to lie to myself, I fail completely in this undertaking' (*BN* 73). So, Sartre asks, 'What must be the being of man if he is to be capable of bad faith?' (*BN* 78). To answer this question he turns to examples which have become some of the best-known vignettes of twentieth-century philosophy: the woman on the date,

---

[17]Pascal, *Pensées* L622/B131. As we saw in Chapter 2, Sartre cites Pascal on diversion in several of his works, e.g. *NM* 258, *BN* 583 and *WD* 250–1.

the waiter and the homosexual.[18] Whether in praise or disdain, English- and French-speaking commentators alike have highlighted this section as *Being and Nothingness*'s 'most famous'[19] or even as the 'most representative of Sartrean philosophy'.[20] Bad faith often follows the pattern of distraction: the woman on a date, who does not want to acknowledge her companion's intentions toward her, can distract her consciousness from the clear expressions of sexual desire to focus only on what is 'respectful and discreet' in his com-munications. She 'disarms words' of their sexual intent in order not to see the situation as it is (*BN* 78). Even when she hears the man state that he is attracted to her, or feels him take her hand, she does not reassess the situation, for, as Sartre puts it, 'the qualities thus attached to the person she is listening to are in this way fixed in a permanence like that of things' (*BN* 78).

Although she is 'profoundly aware of the desire which she inspires', 'the desire cruel and naked would humiliate and horrify her' (*BN* 78).[21] This woman 'uses various procedures' to maintain herself in bad faith. 'While sensing profoundly the presence of her own body – to the degree of being disturbed, perhaps – she real-izes herself as *not being* her own body, and she contemplates it as though from above as a passive object to which events can *happen* but which can neither provoke them nor avoid them because all its possibilities are outside of it' (*BN* 79; emphasis in original).

The basic concept of bad faith involves 'the double property of the human being, who is at once a *facticity* and a *transcendence*' (*BN* 79; emphasis in original). To be human is to be double, a dual-ity, but to say this is not, like Freud, to 'cut the psychic whole in two'.[22] On Sartre's view, the human is constituted both by

[18]Indeed, Morris (2008: 91, n.2) notes that the 'Bad Faith' chapter is the only text of Sartre's that is regularly read by analytic philosophers. Taking the examples out of context has led to clear misreadings (e.g. Phillips 1981, wherein waiters are seen to be particularly susceptible to bad faith!) and subsequent attempts at correction (e.g. Stevenson 1983).

[19]Flynn 2014: 184.

[20]Philonenko 1981: 148.

[21]In this and the following examples of bad faith there is a unifying theme: being reduced to an object in the eyes of another.

[22]See Morris (2008: 79–81) on the different senses in which Sartre uses the word 'duality'. Since, for the purposes of this discussion, the facticity–transcendence dual-ity is most pertinent, it is the only one considered here.

facticity: the factual conditions such as the time, place, body, class, sex, gender, and race into which one is born; and

transcendence: choices which go beyond facts to values, freely chosen commitments in the future and to interpret or surpass my factical constraints.

Sartre writes that while these aspects 'are and ought to be capable of a valid coordination', it is not in the nature of bad faith to wish to coordinate them. Bad faith rather 'seeks to affirm their identity while preserving their differences. It must affirm facticity as being transcendence and transcendence as being facticity, in such a way that at the instant when a person apprehends the one, he can find himself abruptly faced with the other' (*BN* 79).

This may seem no less paradoxical than the paradigms of lying to oneself and the Freudian unconscious (which Sartre dismisses in his discussion). Sartre turns to sincerity, the antithesis of bad faith, in order to demonstrate why his explanation offers an advantage over these others. The reason is simple: bad faith reveals that the human being 'is what it is not and is not what it is'. In other words, bad faith takes us to the root of the problem, namely, that the human is not subject to the principle of identity.

For Sartre, bad faith would not be possible if 'man is what he is'. If that were the case candour would 'cease to be his ideal' and become his being (*BN* 82). But there is an element of *making* ourselves be.

Sartre's waiter famously 'plays at being' a waiter (*BN* 82); he 'realizes the demands' of the public, who expect the following of a certain ceremony in their service:

> There is the dance of the grocer, the tailor, of the auctioneer, by which they endeavour to persuade their clientele that they are nothing but a grocer, an auctioneer, a tailor. A grocer who dreams is offensive to the buyer, because such a grocer is not wholly grocer. Society demands that he limit himself to his function as a grocer, just as the soldier at attention makes himself into a soldier-thing. (*BN* 83)

There are many means by which we try to 'imprison a man in what he is', Sartre writes, 'as if we lived in perpetual fear that he might escape from it' (*BN* 83). But waiters are not waiters in the same sense that inkwells are inkwells. Human beings are not reducible to any single action or attitude.[23] Bad faith is based on an ambiguity, in which 'I affirm here that I *am* my transcendence in the mode of being a thing' (*BN* 80; emphasis in original).

The antithesis of bad faith is sincerity (*BN* 81), but this too is an ideal that is 'impossible to achieve' since to be sincere 'is to be what one is. That supposes that I am not originally what I am' (*BN* 85). Such impossibility is not hidden from consciousness. Rather, Sartre writes, 'it is the embarrassing constraint which we constantly experience; it is our very incapacity to recognize ourselves, to constitute ourselves as being what we are' (*BN* 86).

Sartre's homosexual, for example, 'frequently has an intolerable feeling of guilt, and his whole existence is determined in relation to this feeling' (*BN* 86). He does not want to admit his 'deeply rooted tendency', but rather sees his 'mistakes' as belonging to the past or as due to his lack of satisfaction in beautiful women. His friend, however, 'becomes irritated with this duplicity', asking the homosexual to declare frankly that he is 'a paederast' (the term is Sartre's; *BN* 87). But who is in bad faith here, Sartre asks? Is it the homosexual or the champion of sincerity?

The homosexual does not wish to accept 'a destiny'. 'He does not wish to let himself be considered as a thing. He has an obscure but strong feeling that an homosexual is not an homosexual as this table is a table or as this red-haired man is red-haired' (*BN* 87). Sartre writes that this resistance of the label 'paederast' stems from a recognition of the 'irreducible character of human reality' (*BN* 87). The homosexual is correct to reject the label if he rejects it in the sense of 'I am not what I am' (*BN* 87). But there is a problematic ambiguity in the word *being*. If the homosexual said, 'to the extent that my pattern of conduct conforms to the word "paederast", I am a paederast; but to the extent that human reality cannot be defined by such patterns of conduct, I am not', then he would be correct in rejecting the label. But instead he rejects both senses of its applicability: this is his bad faith.

The 'champion of sincerity', by contrast, 'demands of the guilty one that he constitute himself as a thing, precisely in order no longer to treat him as a thing' (*BN* 88).

---

[23]NB Sartre's example can be adapted to apply to any profession; see Manser 1983 on why Sartre is not (contra Phillips) 'unfair to waiters'.

Who can not see how offensive to the Other and how reassuring for me is a statement such as, 'He's just a paederast', which removes a disturbing freedom from a trait and which aims at henceforth constituting all the acts of the Other as consequences following strictly from his essence? (*BN* 88)

What the 'critic' is demanding of his 'victim' is that 'he should entrust his freedom to his friend as a fief' (*BN* 88). Sartre brings in Hegel's master–slave relation at this point, diagnosing this situation as a double movement where one person appeals to another to demand 'that in the name of his nature as consciousness he should radically destroy himself as consciousness', while simultaneously leading the other 'to hope for a rebirth beyond this destruction' (*BN* 88).

Bad faith is a 'game of mirrors', in which we attempt to escape either our freedom or our facticity. Sincerity, too, has the same essential structure: 'the sincere man constitutes himself as what he *is in order not to be it*' (*BN* 88; emphasis in original). But sincerity, too, is an impossible ideal: in this case, the ideal of being 'what one is' (*BN* 93).

The true problem of bad faith, Sartre writes, is an epistemological problem. Namely, a problem of *belief*: 'if we take belief as meaning the adherence of being to its object when the object is not given or is given indistinctly, then bad faith is belief; and the essential problem of bad faith is the problem of belief' (*BN* 91). A misleading method of thinking arises in bad faith, disordering our ability to evaluate:

Bad faith does not hold the norms and criteria of truth as they are accepted by the critical thought of good faith. What it decides first, in fact, is the nature of truth. With bad faith a truth appears, a method of thinking, a type of being which is like that of objects; the ontological characteristic of the world of bad faith with which the subject suddenly surrounds himself is this: that here being is what it is not, and is not what it is. (*BN* 91)

Bad faith does not admit evidence to the contrary. All such evidence is nonpersuasive because one has already been 'spontaneously determined' not to accept it. For Sartre, belief is a house of cards: to believe is to appear, 'and to appear is to deny itself' (*BN* 92). Upon critical inspection, the house crumbles: 'To believe is to know that one believes, and to know that one believes is no longer to believe' (*BN* 92).

As Jonathan Webber notes, 'The imaginary attitude is a central feature of Sartre's discussions of "bad faith".' We use several strategies of escape in order to avoid believing things we do not want to: 'It is a key tenet of Sartrean existentialism that we often engage in these imaginative games in order to hide aspects of ourselves ourselves and each other.'[24]

It is worth stating the obvious point that all three of the examples given in this section are interpersonal: the woman is in bad faith with respect to the man; the waiter with respect to 'the public' who expect restaurant rituals; and the homosexual with respect to the friend. The selves we *make ourselves be* are made in the knowledge that they will be beheld by others. Like the Pascalian *moi*, the self in bad faith is more concerned with *seeming* (*paraître*) than *being* (*être*).

The antithesis of bad faith is sincerity (*BN* 81), but this too is an ideal that is 'impossible to achieve' since to be sincere 'is to be what one is. That supposes that I am not originally what I am' (*BN* 85). Such impossibility is not hidden from consciousness, Sartre writes: 'it is the embarrassing constraint which we constantly experience; it is our very incapacity to recognize ourselves, to constitute ourselves as being what we are' (*BN* 86).

'The nature of consciousness, Sartre concludes, 'is to be what it is not and not to be what it is' (*BN* 94). The *self*, consequently,

> represents an ideal distance within the immanence of the subject in relation to himself, a way of *not being his own coincidence*, of escaping identity while positing it as unity – in short, of being in a perpetually unstable equilibrium between identity as absolute cohesion without a trace of diversity and unity as a synthesis of multiplicity. This is what we shall call presence to itself. The law of being of the *for-itself*, as the ontological foundation of consciousness, is to be itself in the form of presence to itself. (*BN* 101; emphasis in original)

---

[24]Webber 2004: xxv–vi.

Writing against 'a strong prejudice prevalent among philosophers' which 'causes them to attribute to consciousness the highest rank in being' (*BN* 101), Sartre writes that the coincidence of identity only concerns *external relations* (*BN* 101), relations that are what they are independently of other things.

But human experience includes many relationships that are *internal*. What Sartre means by this distinction is clarified by considering the following:

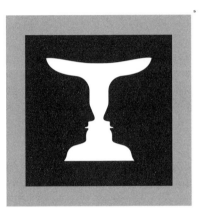

This image illustrates what psychologists call figure/ground ambiguity. If either black or white were removed from it, the urn and the profiles would disappear. The figure and the ground in this image are internally related: neither would be what it is without the other (in Sartrean terms, such an internal relation is a 'duality in unity'). Externally related things, by contrast, are what they are independently. Sartre uses the image of a witness to clarify this distinction. If things are not related internally – for example, your hand and this book – then a witness (in this case, you) must observe them to bring them into relation with one another, to say 'my hand is holding this book'.

Sartre sees many things as internally related which others do not, for example, the past and present of a self. On Sartre's view, it is as inaccurate to say that a = b (where 'a' represents my past and 'b' my present) as it is to say that a ≠ b. Each of these ways of looking at the question, in isolation, is inadequate. A proper understanding, on Sartre's view, involves considering both together.

*Every effort has been made to determine the provenance of this image.

The body and the look

The complexity of the human being's internal relations is only increased when Sartre turns from considering the isolated *for-itself* to consider being with others. The chapter on 'The Body' has been described as 'the pivotal chapter' of *Being and Nothingness*.[25] In it Sartre distinguishes between different *levels* of ontology because he believed that his philosophical predecessors had misunderstood the body on account of confusing the orders of *knowing* and *being*, or *le corps-vu* and *le corps-existé* (cf. *BN* 241 and 325). For Sartre, the ontology of the body is comprised of three levels – 'different modes of manifestation'[26] – each of which is given a subchapter in *Being and Nothingness*:

1) the body as being-for-itself (for which he also uses the term 'facticity') (*BN* 330–62)
2) the body-for-others (*BN* 362–75); and
3) the awkwardly entitled 'third ontological dimension of the body' (*BN* 375–82)

On the first level, the body is the manner in which I exist pre-reflectively; 'the body is *lived* and not *known*' (*BN* 348). Sartre writes that 'my body as it is *for me* does not appear to me in the midst of the world' (*BN* 327; emphasis in original). It is not a thing but rather 'a transparent medium for my experience of the world, but also as somehow *surpassed* toward the world'.[27] It is a conscious structure of consciousness, but a point of view on which I cannot have a point of view – for though I can see my eye reflected in a mirror I cannot, as Sartre puts it, 'see the seeing'. The body at this level is not something one can intuit as an object: following Gabriel Marcel, Sartre is emphatic that I *am* my body (*BN* 342).[28]

Sartre repeatedly emphasizes the given and unchosen nature of embodiment. To have a body, he writes, 'is to be the foundation

---

[25]Catalano 2009: 26.
[26]Moran 2011: 13.
[27]Moran 2009: 43; emphasis in original.
[28]See Marcel's *Metaphysical Journal* (1927) for discussions of incarnation, and Mui 2009 for a discussion of Sartre's indebtedness to Marcel.

of one's own nothingness and not to be the foundation of one's being' (*BN* 350). The body is something to be escaped by nihilation (*BN* 350), and the overwhelming characteristic of corporeality is that it is 'the inexpressible which one wishes to flee' (*BN* 357). On this first, pre-reflective level, therefore, embodiment is an encumbrance,[29] the site of self-alienation. Sartre writes that 'the body is the contingent form which is taken up by the necessity of my contingency. We can never apprehend this contingency as such in so far as our body is *for us*; for we are a choice, and for us, to be is to choose ourselves' (*BN* 352; emphasis in original). But the body conditions the way in which objects appear to me and the way I appear as an object – whether in terms of race, sex, class, nationality, character, physiology or what have you. For Sartre, bodies are the axes of the relationship between being-for-itself and being-for-others.

The second level Sartre expounds is the body as *seen* rather than *lived* (*le corps-vu* rather than *le corps-existé*). This is the domain of the body as utilized and known by others, studied and idealized by the 'objective sciences'. I do not know from my own experience that I have intestine or lymph nodes, for example, but I learn that I have them from others. Sartre uses the imagery of tools to elucidate the distinction between this and the previous ontological order of embodiment. On the first order, the body is the centre of reference, the point of view on which I cannot have a point of view. On the second, however, my body appears as the 'tool of tools' in my instrumental engagement with the world. It appears as 'a thing' which I am.

On the third level, embodiment entails that 'I exist for myself as a body known by the other'. We experience our bodies not only as our own but also as reflected in others' experience: 'the Other is revealed to me as the subject for whom I am an object' (*BN* 375). This is the level on which we experience things like shame and embarrassment. Sartre writes that 'I cannot be embarrassed by my own body as I exist it. It is my body as it may exist for the other which may embarrass me' (*BN* 377).

It is this dimension of the body that exposes us to the omnipresent 'gaze' or 'look' of the other.[30] We are 'imprisoned' by this gaze, because the other deprives us of control over how we see our world

---

[29]On encumbrance, compare Izumi-Shearer 1976: 114.

[30]Although Sartre clearly does not use the term 'omnipresent' in an empirical sense.

and, more importantly, ourselves. Alone in the world I might exist as 'unqualifiable selfness which I have to be forever without relief' (*BN* 315).[31] But 'The Other is present to me everywhere as the one through whom I become an object' (*BN* 303). That is why, as Sartre put it in *No Exit*, 'Hell is other people': because others entrap me as an object in ways that I cannot always resist.

Being with others

On the individual level, my freedom is such that, through negation, I can choose what I want to be. But on the social level, my freedom is only one of many freedoms, and my being is subject to other powers of negation. The 'problem', therefore, of my being in relation to the Other is that *I am not the only being 'by which nothingness comes to the world'* (*BN* 47 and 48; emphasis in original). Sartre develops this point further in 'Concrete Relations with Others', where he discusses ontological *guilt* and describes the 'limit' of the Other's freedom as an 'original situation' (*BN* 431).

The Other as 'limit' appears to us 'in the reality of everyday life' (*BN* 277), where we find an 'original relation to the Other' (*BN* 277). That 'original relation' is *le regard*, usually translated in English as 'the look' or 'the gaze'.

When the Other looks at me, I can no longer see myself at the centre of the world. As Sartre puts it, the Other 'steals' the world, introducing distances and unknowns: when I see an object in the world, I know what I see, but I cannot know what is seen by the Other, and she may contest that I see truly (*BN* 279). Moreover, just as the other 'steals' the world, the Other's freedom can 'steal' my being.[32] The gaze of another reveals that my own consciousness is not the sole arbiter of who I am – I am not the only source of the 'existence' that will determine my 'essence'.

The famous example Sartre gives is of someone spying through a keyhole. Being jealous and thinking there is something behind the door involves something Sartre calls a 'double and inverted determination', in the sense that I am motivated to look because I am

---

[31]'I am condemned to be forever my own nihilation' (*BN* 322).
[32]Though Sartre uses the imagery of theft for the world, he does not explicitly use it for 'one's being'.

jealous, and the jealously would be nothing if there were nothing to be seen. He calls this the *situation*.[33]

> But all of a sudden I hear footsteps in the hall. Someone is looking at me! What does this mean? It means that I am suddenly affected in my being and that essential modifications appear in my structure – modifications which I can apprehend and fix conceptually by means of the reflective cogito. (*BN* 283–4)

Only reflective consciousness has the self directly as an object (*BN* 284). When alone, I can see the fissure between the self-knowing and the self-known. But in the experience of being seen we discover another 'dimension of being' from which we are 'separated by a radical nothingness': the Other's freedom (*BN* 286). The self-known is always indeterminate, because it is always subject to the freedom of others: 'the Other's freedom is revealed to me across the uneasy indetermination of the being which I am for him. Thus this being is not my possible; it is not always in question at the heart of my freedom. On the contrary it is the limit of my freedom' (*BN* 285). In characteristically dramatic language, Sartre writes that in the look there is a 'death of my possibilities', which causes me to 'experience the Other's freedom' (*BN* 294–5). The negating freedom of the Other 'fixes' my possibilities (*BN* 294).

This is why Sartre writes that 'my original fall is the existence of the Other' (*BN* 286). For my 'nature' is not of my making: rather, 'the very stuff of my being is the unpredictable freedom of another' (*BN* 286). Moreover, the alienation of my being involves an alienation of my world, which also falls beneath the Other's gaze. 'The appearance of the Other causes the appearance in the situation of an aspect which I did not wish, of which I am not master, and which on principle escapes me since it is *for the Other*.'

The problem is that 'the Other holds ... the secret of what I am'. In the absence of God, *the other* will define me – before and after death transforms my life into destiny. The other reveals the extent to which the self-known and self-knowing are irreconcilably at

---

[33]See also *BN* 509, where the situation is defined as 'the common product of the contingency of the in-itself and of freedom', which is 'an ambiguous phenomenon in which it is impossible to distinguish the contribution of freedom from that of the brute existent'.

odds, for though 'I am responsible for my being-for-others, … I am not the foundation of it' (*BN* 386).

The alienation of love

Given these views, Sartre has a rather distinctive philosophy of love. He suggests that love is a project of recovery of being:

> Thus to the extent that I am revealed to myself as responsible for my being, I *lay claim* to this being which I am; that is, I wish to recover it, or, more exactly, I am the project of the recovery of my being. I want to stretch out my hand and grab hold of this being which is presented to me as *my being* but at a distance – like the dinner of Tantalus; I want to found it by my very freedom. (*BN* 386; emphasis in original)

But I can only found my freedom if I assimilate the freedom of the Other. 'Thus my project of recovering myself is fundamentally a project of absorbing the Other' (*BN* 386–7). For Sartre, there is no room for two selves; intersubjective relationality is a ruse. We always inevitably turn to the human Other to justify our existence, reducing the Other to a means to my ends. My being can only be recovered, Sartre writes, 'if I get hold of this [the Other's] freedom and reduce it to being a freedom subject to my freedom' (*BN* 388).

That is why the lover wants to be loved, Sartre asserts. It cannot simply be motivated by the usual suspects – physical desire or desire for possession – because such desires can be fulfilled. Rather, the lover's goal is to 'capture a "consciousness".' What the lover really desires is 'a special type of appropriation': 'to possess a freedom as a freedom', to *be God* to the Other. In desiring love,

> the Lover wants to be 'the whole world' for the beloved.… He is and consents to being an *object*. But on the other hand, he wants to be the object in which the Other's freedom consents to lose itself, the object in which the Other consents to find his being and his *raison d'être* as his second facticity. (*BN* 389; emphasis in original).

What we want when we want love, on Sartre's view, is for someone to make an *absolute choice* of us, to have the kind of necessary existence that classical theism only ascribes to God. '*This is the basis for the joy of love when there is joy: we feel that our existence is justified*' (*BN* 393; emphasis added). But this joy is delusional. The 'true ideal of love's enterprise' is alienated freedom – and the mere fact of wanting to be loved alienates man from his freedom (*BN* 397). As Mathieu puts it in *The Age of Reason*, love is 'not something to be felt, not a particular emotion, nor yet a particular shade of feeling, it [is] much more like a lowering curse on the horizon, a precursor of disaster' (*AR* 250).

From within and from without, therefore – by desiring love or by being seen by another – the other alienates me from my freedom. This alienation is featured in several of Sartre's novels and theatrical works. In *Nausea*, though Roquentin would like to be a solipsist, he cannot escape the fact that his body is seen by others. The judgement of the other pierces him 'like a sword'. He describes the gaze of another as 'call[ing] into question my very right to exist. And it was true, I had always realized that: I hadn't any right to exist. I had appeared by chance, I existed like a stone, a plant, a microbe' (*NA* 123–4). And in the plays *No Exit* and *The Respectful Prostitute* false loves are put in the limelight: because in the absence of a divine witness who can see the internal relations of the self for what they are, the Sartrean subject can only be seen by human witnesses – whose vision is partial and obscure.

It is not hard to see why Sartre's philosophy has a reputation for being 'irremediably pessimistic'.[34] Even love – an ideal that has a hard time dying[35] – is presented as unrealizable and, in fact, undesirable. But Sartre's philosophy was also famous for giving hope – in the name of freedom.

The optimistic Sartre: Freedom

The idea that arguably brought Sartre his reputation as '*the* philosopher of his generation',[36] is freedom.[37] His notion of freedom is

---

[34]Howells 1988: 19. For more on Sartre's pessimism, see Flynn 2014: 205; and on the American reception of Sartre in particular, Fulton 1999: 29ff.
[35]See Badiou 2012.
[36]Bernasconi 2006: 5; emphasis in original.
[37]Philonenko 1981: 145.

often described as 'radical' or 'extreme' (a view which finds support
in several moments of Sartrean hyperbole, such as his claim that
'freedom is total and infinite' (*BN* 552) and 'the slave in chains is
as free as his master' (*BN* 570)). In 'Existentialism Is a Humanism'
he also goes on to make very strong claims about responsibility. For
if it is true, as he says, that 'man is what he makes of himself', then
we carry a lot of weight on our shoulders – 'the weight of the whole
world', Sartre says – because we are responsible for the world and
for ourselves as ways of being in the world.

So what does Sartre mean by these claims? He is clearly not
advocating the view that human beings are omnipotent. Rather, he
thinks that success is not important to freedom. A slave in chains
may be unlikely to break free of them, but he is no less free on
that account. But is this view what we would usually call by the
name 'freedom'? To answer this question it is helpful to distinguish
between two senses of the word: 'ontological freedom' and 'freedom in a situation'. To clarify this distinction let us consider the
reasoning behind Sartre's post-war statement that 'we were never
more free than during the German occupation'.

This statement has often been regarded as 'incomprehensible or
stupid'.[38] It is obvious that the freedom of the French people – in
the situation of occupied France – was greatly restricted. They had
to modify their behaviour, being careful in word and deed. But if
we distinguish between freedom of action and freedom of attitude
(or between freedom in situation and ontological freedom), Sartre's
meaning becomes clearer. Their freedom of action was greatly
restricted. However, the attitude in consciousness which the French
took towards the Nazis was free. They were therefore responsible
for their conscious attitude toward the occupiers. Some chose to
acquiesce and collaborate; others chose to fight. As Sartre explains
in *Being and Nothingness*,

> What is an obstacle for me may not be so for another. There is no
> obstacle in an absolute sense ... Human-reality (consciousness)
> everywhere encounters resistance and obstacles which it has not
> created, but these resistances and obstacles have meaning only in
> and through the free choice which human-reality (consciousness)
> is. (*BN* 489)

---

[38]Olson 2012: 109.

This is the reason for the hope many have seen in Sartre's philosophy: because no matter what the level of our unfreedom at the level of the individual situation we confront, at the level of consciousness we are ontologically free.

But Sartre's message of freedom is also a message of responsibility. Freedom is 'the stuff of my being', and the first step Sartre makes towards making 'this comprehension' explicit is to revisit his discussion of bad faith, reminding his reader that since human reality is its own nothingness the human person is 'condemned to exist forever beyond [his or her] essence' (*BN* 461). For if the 'being of man is to be reabsorbed in the succession of his acts' (*BN* 453), then 'no limit can be found to my freedom except for freedom itself … we are not free to cease being free' (*BN* 462).

He writes that this condemnation to freedom is what he defined earlier as *facticity*. 'I can neither abstain totally in relation to what I am (for the Other) – for to refuse is not to abstain but still to assume – nor can I submit to it passively (which in a sense amounts to the same thing). Whether in fury, hate, pride, shame, disheartened refusal or joyous demand, it is necessary for me to choose to be what I am' (*BN* 550).

But there are aspects of Sartre's account of freedom that seem not to merit the label 'optimistic'. As we shall see in the following chapters, precisely whether Sartre's view constituted pessimism, optimism or realism (whole or partial) became a matter of theological debate. For in *Being and Nothingness* Sartre describes freedom as 'really synonymous with lack' (*BN* 586). To be conscious is to exist in a state of perpetual knowledge of nothingness, of falling short. And Sartre explicitly (and famously) refers to this state as one of condemnation: we are 'condemned to be free'.[39]

> Freedom coincides at its roots with the non-being which is at the heart of man. For a human being, to *be* is to choose himself; nothing comes to him either from without or from within himself that he can receive or accept. He is wholly and helplessly at the mercy of the unendurable necessity to make himself be, even in the smallest details of his existence. Thus freedom is not a being, it is the being of man, that is to say his non-being. If

---

[39]That freedom is a state of condemnation is reiterated twenty times in *Being and Nothingness*: for some of the most famous passages, see *BN* 152, 462, 506 and 530.

we begin by conceiving of man as a fullness it becomes absurd to look in him for psychic moments or regions of freedom; we might as well look for an empty space in a vessel which we have filled to the brim. Man cannot be at times free and at other times a slave: either he is always and entirely free or he is not free at all.[40]

In the *War Diaries* Sartre wrote that 'freedom is the apparition of Nothingness in the world'.[41] In *Being and Nothingness* he uses explicitly Christian terminology for sin – the *sicut Deus* of Genesis 3:5 and Augustinian tradition – to describe freedom as 'a choice of being God and all my acts, all my projects translate this choice and reflect it in a thousand and one ways' (*BN* 620). The desire to be God is so central to Sartre's anthropology that he defines man as 'the being whose project is to be God'; 'To be man means to reach toward being God. Or if you prefer, man fundamentally is the desire to be God' (*BN* 587).

At this point Sartre anticipates his objectors, for whom such statements may sound suspiciously like a declaration of human essence.[42] What becomes of freedom if we can choose 'only to be God'? Sartre's answer is that, while the meaning of every desire is 'ultimately the project of being God, the desire is never constituted by this meaning. On the contrary, it always represents a particular discovery of its ends' (*BN* 587). The desire to be God can never be realized, and humanity is a 'useless passion':

Each human reality is at the same time a direct project to metamorphose its own For-itself into an In-itself-For-itself and a project of the appropriation of the world … Thus the passion of man is the reverse of that of Christ, for man loses himself as man in order that God may be born. But the idea of God is contradictory and we lose ourselves in vain. Man is a useless passion. (*BN* 636)

[40]Emphasis in original. It is interesting to note Marcel's comment on this passage: 'one of the significant and explicit [passages] in all Sartre's work. I do not believe that in the whole history of human thought, grace, even in its most secularised forms, has ever been denied with such audacity or such impudence' (Marcel 2002: 79).
[41]Sartre, *WD* 132–33.
[42]Indeed, Howells writes that for Sartre 'man's essence is defined as his liberty' (1988: 1).

The ambivalent Sartre?

We have seen now that the account Sartre presents in *Being and Nothingness* offers both pessimistic and optimistic elements. The knowledge of itself that consciousness seeks is eternally elusive. Sartre describes recourse to two different sources of information where 'knowing thyself' is concerned: consciousness and the judgements of others. But these have irreconcilable natures, for in the case of the latter we can feel we have been misjudged. The gaze of the other threatens the Sartrean consciousness, providing the possibility of ascribing greater reality to what is said than what is lived. The root of both of these problems is *nothingness*: I suffer its ambiguous consequences not only in the ambiguity of my internal relationships (in the domain of self-knowledge and self-deception) but also in the domain of relationships mediated by the other. Freedom is therefore both liberating and a liability – on this view it is little wonder that Sartre has Orestes protest to Zeus 'you should not have made me free!'[43]

In a famous footnote Sartre writes that 'these considerations do not exclude the possibility of an ethics of deliverance and salvation. But this can be achieved only after a radical conversion which we cannot discuss here.'[44] This 'astounding'[45] footnote has drawn much comment, as has the fact that Sartre did not publish such an ethics during his lifetime.[46] Themes of Fall and salvation recur in *Being and Nothingness* and elsewhere in his work, informing one of his earliest definitions of 'human reality': 'There is an original fall and striving for redemption – and that fall with that striving constitutes human reality' (*WD* 110).

Sartre concluded *Being and Nothingness* with a two-page section entitled 'Ethical Perspectives', in which he asserted that ontology does not formulate ethical precepts: 'It is concerned solely with what is, and we can not possibly derive imperatives from ontology's indicatives' (*BN* 645). Even so, he suggests, we can glimpse the ethics implied by considering *human reality in situation*. By means of existential psychoanalysis Sartre proposes that human beings will

---

[43]*F* 117.
[44]*BN* 412, n.414.
[45]Ramsey 1962: 71.
[46]The *Notebooks for an Ethics* were published posthumously in 1983.

be reacquainted with their passions. Again speaking of his method as one that promises 'deliverance and salvation' in the pursuit of being, he says that human beings must be liberated from the 'spirit of seriousness', to see that 'all human activities are equivalent … and that all are on principle doomed to failure': 'Thus it amounts to the same thing whether one gets drunk alone or is the leader of nations' (*BN* 646–7). Human beings are the beings by whom values exist. And once we recognize this our freedom will 'become conscious of itself and will reveal itself in anguish as the unique source of value and the nothingness by which the world exists' (*BN* 647).

We shall see in Part 3 that many theologians engage with Sartre's anthropology as a bleak but realistic depiction of fallenness – but they argue that the portrait Sartre paints is incomplete. But before proceeding to consider their reactions we must first consider the way Sartre responded to the earliest critics of *Being and Nothingness* in his famous lecture 'Existentialism Is a Humanism' – for his responses here shaped subsequent receptions of the work.

5

'Existentialism Is a Humanism'

On 29 October 1945 Sartre delivered a lecture at Club Maintenant, in Paris. The organizers were worried that no one would show up, but the venue was so full that there was standing room only. The paper delivered, unlike the version published, was given an interrogative title – 'Existentialisme, est-il un humanisme?' In the process of asking this question Sartre condensed and clarified several of his important concepts (including anxiety, abandonment and despair) and also drew out the moral and political implications of existentialism in ways that *Being and Nothingness* itself did not.

The lecture's content was provoked, at least in part, by an attack on Sartre's philosophy in the communist weekly *Action* (in June 1945), which denounced existentialism as 'idealist' (in the sense that it was opposed to dialectical materialism, that is, Marxism, rather than the idealism of Kant or Husserl). As Leak writes, after the publication of *Being and Nothingness*, Sartre was frequently criticized for being a 'bourgeois lackey/hyena/running dog'.[1] Concerned by this interpretation of his work, Sartre wanted to make clear that existentialism was for people of action. Existentialist freedom did not involve renouncing duty and the ties that bind us to others. Although Delarue did hold this view in the first two volumes of *The Roads to Freedom* trilogy (which were published in September 1945), he renounced it in the third.

Sartre opened the lecture with a statement of purpose, namely, to defend existentialism against the following charges: (1) being a

---

[1]Leak 2006: 73.

quietism of despair (so charged the communists); (2) 'emphasizing what is despicable about humanity … exposing all that is sordid, suspicious, or base, while ignoring beauty and the brighter side of human nature' (so charged some Catholics) (*EH* 17); (3) failing to recognize human solidarity and considering only the isolated individual (so charge the Catholics and the communists); (4) denying the reality and seriousness of human affairs by rejecting transcendent values and reducing ethics to matters of individual will (so charged the Christians).

Having stated the objections against which he would defend existentialism, Sartre proceeded to define the sense in which he uses the term 'humanism' (*EH* 18). This is significant, and he acknowledges that it will surprise some readers, for the Sartre of the 1930s (the author of *La Nausée*'s autodidact) was decidedly *not* a humanist. (His earlier assessment, in fact, was that 'humanism is shit' (*EM* 32).)

The 'humanism' of 'existentialism' as he defines it here consists in its being a doctrine that (1) 'makes human life possible' (*EH* 18) and (2) 'affirms that every truth and every action imply both an environment and a human subjectivity' (*EH* 18). What his objectors' charges boil down to, on Sartre's account, is the accusation that existentialism overemphasizes the evil side of life. But their objections are misdirected, Sartre thinks: what his opponents really find gloomy is not existentialism's pessimism but its optimism, namely, that it confronts man with a 'possibility of individual choice' (*EH* 20).

Bemoaning the fact that the word 'existentialist' is 'so loosely applied to so many things that it has come to mean nothing at all' (*EH* 20), Sartre clarifies that the question of definition is complicated because there are 'two kids of existentialists': Christian and atheist.[2] What they have in common is the belief that for human beings 'existence precedes essence' (*EH* 20).

In order to clarify his position Sartre provides the example of a paper knife: a paper knife has been made by a manufacturer – an artisan – who set out to produce this particular object to serve the purpose of cutting paper. In the case of the paper knife, Sartre says, 'production precedes essence' (*EH* 21). When we think of

---

[2]Although some early English critics would charge that 'existentialism' and 'Christianity' were strictly incompossible (O'Doherty 1954), clearly Sartre himself did not take this view.

the creator God, Sartre says, most of the time we imagine him to be a superartisan. Whether the God in question is Descartes's or Leibniz's, the divine will follows divine understanding, such that all of God's creations are deliberate and flawless. If such a God were the maker of humanity, each human would be conceived in the mind of God and brought into existence for a purpose. Like the artisan makes the paper knife, so God realizes his ideas to play their part in the world. Sartre notes that the atheists of the eighteenth century, although they rejected the concept of God, nevertheless kept the notion that essence is prior to existence: man was still thought to have a 'human nature' even though there was no divine architect behind the blueprint.

Atheistic existentialism, by contrast, offers a more consistent position, claiming that

> it states that if God does not exist, there is at least one being in whom existence precedes essence – a being whose existence comes before its essence, a being who exists before he can be defined by any concept of it.... What do we mean here by 'existence precedes essence'? We mean that man first exists: he materializes in the world, encounters himself, and only afterward defines himself. If man as existentialists conceive of him cannot be defined, it is because to begin with he is nothing. He will not be anything until later, and then he will be what he makes of himself. Thus, there is no human nature since there is no God to conceive of it.... man is nothing other than what he makes of himself. This is the first principle of existentialism. (*EH* 22)

This, Sartre says, is why people reproach existentialism for its 'subjectivity'. But Sartre argues that his view gives humanity much more dignity than a stone or a table – human beings are projects who possess subjective lives and must will themselves into existence: 'Thus, the first effect of existentialism is that it puts every man in possession of what he is, and to make him solely responsible for his existence' (*EH* 23).' In a famously Kantian move, Sartre's defence of existentialism against the charge of subjectivity moves from individual responsibility to choosing for all humankind: 'I am therefore responsible for myself and for everyone else, and I am fashioning a certain image of man as I choose him to be. In choosing myself I choose man' (*EH* 24–5). This, Sartre writes, should help us understand the meaning of the existentialist terms anguish, abandonment and despair. He restates the line from *Being and Nothingness* that 'man is anguish', clarifying that

> a man who commits himself, and who realizes that he is not only the individual that he chooses to be, but also a legislator choosing at the same time what humanity as a whole should be, cannot help but be aware of his own full and profound responsibility. True, many people do not appear especially anguished, but we maintain that they are merely hiding their anguish or trying not to face it. (*EH* 25)

In Sartre's elaboration on anguish in 'Existentialism Is a Humanism', however, he appeals to Kierkegaard's example of Abraham.[3] Many people think their choices affect only themselves. And if you were to ask, 'what if everyone did that?' their reply would likely be 'everyone does not.' But, Sartre says, 'one ought always to ask oneself what would happen if everyone did as one is doing; nor can one escape from that disturbing thought except by a kind of self-deception' – and this very self-deception reveals anguish, Sartre says, 'that Kierkegaard called "the anguish of Abraham"':

> You know the story: An angel orders Abraham to sacrifice his son. This would be okay provided it is really an angel who appears to him and says, 'Thou, Abraham, shalt sacrifice thy son.' But any sane person may wonder first whether it is truly an angel, and second, whether I am really Abraham. What proof do I have? There was once a mad woman suffering from hallucinations who claimed that people were phoning her and giving her orders. The doctor asked, 'But who exactly speaks to you?' She replied: 'He says it is God.' How did she actually know for certain that it was God? If an angel appears to me, what proof do I have that it is an angel? Or if I hear voices, what proof is there that they come from heaven and not from hell, or from my own subconsciousness or some pathological condition? Who can prove that they are intended for me? (*EH* 26)

---

[3]This is not discussed in *The War Diaries* or *Being and Nothingness*, although it is listed on Sartre's 'Readings of Youth' manuscript.

Sartre's point is simple: can you prove that you are the appropriate person to impose on humanity, through your choice, your conception of the human? If a voice speaks to you, it is still you who decide whether or not the voice belongs to an angel. If you must choose to act or not act, it is you who decide whether action or inaction is the better course.

Sartre is careful to emphasize that this anguish could not lead 'to quietism or inaction, but rather that it is well known to those who have borne responsibility: 'All leaders have experienced that anguish, but it does not prevent them from acting. To the contrary it is the very condition of their action, for they first contemplate several options, and, in choosing one of them, realize that its only value lies in the fact that it was chosen' (*EH* 27). Anxiety does not separate us from action, Sartre asserts, but is a condition of it.

As concerns 'abandonment', Sartre states that 'we merely mean to say that God does not exist, and we must bear the full consequences of his absence right to the end' (*EH* 27).[4] Writing against the secular morality that emerged around 1880, Sartre rejects the need or even possibility of a priori ideals. Atheists need to recognize that on the human plane such ideals are no longer defensible.

Sartre cites Dostoevsky's famous line that 'if God does not exist, everything is permitted' as 'the starting point' for existentialism:

> Indeed, everything is permissible if God does not exist, and man is consequently abandoned, for he cannot find anything to rely on – neither within nor without. First, he finds there are no excuses. For if it is true that existence precedes essence, we can never explain our actions by reference to a given and immutable human nature. In other words, there is no determinism – man is free, man is freedom. If, however, God does not exist, we will encounter no values or orders that can legitimize our conduct. Thus, we have neither behind us, nor before us, in the luminous realm of values, any means of justification or excuse. We are left alone and without excuse. That is what I mean when I say that man is condemned to be free: condemned, because he did not create himself, yet nonetheless free, because once cast into the world, he is responsible for everything he does. (*EH* 29)

[4]Modified translation; Sartre's French refers to the absence of God here, while the English translation has only 'bear the consequences of this assertion'.

As for despair, Sartre writes that its meaning is extremely simple: we must limit ourselves to rely upon only that which is within the scope of our will and 'act without hope' that salvation will come to us from without. As we saw at the conclusion of the last chapter, in the *War Diaries* Sartre wrote that 'There is an original fall and striving for redemption – and that fall with that striving constitutes human reality' (*WD* 110). But, Sartre argues, some ways of striving are better than others.

To the Marxist reply that one can rely on others to carry forward one's action to its accomplishment Sartre argues that although we should certainly be engaged in common causes with others, 'I cannot count on men whom I do not know based on faith in the goodness of humanity or in man's interest in society's welfare, given that man is free and there is no human nature in which I can place my trust' (*EH* 35–6).

Again Sartre emphasizes that he is not endorsing quietism; he is not saying one should lazily or complacently assume that 'Others can do what I cannot do' (EH 36). On the contrary, he argues, his doctrine declares that 'there is no reality except in action'. He understands that this aspect of existentialism strikes many as horrifying, because many have 'one resource to sustain them in their misery', namely to consider themselves passive victims of circumstance. Some find solace in thinking to themselves,

> 'I deserve a much better life than the one I have. Admittedly, I have never experienced a great love or extraordinary friendship, but that is because I never met a man or woman worthy of it; if I have written no great books, it is because I never had the leisure to do so; if I have had no children to whom I could devote myself, it is because I did not find a man with whom I could share my life. So I have within me a host of untried but perfectly viable abilities, inclinations, and possibilities that endow me with worthiness not evident from any examination of my past actions.' In reality, however, for existentialists there is no love other than the deeds of love; no potential for love other than that which is manifested in loving. There is no genius other than that which is expressed in works of art. (*EH* 37)

This is not to say that the artist is reducible to his art ('for a thousand other things contribute no less to his definition as a man') but rather to say that the human is the sum of her actions.

The problem, Sartre says, is not his pessimism but instead 'the sternness of our optimism' (*EH* 38) – *you* are free to make what you will of your life, but you must *act*. Having defended existentialism against his objectors, Sartre goes on to outline some of its virtues, claiming that *this theory alone* 'endows man with any dignity'; it is 'the only one which does not turn him into an object' (*EH* 41).

Although it is impossible to find in each human being a universal essence, Sartre writes that there is nevertheless a universality of *condition*. 'It is no accident,' he writes, 'that today's thinkers are more likely to speak of the condition of man rather than of his nature' (*EH* 42). There are limitations which a priori define the situation of human beings, such as their historical situation, but everyone has to be in the world, live and die. These limitations have both an objective and a subjective aspect: they are objective in that they occur in each human existence and subjective in that they have to be *lived* by particular human existences.

Existentialism is a humanism, Sartre says, because it reminds human beings that there are no legislators but themselves. You are abandoned and must judge for yourself. And you must always seek, beyond yourself, an aim which is one of liberation in order to 'realize [your]self as truly human' (*EH* 53).

Sartre's concluding paragraph summarizes existentialism as 'an attempt to draw all of the conclusions' entailed by 'a consistently atheistic position' (*EH* 53). But this atheism is not interested in 'exhaust[ing] itself in demonstrations of the non-existence of God'.

> Rather, it affirms that even if God were to exist, it would make no difference – that is our point of view. It is not that we believe that God exists, but we think that the real problem is not one of His existence; what man needs is to rediscover himself and to comprehend that nothing can save him from himself, not even valid proof of the existence of God. In this sense existentialism is optimistic. It is a doctrine of action, and it is only in bad faith – in confusing their own despair with ours – that Christians are able to assert that we are 'without hope'. (*EH* 53–4)

Conclusion

In 'Existentialism Is a Humanism' Sartre does not always provide arguments for his assertions. It is far from certain that he achieved his stated aims, namely, to defend existentialism against the ethical concerns that 'if God doesn't exist, anything is permitted' and to prove that existentialism is, indeed, a humanism. Increasing the scope of responsibility for my decisions from its usual domain (me) to all of humankind is also contentious. Why must what I choose to value be 'better for all'? This seems counterintuitive and, frankly, impractical: it is simply not sustainable for all of humanity to spend their time writing books about Sartre, for example.

Sartre soon regretted having published the lecture: too many readers assumed it was an adequate introduction to the philosophy of *Being and Nothingness*.[5] But despite its superficiality (or perhaps, because of it) the lecture became the representative text of Sartrean existentialism. Early Anglophone receptions of Sartre interpreted it as a challenge to 'get rid of promised lands, and myths of survival, and face the nothingness which you are and will be'. One writer called it 'the first consistent unrelenting attempt to formulate total atheism':

> Those who in the past denied the existence of God, tried nevertheless to retain rationality, to retain morality, to retain hope. They tried to substitute something else for the God they rejected … to give a meaning to the notion of truth, … to the value of living …. The only thing which is new in existentialism, and that which gives it, or gave it its strength, is the fact that it relentlessly, consistently, and in its own way triumphantly draws all the consequences of the denial of God's existence.[6]

In France, too, it prompted books asking whether Sartre was possessed – and earned him the epithet 'the Socrates of nothingness'.[7]

As we shall see in Part 3, it provoked a wide spectrum of theological responses: Sartre's philosophy was to be decried as Luciferian and celebrated as the highest moment of Western theology.

[5]See *EH* xiii.
[6]O'Doherty 1954: 56–7.
[7]This expression was employed by Pierre Boutang, in *Sartre est-il un possédé?*, Paris: La Table ronde, 1947, p. 35.

PART 3

Sartre's theological legacy

6

Sartre and Protestant theology: Barth and Tillich

There never actually has been a philosophia christiana, for if it was philosophia it was not christiana, and if it was christiana it was not philosophia.[1]

KARL BARTH

Whether or not Sartre can comfortably be said to have 'influenced' Protestant theology depends on the methodological commitments of the theological reader. For Protestant theology in the twentieth century is a tale of – if not two cities – two districts. On the one hand, we have Barth's proclamation that 'if it was *philosophia* it was not *christiana*', and on the other we have Tillich's insistence that theology's task is precisely to answer the questions posed by philosophy. In order to demonstrate that Sartre informed Protestant theology, therefore, this chapter outlines the ways in which both Barth and Tillich engage with Sartre in their systematic theologies.

Sartre and Karl Barth

In Barth's *Church Dogmatics* he mentions Jean-Paul Sartre 67 times. All of these instances are found in volume 3, on the doctrine of creation. The first part of volume 3 was composed in a period ending in

---

[1] Barth *CD* I.i.6; emphasis in original.

1945,[2] and the complete volume was published in English between 1958 and 1961. The location of Barth's discussion of Sartre is theologically significant, but in order to see precisely why it is necessary to briefly outline Barth's Christological method and, in particular, the role of nothingness (*das Nichtige*) in his theology. This kind of methodological overview is not possible for all of the theologians considered in Part 3, but it is necessary here for reasons that will become apparent.

Barth's theological method is Christological. According to the first volume of *Church Dogmatics* the criterion of truth of Christian utterance is Jesus Christ.[3] This may have helped Barth overcome the obstacles raised by Enlightenment rationalism, Romanticism and the quest for the historical Jesus. But it presented him with a challenge when it came to presenting sin. For how can we look to the only sinless God-Man, Jesus Christ, for answers to this question? Barth's answer is Augustinian: sin is nothingness, *das Nichtige*.

Das Nichtige

Barth's *das Nichtige* is famous for stretching the limits of consistency. His account of nothingness is found in the context of his broader doctrine of creation – where one might usually expect to find a doctrine of sin. For Barth, the doctrine of creation must bring about the confession that 'God is before the world in the strictest sense that He is its absolute origin, its purpose, the power which rules it, its Lord. For He created it'.[4] Barth does not, however, unequivocally appeal to the *ex nihilo* doctrine, writing that 'it may well be that the concept of a *creatio ex nihilo*, of which there is no actual hint in Genesis 1:2, is the construct of later attempts at more precise formulation.' The biblical text, for Barth, takes precedence over the classical formula. 'But its antithesis – the mythological acceptance of a primeval reality independent of God – is excluded in practice by the general tenor of the passages as well as its position within the biblical context.'[5]

---

[2] Barth's preface is dated October of that year. See Barth, *CD* III.1, preface.
[3] Barth, *CD* I.i.4.
[4] Barth, *CD* III.1.7.
[5] Barth, *CD* III.1.104.

Barth's account of nothingness is haunted by the same theological dilemma Augustine confronted, namely, how to account for evil in a way that exculpates God and respects the dignity of the human creature (as God's creation). It is also haunted by the problem of how we come to know *das Nichtige*, for on Barth's account 'there is no accessible relationship between the creature and nothingness'.[6] As such, our knowledge of nothingness – like that of sin – must be derived from 'the source of all Christian knowledge': Jesus Christ.

> In Him there is revealed not only the goodness of God's creation in its twofold form, but also the true nothingness which is utterly distinct from both Creator and creation, the adversary with whom no compromise is possible, the negative which is more than the mere complement of an antithetical positive, the left which is not counterpoised by any right, the antithesis which is not merely within creation and therefore dialectical but which is primarily and supremely to God Himself and therefore to the totality of the created world.[7]

Barth emphasizes that this antithesis has no substantive existence. It is not a creature but rather an alien, opposing element.

For Barth nothingness is not defined in contrast to being as the term for actuality, but vis-à-vis the will of God. Sin is the most concrete form of nothingness as that which 'God has not willed and does not will and will not will, of that which absolutely is not, or is only as God does not will it, of that which lives only as that which God has rejected and condemned and excluded'.[8] Nothingness, as that which God has negated, tempts the human being in such a way that when a man (or woman) sins, (s)he not only willingly cooperates with nothingness but also is its victim. Barth defines sin as a wilful human act of 'surrender to the alien power of an adversary',[9] for the reality of nothingness is not sufficiently grasped 'if sin is understood only generally as aberration from God and disobedience to his will'.[10]

[6]Barth, *CD* III.3.350.
[7]Barth, *CD* III.3.302.
[8]Barth, *CD* IV.1.409.
[9]Barth, *CD* III.3.310.
[10]Barth, *CD* III.3.308.

But for Barth, nothingness is a broader category than sin: 'There is real evil and real death as well as real sin.'[11] In a frequently cited passage Barth writes, 'there is not only a Yes but also a No; not only a height but also an abyss'.[12] Though his antithetical rhetoric could easily be interpreted otherwise, Barth's nothingness is not conceived as the dialectical counterpart of good. Like Augustine's privative view, Barth presents *das Nichtige* as having no power – or being – before God. But if nothingness is 'not an adversary to God',[13] how is it that 'it is His enemy no less than ours',[14] 'an adversary with whom God and God alone can cope'?[15]

Though this tension cannot easily be resolved, one answer Barth offers is that because creation is helpless against it, God takes nothingness seriously, making the cause of the creature God's own. Because nothingness threatens God's glory by threatening the creature, God is its 'primary victim and foe'.[16] He has overcome it in the event of the cross,[17] but though it is a thing of the past God allows it to have a limited existence now, such that we live ' "as if" He had not yet mastered it for us'.[18]

Nothingness is characterized as an 'impossible possibility', or an 'ontological impossibility': because the ontology of God makes nothingness in the ontology of man unfathomable.[19] In order to reflect further on nothingness we must turn to what nothingness is not, that is, Barth's ontology of God and humanity. But before we do let us return to section 50 of *CD* III.3 ('God and Nothingness'), where the vast majority of Barth's direct citations of Sartre are to be found.

Sartre and *das Nichtige*

In that section, although Barth frequently uses their names in the same breath, it is very clear that Barth had read Heidegger and

[11]Barth, *CD* III.3.310.
[12]Barth, *CD* III.3.297.
[13]Barth, *CD* III.3.77.
[14]Barth, *CD* III.3.103.
[15]Barth, *CD* III.1.305.
[16]Barth, *CD* III.3.360.
[17]Barth, *CD* III.3.305.
[18]Barth, *CD* III.3.367.
[19]Barth uses similar language to describe the incarnation: where sin is inexplicable, the incarnation is inconceivable. The latter, however, is not absurd (*CD* I.2.160).

Sartre carefully enough to see the nuances between their positions. He spends several pages setting out his assessment of their differences,[20] for example, writing that nothingness is 'Heidegger's goal and Sartre's starting point'.[21] This passage shows that Barth had read several of Sartre's works: he makes reference to French editions of *The Reprieve* and *No Exit* as well as *Being and Nothingness* and 'Existentialism Is a Humanism', the latter of which he takes to be a 'commentary' on the former, which 'answers his opponents' and 'offers an exact and definitive statement of his system'.[22]

Barth writes that Sartre 'has behind him (as though obsessed by nothing and unable to see anything except in the light of it) what Heidegger still has before him (as though obsessed by nothing and unable to look to any other goal)'.[23] Both are concerned with the principle of nothingness, and with nothingness as a dimension of human life:

> But whereas Heidegger's purpose is almost entirely to demonstrate the potency of nothing against existence, that of Sartre is almost entirely to demonstrate human existence as conditioned by it. In both cases I have said 'almost entirely', for naturally there is overlapping. Heidegger's own teaching foreshadows the inevitable and ultimate tendency of the development of his thought if his conclusions regarding the constraint and compulsion of nothing are accepted and human existence is positively interpreted in accordance with his view. Indeed, this tendency is already evident in his own thought.[24]

One difference Barth takes as separating Heidegger and Sartre is that the latter has a 'decisive presupposition' that the former does not, namely, his emphatic denial of God's existence. This gives him a radical awareness that Heidegger does not have

---

[20]Barth, *CD* III.3.338 ff.
[21]Barth, *CD* III.3.344.
[22]See *CD* III.3.338; Barth and Tillich both took *EH* to be an authoritative statement of Sartre's existentialist position despite Sartre's shift from an anti-humanist to a humanist stance between 1943 and 1945 and later expressions of frustration with the lecture's popularity.
[23]Barth, *CD* III.3.338.
[24]Barth, *CD* III.3.338.

awareness of dread, *délaissement*, and despair. In 1938, when the French were faced by a probable war which was only postponed, Sartre depicted it in *Le Sursis* in all the colours of a mythical monster: *on était solidaire d'un gigantesque et invisible polypier*. His description of hell in *Huis Clos* is overpowering just because it is ultimately no more than a portrayal of the dreadful banality that prevails in man's relationship with man. And many more examples might be given.[25]

Barth writes that because Sartre is 'so eloquent and illuminating on this subject Sartre has often been misunderstood', defending Sartre against those accusers who thought he was merely intent on exposing the ugly face of humanity, writing that Sartre's unsightly depictions of human life reveal that 'his passionate concern is to be sought in his description of man, ... the man who realises that he must live without God ... the man who knows dread, *délaissement*, despair, war and hell'.[26] Barth commends his ability to describe, his phenomenological renderings of a life without God, suggesting that Sartre recognizes that the 'awful No derived from nothing is an actuality, but out of it there strangely grows the peculiar and categorical Yes of human existence. This Yes is Sartre's concern.'[27]

In fact, on Barth's assessment, Sartre is 'the most virile' of the modern existentialists because his teaching is not that humanity is in suspense but rather that 'he should stand and advance to a goal'.[28] Barth thinks this is what Sartre means by claiming that existentialism is a doctrine that 'renders life possible' in 'Existentialism Is a Humanism':

> His existentialism is a doctrine of freedom. Man *hic et nunc* – this or that particular man – cannot and may not find freedom anywhere at all. But he can and may exercise and therefore possess it. Indeed, he can and may become it himself. Hence his freedom is not an idea. It is not a potentiality which he controls. It is not a gift which he is granted. It is not an assumption on which he may proceed. It is not a capital sum on which interest accrues and

---

[25]Barth, *CD* III.3.339.
[26]Barth, *CD* III.3.339.
[27]Barth, *CD* III.3.339.
[28]Barth, *CD* III.3.339.

with which he can start something. He cannot start anywhere or with anything. There is no corresponding something. He can start only with nothing.[29]

'*All that is lacking*', Barth says, 'is the slightest trace of the biblical concept of God.'[30] Of course, that is enough to damn him and his philosophy. As Gilson wrote, 'All the Barthian Calvinist asks of philosophy is that it recognize itself as damned and remain in that condition.'[31]

Sartre and the other

Nevertheless, we see further suggestions of Sartrean influence in Barth's discussion of sin ('the concrete form of nothingness'), particularly with reference to being with others. Again, Barth's methodological commitments require him to look to Jesus as the type of humanity. For Barth, Jesus's being a 'real man' consists in his being 'man for God' and 'man for other men'.[32] To say that Jesus (and by implication, humanity) exists for God is equivalent to saying that he does not live for himself.[33] This means that he is 'man for other men'. This is why, on Barth's reading, so little attention is given to Jesus's 'private life' in the Gospels – even his intimate life with God is *for others*.[34] 'If we see Him alone', Barth writes, 'we do not see Him at all.'[35]

And yet this self-for-others is not *selfless*; he is supremely himself. 'What emerges in [the New Testament] is a supreme I wholly determined by and to the Thou.'[36] There is a correspondence between Jesus's being for God and for man: the *analogia relationis* between the relation in God and between God and man.[37] On Barth's Christological (and therefore Trinitarian) definition, humanity is

---

[29]Barth, *CD* III.3.340.
[30]Barth, *CD* III.3. 342–3.
[31]Gilson 1939: 47.
[32]Barth *CD* III.2, §§44.1, 45.1.
[33]Barth *CD* III.2.133.
[34]Barth, *CD* III.2.209.
[35]Barth, *CD* III.2.216.
[36]Barth, *CD* III.2.216.
[37]Barth, *CD* III.2.219–22.

essentially relational: vertically, 'to be a man is to be with God',[38] and on the horizontal axis, to be human is to be with human others. We do not see humanity at all if the individual man is viewed only 'in and for himself', or as isolated from, opposed to, neutral towards or only accidentally related to others.[39] Our humanity consists in our being with others.

Though we cannot be for others as Christ can, we can be for others in an analogous, secondary sense. 'We can support but not carry [the other], give him encouragement but not victory, alleviate but not liberate.'[40] In order to be for another in this way, we must 'encounter' him. Barth's discussion of what it means to be with and for the other draws heavily on the thought of Buber.[41] For both, to be human is to be in relation to another. But this relation is not static; it is an encounter, such that '"I am" … may thus be paraphrased "I am in encounter"'.[42] For Barth, encounter is the image of Christlikeness, the form of the Trinity, and is thus the true model for human relations.

Being in encounter involves four components:

(1) looking the other in the eye (including being open to others and letting oneself be seen)
(2) mutual speaking and listening
(3) mutual assistance
(4) mutual gladness throughout (which Barth calls 'the secret of the whole').[43]

On Barth's view we have already been exalted to fellowship with God and each other in Christ. Sin is therefore not the failure to reach an abstract ideal – Adamic perfection – but rather the attempt to be other than we are, failure to conform to the reality of our humanity as given in Christ. This is not merely morally wrong but

[38]Barth, *CD* III.2.135.
[39]Barth *CD* III.2.226–7.
[40]McLean 1981: 41.
[41]For analyses of their relationship, see Selinger 1998: 126–34; Mikkelsen 2010: 97–120.
[42]Barth, *CD* III.2.245–8.
[43]Barth, *CD* III.2.250–65.

also mistaken about what it means to be human. It is worth quoting Barth at length on this point:

> The error of man concerning himself, his self-alienation, is that he thinks he can love and choose and will and assert and maintain and exalt himself – *sese propter seipsum* – in his being in himself, his self-hood, and that in so doing he will be truly man. Whether this takes place more in pride or in modesty, either way man misses his true being. For neither as an individual nor in society was he created to be placed alone, to be self-controlling and self-sufficient, to be self-centred, to rotate around himself. Like every other creature he was created for the glory of God and only in that way for his own salvation ... He is a man, himself, as he comes from God and moves towards God. He is a man as he is open to God, or not at all. If he chooses himself in any other way, *incurvatus in se*, in self-containment, then he misses the very thing that he seeks.[44]

To sin, on Barth's view, is to deny our relatedness to God and others, to attempt to be a 'relationless man',[45] who exists in 'graceless being for ourselves'.[46]

Sartre's and Barth's methodology

Barth's position on Sartre is clear: *being-for-itself* is graceless, and his concept of nothingness is not seen with the eyes of faith. The 'atheistic blindness' of Heidegger and Sartre precluded them from seeing truly: 'in view of the state of their knowledge of God, we cannot expect from these two philosophers a knowledge of nothingness which is finally acceptable' – *but*, he says, 'for all the speculation something instructive and worthwhile is introduced'.[47]

This leaves the Barthian with something of a conundrum. If one takes Barth to be consistent in his Christological method, then a Sartrean influence is a non sequitur. But if one takes Barth's method to be less-than-consistently employed – for example, because he

[44]Barth, *CD* IV.1.421.
[45]Barth, *CD* III.2.96–109.
[46]Barth, *CD* IV.2.458.
[47]Barth, *CD* III.3.344.

does say that 'in our present discussion of Heidegger and Sartre we are concerned to learn about nothingness',[48] again implying that there is something *to be learned* from them – then admitting a Sartrean legacy is less problematic.

Barth himself recognized that 'the conventional Western figure of God is almost completely delineated' in Sartre's account, 'with the one difference that the existence of God is denied, and "atheistic" man, man discarding acknowledgement of any Supreme Being other than himself, stands forth clothed in the garments of the conventional figure of God'.[49] Elsewhere in Barth's discussion of Sartre he comes very close to the conclusion that knowledge of nothingness is possible outside the domain of faith, writing that Heidegger and Sartre provide evidence that 'nothingness is really present and at work'[50], and that their thought is 'determined in and by real encounter with nothingness'. Barth even goes so far as to claim that 'no one today can think or say anything of value without being an "existentialist" and thinking and speaking as such, i.e. without being confronted and affected by the disclosure of the presence and operation of nothingness as effected with particular impressiveness in our day'.[51] He does qualify his praises by insisting that 'it must be stated most emphatically that seeing they do not really see'.[52] But it is difficult not to read these repetitive dismissals as a case of *qui s'excuse s'accuse*, and Barth's theology as 'answering' (in the Tillichean sense) more than he wished to admit.

Despite invoking categories such as 'nothingness', 'relationless man' and 'graceless being for ourselves' to describe the experience of fallen human existence, at points in *Church Dogmatics* Barth's official line is clear: Christian theology can learn nothing about true nothingness from the existentialists:

> But in spite of our indebtedness to them for bringing us to this point, we cannot agree that, with their doctrine of nothing, our existentialists have even entered the dimension in which

---

[48]Barth, *CD* III.3.344.
[49]Barth, *CD* III.3. 342–3.
[50]Barth, *CD* III.3.345.
[51]Barth, *CD* III.3.345.
[52]Barth, *CD* III.3.346.

nothingness is to be seen and described as true nothingness by Christian insights. This is naturally of a piece with their ignorance of God, in consequence of which they cannot adopt the standpoint from which one must see and think and speak in this matter. They see and think and speak as true, alert and honest children of our time who have experienced themselves the shock sustained by modern man.[53]

Sartre and Tillich

Anne Marie Reijnen writes that 'if there is indeed a dividing line in Western theology between those who ask the modern or "liberal" question of Jesus' place in our story and other theologians – postmodern or pre-modern – who choose to enquire only "into our place in his", Tillich certainly belongs to the former'.[54] Tillich approaches sin from a diametrically opposite starting point to the Christological method of Barth, writing that it is flatly 'wrong to derive the question implied in human existence from the revelatory answer'. In fact, he asserts, it is impossible to do so, because 'the revelatory answer is meaningless if there is no question to which it is the answer. Man cannot receive an answer to a question he has not asked.'[55] From Tillich's perspective, Barth's Christological approach is the theological equivalent of hurling the Gospel at man 'like stones to his head'.[56]

Given Tillich's theological method it is no surprise that he would have considered Sartre's thought worthy of serious consideration. But to what extent, if any, can Tillich's theology be said to answer distinctively Sartrean questions? In what follows, Tillich's theological method, ontology and hamartiology (doctrine of sin) are introduced before I argue that the threat of anxiety in Tillich – and in particular, the anxiety of meaninglessness – explicitly 'answers' the philosophy of Sartre.

[53]Barth, *CD* III.3. 346.
[54]Reijnen 2009: 56.
[55]Tillich 1957: 13.
[56]Thomas 2000: 49; cf. Tillich 1953: 7.

Tillich's method

For Tillich, the 'besetting sin of theology' is that 'it becomes entirely occupied with its own concepts and ceases to have any relevance to the social situation which is its context'.[57] Desiring to rescue theology from what he perceived as an arid, atrophied orthodoxy, Tillich proposed a method of correlation which 'explains the contents of the Christian Faith through existential questions and theological answers in mutual interdependence'.[58] On Tillich's view, theologians must not ignore the cultural context they address (and are informed by), for 'philosophy formulates the questions implied in human existence, and theology formulates the answers implied in divine self-manifestation under the guidance of the questions implied in human existence'. The two tasks are not exclusive. Faith as 'ultimate concern' requires that theological answers must be correlated to and *answer* the ontological question that exists and is developed independently from the answer itself.

Tillich's method of correlation distinguishes between form and content in the answers of theology. While revelation determines the content of theological answers, Tillich suggests, the formulation of the questions determines the form of the answer. This is because – in stark contrast to Barth, who rejected apologetics as 'anxiety concerning the victory of the Gospel'[59] – theology must always be apologetic.[60] Bayer writes that 'in no other twentieth-century theological system is apologetics such a defining consideration as it is for Tillich'[61] – theology must be 'answering theology'.[62] As early as his lectures on dogmatics of 1925–27, Tillich was emphatic that 'theology must go on the offensive' (*Theologie muß Angriff sein*).[63]

Shortly after these lectures, the language (and concepts) Tillich used to articulate his theological work began to change, a most pertinent example being his replacement of 'sin' (*Sünde*) with 'lack of being' (*Seinsverfehlung*). Through appropriating the ontological

[57]Thomas 2000: 31.
[58]Tillich 1953: 60.
[59]Barth 1933: 35.
[60]Although Tillich rejected the idea of 'apologetics' as *apologizing* for faith (cf. Thomas 2000: 53).
[61]Bayer 2009: 20.
[62]Tillich 1953: 6.
[63]As he put it in the epigraph to said lectures.

language of contemporary philosophy, Werner Schüßler writes, he attempted 'to reach "spiritual seekers" who had turned away from the church'.[64] God is called the 'ground of being' because God definitively answers the question asked by man's existence: the ontological threat of nonbeing.

Tillich's ontology

Tillich's concept of nothingness, or nonbeing, clearly draws on ontologies other than Sartre's. But it is worth highlighting the importance Tillich assigns to ontology – he considers it to be the true subject of our 'ultimate concern'. Being, far from an empty abstraction, is the most meaningful of concepts because it is 'the power of being in everything that has being'.[65]

Tillich presents a very different ontology from that of traditional medieval theology as exemplified in Anselm and Aquinas.[66] According to the latter, God is understood as the supreme Being – that than which nothing greater can be thought – and he is characterized by the predicates of omnipotence, omniscience, benevolence and so on. Philosophical arguments for God's existence are premised upon such an understanding of Him, but Tillich is highly critical of this mode of discourse (which he calls 'theological theism'). If God is a Being (*das Seiende*), Tillich objects, even if 'the highest', He cannot be called the source of being.

Tillich argues that the theological theists' God is responsible for much revolt against faith. As 'Being-Itself', Tillich's ontological view of God is the foundation that 'precedes' all beings; no human person can be outside God. The famous 'unknown God' of Athens witnessed to the Athenians' (and, more generally, humanity's) 'religious knowledge in spite of their religious ignorance'.[67]

On Tillich's view, humanity would not ask questions about God if it were not the case that we are separated from Him as infinite essence. We do ask such questions, however, which reveals that we remain bound to God. Tillich therefore makes a significant move

[64]Schüßler 2009: 8.
[65]Tillich 1957: 11.
[66]Tillich 1957: 225–33. Although McKelway (1964: 33) suggests that Tillich proposes an existential interpretation of classical ontology similar Gilson's.
[67]Tillich 1948: 130.

in assuming an original 'essential unity' of God and humanity. The differentiation between God and humanity (and all creation) is a sign of estrangement and sin. It would not exist if we were unified with our origin (that is, God).[68] Therefore, along with natural knowledge of God comes natural knowledge of his absence.[69] Tillich writes,

> Although mankind is not strange to God, it is estranged from Him. Although mankind is never without God, it perverts the picture of God. Although mankind is never without the knowledge of God, it is ignorant of God. Mankind is separated from its origin; it lives under a law of wrath and frustration, of tragedy and self-destruction, because it produces one distorted image of God after another, and adores those images.[70]

On this point, his apologetic dogmatics has a polemical edge. The theologian's purpose is not simply to clarify theoretical points of doctrine but to 'discover the false gods in the individual soul and in society'.

> Theological polemic is not merely a theoretical discussion, but rather a spiritual judgment against the gods which are not God, against those structures of evil, those distortions of God in thought and action....[...] In spite of the dangers inherent in so judging, the theologian must become an instrument of the Divine Judgment against a distorted world.[71]

---

[68]In light of this equation of estrangement and differentiation from God, Tillich suggests that there is a 'point of indifference' (*Indifferenzpunkt*) where 'question and answer are not separated' (I.61). It belongs 'to man's essential being, to the unity of his finitude with the infinity in which he was created, and from which he is separated' (I.61). This formulation is highly indebted to Schelling, who proposes a point of indifference where 'Nature and Spirit, God and humanity, recognizing subject and recognized object, ultimately come together and are ultimately one and the same' (Bayer 2009: 24).

[69]McKelway (1964: 33) notes that, while Tillich does not think a natural theology is possible, his 'doctrine of revelation implies a natural, ontological, and noetic relation between man and the divine which differs from a developed natural theology only in degree'.

[70]Tillich 1948: 131.

[71]Tillich 1948: 131–2.

Before turning to consider Sartre's role in Tillich's depiction of the
'distorted world', however, it must be noted that on Tillich's view,
no matter how disfigured humanity has become there is nonetheless a unity of being between the sinner and God such that 'God is
nearer to us than we ourselves'.[72]

Tillich's hamartiology

Tillich's analysis of creation and fallenness begins with the Genesis
myth, 'the profoundest and richest expression of man's awareness
of existential estrangement'.[73] Tillich can be said to stand in the
Augustinian stream of Christian thought, though his account of the
Fall makes substantial departures from it.[74] 'In myth and dogma',
Tillich writes, 'man's essential nature has been projected into a past
as a history before history, symbolized as a golden age or paradise.'[75]
In contrast to Augustine, for Tillich 'creation and fall coincide': to
exist is to be fallen.[76] It is absurd that 'man' should be held directly
responsible for 'a moment in time in which man and nature were
changed from good to evil'.[77] Rather, the fall must be interpreted
symbolically and *trans-* (or *supra-*) historically.[78]

Tillich asserts that humanity's 'essential nature' is good: it is
a 'dreaming innocence of undecided potentialities'. But because
we are fallen we never experience this in undistorted form – how
things were in the 'time before time' must be revealed or inferred.
The classical statement of creation as *creatio ex nihilo* reveals that
humanity also has a heritage of nonbeing.[79] On account of this
heritage we are – like all creation – limited by nonbeing. This
manifests itself in our finitude, which Tillich defines etymologi-
cally as having 'a definite end (*finis*)'.[80] But the distinctive nature
of human finitude lies in our ability to experience 'the shock of

---

[72]Tillich 1948: 131.
[73]Tillich 1957: 35.
[74]Slater 1985: 196.
[75]Tillich 1957: 33.
[76]Tillich 1957: 44.
[77]Tillich 1957: 41.
[78]See Tillich 1957: 40 and 33.
[79]Tillich 1953: 209.
[80]Tillich 1953: 210. On Tillich's reliance on etymology, see Thomas 2000: 88–9.

non-being'.[81] Humanity is conscious of the inevitable approach of its own death; it is anxiously aware that its existence will end in nonbeing.[82] Only humanity, as aware of this finitude, has the ability to transcend it.

According to Tillich's idiom, the fall symbolizes the 'transition from essence to existence'.[83] The distinction between essence and existence 'underlies Tillich's entire theological system'.[84] In language reminiscent of Barth on the origin of sin, Tillich refers to the transition from essence to existence as 'the original fact'.[85] This fall from essence is described by some scholars as 'an ongoing process, a tension between the essential and the existential'.[86] In it we are estranged, dehumanized, 'filled with anxiety and threatened by meaninglessness'[87]:

> Estranged from the power of being, Man is determined by his finitude. He is given over to his natural fate. He came from nothing and he returns to nothing. He is under the domination of death and is driven by the anxiety of having to die.[88]

It is clear from the foregoing that on Tillich's view to be a self – essentially – is to be in relation. Indeed, 'relation is a basic ontological category'.[89] But in the state of sin – in the tragic sense of the 'estrangement' of man from his true being – our relationships propel us further from our essence. Tillich asserts that this is not something that can be diagnosed and treated psychologically. He is critical of the Freudian approach taken by many of his contemporaries in psychology. They attempted to overcome 'existential negativity, anxiety, estrangement, meaninglessness, and guilt' as though they were illnesses which could simply be treated and therefore deprived of power. 'But this is impossible. The existentialist structure cannot be healed by the most refined techniques. They are

[81]Tillich 1953: 207.
[82]Tillich 1957: 77.
[83]Tillich 1957: 29ff.
[84]Parrella 2009: 76.
[85]Tillich 1957: 36.
[86]Dreisbach 1980: 521.
[87]Tillich 1957: 25.
[88]Tillich 1957: 66.
[89]Tillich 1953: 300.

objects of salvation'.[90] Only a religious understanding of estrange-ment reveals existence for what it is, and only New Being can trans-form the suffering nothingness entails. As Meszaros shows, Tillich's ontology – unlike Sartre's ontology of conflict – is an ontology of participation.[91]

This is Tillich's answer to the threat of nonbeing. The 'third and final part of the theological answer' and apologetic dogmatics is the overcoming of estrangement through Jesus Christ. 'For we are real theologians', he writes, 'when we state that Jesus is the Christ, and that it is in Him that the Logos of theology is manifest.'[92] To repeat a passage already cited, it is not only estrangement but also the doctrine of the Christ which constitutes 'the heart of any Christian theology'.[93]

Sartre in Tillich

Given Tillich's methodological approach and ontological con-cerns it is no surprise that he found Sartre's work noteworthy. Sartre appears by name in several of Tillich's works: twelve times in *The Courage to Be*, three times in volumes one and two of *Systematic Theology* and once in volume three.[94] In these pas-sages Tillich demonstrates knowledge of several of Sartre's works, both philosophical and literary: in addition to references to *Being and Nothingness*, 'Existentialism Is a Humanism' and the *Transcendence of the Ego*,[95] one also finds the play *No Exit*[96] and the novel *The Age of Reason*. However, simply counting index listings does not accurately reflect the importance of Sartre's phil-osophical question for Tillich's theological answer. For, in addi-tion to instances of Sartre's name there are several discussions of

[90]Tillich 1964b: 88–9.
[91]See Meszaros 2016, especially chapters 3 and 4.
[92]Tillich 1948: 132.
[93]Tillich 1957: vii.
[94]It is worth reminding the reader that Sartre's *Being and Nothingness* was published in 1943. The fact that the proportion of references to Sartre decreases with distance from this date is unlikely to be coincidental (with *The Courage to Be* published in 1952 and the three volumes of *Systematic Theology* published in 1951, 1957 and 1963 respectively).
[95]*CB* 132: discussion of the *sum* behind the *cogito*.
[96]Tillich 1957: 86.

'existentialism'[97] or 'existentialist' themes such as anxiety, freedom and destiny, loneliness and estrangement.

Of course, Sartre is far from being the only existential philosopher who influenced Tillich – so these latter passages might reasonably be claimed to have ambiguous ancestry.[98] In particular, for those readers who see Sartre as more philosophaster than philosopher, and his work as derivative of Heidegger, it is important to establish that Tillich himself (like Barth) differentiates between the two. This distinction is significant. Sartre introduces a difference in Tillich's approach to existentialism which can be observed by comparing a text such as 'The Conception of Man in Existential Philosophy' (1939) to later works like *The Courage to Be* (1952) and *Systematic Theology* (1950–1963).

In 'The Theological Significance of Existentialism and Psychoanalysis', Tillich describes Sartre's philosophy as 'pure existentialism' and praises his 'sensitive psychological analysis'.[99] Indeed, while his claim that Sartre's greatness consists in his being 'the psychological interpreter of Heidegger' could be construed as diminutive, Tillich is emphatic that Sartre's 'psychological insights are profound'.[100] And in chapter 8 of the first volume of *Systematic Theology* (entitled 'Being, Finitude and the Question of God') Sartre is described as extending the 'threat of nothingness' to the threat of meaninglessness.[101] In the context of introducing the question of being, which is produced by 'the shock of non-being',[102] Tillich writes that 'man, who is this being, must be separated from his being in such a way as to enable him to look at it as something strange and questionable'.[103] On this subject it is worth quoting at length:

> Recent existentialism has 'encountered nothingness' (Kuhn) in a profound and radical way. Somehow it has replaced being-itself

[97]Although the term 'existentialism' was coined by Marcel to refer to Sartre's philosophy and was eventually rejected by others such as Heidegger (see Fulton 1999: 12–13), Tillich does not seem to follow this nomenclature rigorously.

[98]Tillich's intellectual debt to German idealism – especially Schelling and Kant – goes without saying, so where 'existentialist' content can be found in these thinkers a further possible line of influence emerges.

[99]Tillich 1964b: 120.

[100]Tillich 1964b: 120.

[101]Tillich 1953: 210.

[102]Tillich 1953: 207.

[103]Tillich 1953: 208.

by non-being, giving to non-being a positivity and a power which contradict the immediate meaning of the word. Heidegger's 'annihilating nothingness' describes man's situation of being threatened by non-being in an ultimately inescapable way, that is, by death. The anticipation of nothingness at death gives human existence its existential character. Sartre includes in non-being not only the threat of nothingness but also the threat of meaninglessness (i.e., the destruction of the structure of being). In existentialism there is no way of conquering this threat. The only way of dealing with it lies in the courage of taking it upon one's self: courage![104]

It is this distinction – the threat of meaninglessness – that I believe makes Tillich's 'answer' a response to Sartre's question. For Sartre, whose stated aim (and indeed definition of existentialism) was 'an attempt to draw all the consequences of a coherent atheistic position', the separation of essence and existence results in an analysis of the human condition which, as we have seen, some commentators have called irredeemably pessimistic or pathologically negative.[105] We find in his philosophy an alienation from self and other which, from a theological perspective, might be viewed as a realized eschatology of damnation. We have already seen in Chapter 4 that Sartre thinks identity is impossible, and that unity with the other is an unrealizable ideal. In Tillichean terms, the impossibility of identity can be read as the source of spiritual anxiety, and the impossibility of community as the source of loneliness or moral anxiety. We consider each of these in turn.

The impossibility of identity

We saw in Chapter 4 that on the view Sartre developed in *The Transcendence of the Ego* and *Being and Nothingness*, every negation – every exercise of freedom – is an *estrangement* from being.

---

[104]Tillich 1953: 210. The text referred to here is Helmut Kuhn's *Encounter With Nothingness: An Essay on Existentialism* (Hinsdale, IL: Henry Regnery Co., 1949), which was reviewed by Jean Wahl in the University of Chicago journal *Ethics* in 1950 (60 (3): 215–217).

[105]Indeed, Tillich notes that 'existentialism has been criticised as being too "pessimistic"' (Tillich 1957: 31).

Sartre asserts that 'anguish as the manifestation of freedom in the face of self means that man is always separated by a nothingness from his essence' (*BN* 59). Without recourse to divine grace, there is nothing that can 'ensure me against myself, cut off from the world and from my essence by this nothingness which *I am*' (*BN* 63; emphasis in original). Any meaning I now claim for my life today may be meaninglessness tomorrow.

In *The Courage to Be*, where Tillich outlines the differences between and history of the 'existentialist point of view', 'existentialist protest' and 'existentialist expression', he demonstrates familiarity with *The Transcendence of the Ego*. He writes that Descartes's writings have an 'anti-Existential bias, where existence of man and his world is put into brackets. Man becomes pure consciousness, a naked epistemological subject; the world (including man's psychosomatic being) becomes an object of scientific enquiry and technical management.'[106] He goes on to say that 'recent philosophical Existentialism showed that behind the *sum* (I am) in Descartes' *cogito ergo sum* lies the problem of the nature of this *sum* which is more than mere *cogitation* (consciousness) – namely existence in time and space and under the conditions of finitude and estrangement'.[107]

For Sartre, the anxiety-arousing impossibility of identity – the estrangement of the self from its essence – is the consequence of the radical freedom of consciousness. And on Tillich's view the duality of 'essential and existential', which Tillich explicitly associates with Sartre in the first volume of *Systematic Theology*, is seen in all ontologies.[108] He continues to say that in all ontologies the question of the relation of essence to existence is being asked, and that its answer is found by the polarity of 'freedom and destiny on the second level of ontological analysis. However, freedom as such is not the basis of existence, but rather freedom in unity with finitude. Finite freedom is the turning point from being to existence'.[109] In Tillich's hamartiology (as expressed in the second volume of *Systematic Theology*), 'the transition from essence to existence is the original fact'.[110]

[106] Tillich 1952: 131.
[107] Tillich 1952: 132; emphasis in original.
[108] Tillich 1953: 183.
[109] Tillich 1953: 183–4.
[110] Tillich 1957: 41.

In the *Courage to Be* Sartre is described as carrying

> through the consequences of Heidegger's Existentialist analyses without mystical restrictions. This is the reason he has become the symbol of present-day Existentialism, a position which is deserved not so much by the originality of his basic concepts as by the radicalism, consistency, and psychological adequacy with which he has carried them through. I refer above all to his proposition that 'the essence of man is his existence'. This sentence is like a flash of light which illuminates the whole Existentialist scene. One could call it the most despairing and the most courageous sentence in all Existentialist literature. What is says is that there is no essential nature of man, except in the one point that he can make of himself what he wants.... Man is what he makes of himself'.[111]

Clearly, for Sartre and for Tillich, the consequence of the separation of essence and existence is anxiety. But it is also clear that anxiety is not solely a Sartrean theme, and that Tillich wrote on it before Sartre rose to prominence.[112] Although Tillich's discussion of anxiety in the second volume of *Systematic Theology* (39ff.) focuses on the term's use in German and Danish philosophy (which is to say Kierkegaard and Heidegger), his discussion in *The Courage to Be* has a distinctly Sartrean inflection, where the threat of meaninglessness looms largest. In 'Existentialism Is a Humanism' Sartre made clear that human beings are the beings through which value comes to the world. But is such self-derived meaning meaningful enough to fulfil human desire?

In *The Courage to Be* Tillich writes that 'we need an ontological account of anxiety'.[113] On Tillich's view, there are three types of anxiety which correspond to three ways in which nonbeing threatens being: 'Nonbeing threatens man's ontic self-affirmation, relatively in terms of fate, absolutely in terms of death. It threatens man's spiritual self-affirmation, relatively in terms of emptiness, absolutely in terms of meaninglessness. It threatens man's moral

---

[111]Tillich 1952: 149–50.
[112]See Tillich 1939: 208.
[113]Tillich 1952: 65.

self-affirmation, relatively in terms of guilt, absolutely in terms of condemnation'.[114]

Tillich's second, 'spiritual' anxiety – the 'anxiety of meaningless-ness' – is described as 'anxiety about the loss of an ultimate concern, of a meaning which gives meaning to all meanings. This anxiety is aroused by the loss of a spiritual center, of an answer, however symbolic and indirect, to the meaning of existence.'[115] It is this anxi-ety that Tillich believes to be 'dominant' in his age.[116] He writes, that 'we are under the threat of spiritual non-being. The threats of moral and ontic non-being are, of course, present, but they are not independent and not controlling.'[117]

At the end of the book he repeatedly emphasizes the dominance of this anxiety of meaninglessness.[118] This is the question his theol-ogy sought to answer:

> The anxiety which determines our period is the anxiety of doubt and meaninglessness. One is afraid of having lost or of having to lose the meaning of one's existence. The expression of this situation is the Existentialism of today. Which courage is able to take nonbeing into itself in the form of doubt and meaninglessness? This is the most important and most disturbing question in the quest for the courage to be. For the anxiety of meaninglessness undermines what is still unshaken in the anxiety of fate and death and of guilt and condemnation.[119]

The impossibility of community

We also saw in Chapter 4 that a third of the way through *Being and Nothingness*, Sartre turns from considering individual conscious-ness to the existence of others because the Sartrean self is syncat-egorematic: it has no meaning without others. As King puts it, 'In

---

[114]Tillich 1952: 40–1.
[115]Tillich 1952: 47.
[116]Tillich 1952: 62.
[117]Tillich 1952: 62. See also *CB* 56 on the prominence of the anxiety of meaninglessness.
[118]Tillich 1952: 171–3.
[119]Tillich 1952: 173–4.

order to think of myself, I have to implicitly think of the Other for whom I am that self.'[120]

In order to bring back to mind the important role the other plays in the distance between consciousness and the ego, consider one of the adjectives that most of us might like to use to describe ourselves: 'intelligent'.[121] What others tell you about yourself is what you are in respect to them. But statements like 'you are intelligent' are not soluble in consciousness. In your consciousness you can know that you are thinking; you can know it with certainty. But knowing you are *intelligent* – or charming, or lovable, or what have you – is always more or less doubtful: it is dependent on the estimations of others.

On Sartre's view, 'a consistent atheist position' involved admitting that we are subject to each other's objectifying gazes, and that there is no God's-eye view from which to see things as they 'really are'. Attempts at self-definition are thus defined as movements in a combat, a 'battle to the death' for my identity – for if my essence follows from my existence, I have to fight to maintain creative rights. The consciousness of 'being seen' by another as other than we desire to be gives rise to the experience of others as 'hell'; we realize that we are not merely subject to the nihilating power of our own freedom but to that of others.

This too provided a question Tillich sought to answer. In the third volume of *Systematic Theology* Tillich writes that the 'ambiguity of self-determination is rooted in the fact that the self as subject and the self as object are split and that the self as subject tries to determine the self as object in a direction from which the self as subject is itself estranged'.[122] Here he echoes Sartre's view of the noncoincidence of the self, writing that 'no centred self under the conditions of existence is fully identical with itself.' What is needful is that 'the split of the self into a controlling subject and a controlled object' be overcome through 'the vertical dimension'.[123] If one remains on the horizontal plane, he writes, any effort to overcome the split between subject and object in interpersonal encounters will result in defeat, in surrender: either of 'oneself to the other one or by taking

---

[120]King 1974: 76.
[121]Sartre discusses this in *Genet*; cf. King 1974: 77.
[122]Tillich 1964a: 276.
[123]Tillich 1964a: 276.

the other one into one's self'. But 'both are failures', because 'they destroy the persons they seek to unite'.[124] In this context, indeed, we read that 'Sartre's assertion of the mutual objectivation of human beings in all their encounters cannot be denied except from the point of view of the vertical dimension'.[125]

Conclusion

It is clear from the foregoing that there are textual and conceptual reasons to think Tillich's later theology intentionally answers Sartre. In concluding, however, a final difficulty must be noted. Due to Tillich's style of scholarship it is challenging to ascertain precisely when or what he read of 'the Socrates of nothingness'. His discussions of Sartre, as we have seen, suggest familiarity with several works. But did he read *Being and Nothingness*? *L'Etre et le néant* came out in French in 1943, but it was not available in German until 1952[126] and in English until 1956. Although some of Sartre's works were published in English in the United States in the mid-1940s, it is probable that Tillich came to Sartre through less scholarly media.[127] Like most American academics at the time, Tillich is likely to have become acquainted with Sartre 'through newspapers, popular magazines, and journals of opinion'.[128]

As Tillich defines it in the first volume of his *Systematic Theology*, the task of theology is to interpret the Christian message in such a way that it was 'relevant to the present situation'.[129] And in his present situation he believed it was

---

[124]Tillich 1964a: 277.

[125]Tillich 1964a: 278.

[126]The 1952 German translation published by Rowohlt Verlag was an abbreviated edition, which omitted the section on the phenomenology of the body, among other things (see Heinemann 1953: 356).

[127]Sartre delivered two lectures at Yale in 1945: the first on philosophy, and the second on literature. Many of Sartre's plays and novels were available in English: *The Flies* (1947), *No Exit* (1947), *The Age of Reason* (1947) and *The Reprieve* (1947), but few of his philosophical works were published in English in the 1940s: *Existentialism*, in 1947 (*Existentialisme est un humanisme* was published in France in 1946) (see Fulton 1999: 22–3).

[128]Fulton 1999: 27.

[129]Tillich 1953: 59.

not an exaggeration to say that today man experiences his present situation in terms of disruption, conflict, self-destruction, meaninglessness, and despair in all realms of life. This experience is expressed in the arts and in literature, conceptualised in existential philosophy, actualised in political cleavage of all kinds, and analysed in the psychology of the unconscious. It has given theology a new understanding of the demonic-tragic structures of individual and social life.[130]

In a sermon on 'Salvation', Tillich writes that 'the words which are most used in religion are also those whose genuine meaning is almost completely lost and whose impact on the human mind is nearly negligible'.[131] Such words, he continues, must be either reborn or thrown away. The 'gift' that existentialism gives theology is 'a rediscovery of the word sin' – 'especially in the description of hell and purgatory, and of the inner self-destructiveness of man in his estrangement from his essential being'.[132]

However Tillich discovered Sartre, the latter's 'profound psychological insights' demonstrated the threat of meaningless under the conditions of estrangement from self and other. But Tillich does not leave it at that. He also argues that Sartre's account of existentialism is contradictory:

Sartre says man's essence is his existence. In saying this he makes it impossible for man to be saved or to be healed. Sartre knows this, and every one of his plays shows this too. But here also we have a happy inconsistency. He calls his existentialism humanism. But if he calls it humanism, that means he has an idea of what man essentially is, and he must consider the possibility that the essential being of man, his freedom, might be lost. And if this is a possibility, then he makes, against his own will, a distinction between man as he essentially is and man as he can be lost: man is to be free and to create himself.[133]

---

[130]Tillich 1953: 55.
[131]Tillich 1963: 94.
[132]Tillich 1964b: 122.
[133]Tillich 1964b: 120. See also Tillich 1956: 742, where he writes that 'it is the basic shortcoming of Sartre that he did not acknowledge this dependence [of positive philosophy on negative philosophy], although his own writings confirm it on every page'.

As we shall see in the chapters that follow, Tillich was not alone in making this objection. Sartre, on this reading, is a 'hidden theologian' of original sin who shaped the Tillichean answer.[134] Whereas in 1939 Tillich could write of 'existential philosophy' that 'we know a feeling in which the very fact that we are able to face our nothingness includes the certainty that we are beyond it',[135] Sartre's 'threat of nothingness' went further than his predecessors': for there is no possibility of redemptive grace, and belief in such a notion must be rejected as bad faith. Such a question required of Tillich a different – or at least differently inflected – answer.

---

[134]Tillich 1953: 29.
[135]Tillich 1939: 210. It is also interesting to compare what Tillich writes about freedom and reason in the 1939 piece (1939: 203) to his discussion of freedom and destiny in the second volume of *Systematic Theology* – in the latter, destiny could be read as a revised version of Sartrean facticity, which (contra Sartre) includes the divine and grace (Tillich 1957: 72–3).

7

Sartre and Catholic theology: Marcel and Wojtyła

The relation between God and myself is that of one freedom to another.[1]

GABRIEL MARCEL

In his 1950 Encyclical *Humani Generis*, Pope Pius XII explicitly addressed 'the new erroneous philosophy', existentialism, among other 'false opinions threatening to undermine the foundations of Catholic doctrine'. The encyclical sends a rather mixed message. On the one hand Catholic theologians and philosophers are urged to understand it:

> Catholic theologians and philosophers, whose grave duty it is to defend natural and supernatural truth and instil it in the hearts of men, cannot afford to ignore or neglect these more or less erroneous opinions. Rather they must come to understand these same theories well, both because diseases are not properly treated unless they are rightly diagnosed, and because sometimes even in these false theories a certain amount of truth is contained, and, finally, because these theories provoke more subtle discussion and evaluation of philosophical and theological truths.[2]

And on the other hand, we read that bishops are to take 'most diligent care' that such opinions not be 'taught in any manner

[1]Marcel 1935: 58.
[2]Pius XII 1950: 9.

whatsoever to the clergy or the faithful'.[3] Officially the latter message prevailed: in 1959 Sartre's complete works were added to the *Index Librorum Prohibitorum*. But Catholic philosophers and theologians continued to read and respond to Sartre. In this chapter, we look at the engagement of two twentieth-century Catholics, Gabriel Marcel and Karol Wojtyła, both of whom – despite their differences of situation – saw Sartre's depiction of being with others as descriptively accurate of *part* of human experience, but as lacking its highest perfection: participation in love.

Sartre and Marcel

Marcel's reception of Sartre, unlike that of Barth and Tillich, was not mediated by the same distances – of geography, time or language. In fact, the two met in Marcel's home (at the 'Friday evenings' Marcel hosted), saw each other's plays and labelled each other's philosophies – for it was Marcel who christened Sartre's philosophy 'existentialism',[4] and Sartre who christened Marcel's 'Christian existentialism'.[5] Sartre and Marcel have been called 'the two "enemies" of French existentialism',[6] and it is not hard to see why: Marcel offered consistent criticism of Sartre over a period that spanned decades.

Marcel was born in Paris on 7 December 1889, making him roughly fifteen years Sartre's senior. He passed his *agrégation* in 1910 and then taught lycée philosophy in various parts of France before becoming a drama critic, lecturer and editor. In 1927 Marcel published his *Metaphysical Journal* (*Journal métaphysique*), an original form of philosophical analysis intended to demonstrate his conception of the true self as a gradual awakening to the 'appeal' of being. The text is not systematic. As Copleston said in his 1954

---

[3]Pius XII 1950: 41.
[4]Although Protevi has shown that the term was in use in Italian, French, English and German prior to its post-war Parisian heyday (see Protevi 2006: 194–5).
[5]Marcel thought it inappropriate to apply the label 'Christian' to his philosophy, since he thought non-Christian existentialists might also find it preferable to Sartre's on philosophical grounds (Marcel 2002: 91), and preferred the term 'neo-Socratism' (In the *Metaphysical Journal*, Autumn 1950, he elaborates that neo-Socratism is 'an attitude of interrogation which is constant but in no way skeptical'.)
[6]Deranty 2015.

review of an English translation, 'M. Marcel's way of going about things is certainly not everyone's cup of tea.'[7] (But even so, Copleston went on to say, it offered stimulation and illumination analogous to Platonic dialogues.)

Two years after publishing the *Metaphysical Journal*, at the age of 40, Marcel converted to Catholicism. His conversion story is worth recounting: it was prompted by a letter from the novelist François Mauriac. Mauriac had noticed several religious themes in Marcel's writings, such as forgiveness and the religious justification of morality, so he wrote to Marcel and explicitly asked him whether he thought he should join the Catholic Church. Marcel reflected on the question for a while and decided that, in fact, he should.

Whether pre- or post-conversion, Marcel's writings on religion are regarded by some as his best philosophical contributions: 'From the beginning of his philosophical career, Marcel's main interest has been the interpretation of religious experience, that is, of the relation between man and ultimate reality.'[8] In 1949–50 he gave the Gifford Lectures in Aberdeen (which later appeared as the two-volume work *The Mystery of Being*) and in 1961–62 he gave the William James Lectures at Harvard University (later published as *The Existential Background of Human Dignity*).[9] He also wrote thirty plays – more than any other existentialist – although he is not well remembered for them. One of them (*La Dimension Florestan*) ridiculed Heidegger:

THE COUNTESS: You said, the pear pears, and you added, with an even more imperious authority, that the apple apples.

FRAU MELITTA (sardonically): Somebody might be tempted to ask whether the peach is the act of peaching.[10]

The one time Sartre met Heidegger, in fact, Marcel's play was 'all they talked about': Heidegger was unaccustomed to seeing himself in satire and Sartre apologized on behalf of his compatriot.[11]

---

[7]Coplestone 1954: 170.
[8]Cain 1995: 87.
[9]A full bibliography of Marcel's extensive works is: Francois H. and Claire Lapointe (eds.), *Gabriel Marcel and His Critics: An International Bibliography (1928–1976)* (New York and London: Garland Publishing, 1977).
[10]Marcel 1958: 11.
[11]Beauvoir 1977: 288–9.

Before assessing Marcel's direct engagement with Sartre it is worth noting that his conversion to Catholicism did not significantly alter his philosophy. There is no Heideggerian 'turn' or Wittgensteinian early/late distinction to be made on such grounds. Marcel's later works do give greater attention to moral experiences as possible disclosures of transcendence, but much of what he wrote in *Being and Having* and the *Metaphysical Journal* was still affirmed by the post-conversion Marcel. On his own assessment his philosophy and Christianity were independent of each other:

> It is quite possible that the existence of the fundamental Christian data may be necessary *in fact* to enable the mind to conceive some of the notions which I have attempted to analyze; but these notions cannot be said to depend on the data of Christianity, and *they do not presuppose it* ... I have experienced [the development of these ideas] more than twenty years before I had the remotest thought of becoming a Catholic.[12]

It is worth underscoring this point, because, although Marcel's criticisms of Sartre are often presented as reactions against the latter's atheism, as Tattam notes, Marcel insists that a philosophically responsible reaction must not presuppose a specifically Christian worldview. The problem with Sartre's philosophy is *not* just that it is not Christian.[13] The problem is that it is wrong on several counts – ontology, the nature of freedom, the self, being with others and God, to name but a few. For some, this may render Marcel's inclusion as a 'theologian' questionable. But given that others may define 'theology' more broadly, and that many of his criticisms anticipate the criticisms that self-proclaimed 'theological' respondents would make, he has been included.

Marcel discusses Sartre in several of his works, including the plays *Rome n'est plus Rome* and the essays and *L'Homme contre l'humain*, but this chapter focuses on his early analyses of Sartre in 'Being and Nothingness' (November 1943), 'Existence and Human

---

[12]Marcel 2002: 44–5; emphasis in original. In the preface to a 1950 edition of the *Journal Metaphysique* Marcel admits that he has revised his view that being is beyond truth, but otherwise he accepts the opinion of Hippolyte that the seeds of his life's philosophy are present in this work.
[13]See Tattam 2016: 23.

Freedom' (January 1946), 'Testimony and Existentialism' (February 1946) and *The Mystery of Being* (1949–50), since these express Marcel's central objections to Sartre and show the course of their development.

'Being and Nothingness' (1943)

The year Sartre's *Being and Nothingness* appeared, so did Marcel's first reply, under the same title. Marcel is one of the first Christian writers to say that 'the importance of M. Sartre's book is incontestable'. At first glance, he tells his reader, it looks as though it is a repetition of Heidegger. But closer inspection reveals that Sartre diverges from *Being and Time* on very important points, and that 'the central intuition of the young French philosopher is his own'.[14] Eventually Marcel will tell us that this intuition is 'a form of metaphysics which denies or refuses grace', which sets before us 'the image of an atrophied and contradictory world where the better part of ourselves is finally unable to recognize itself'.[15] But before doing so he takes his reader through the structure of *Being and Nothingness*, pointing out places where Sartre takes false steps.

In this 1943 commentary we read a criticism that will recur in Marcel's subsequent criticisms of Sartre: namely, that he is a sophist.[16] He uses complicated words to explain simple ideas, leading Marcel (with rhetorical flourishes that give his charges of sophistry an ironic tinge) to describe Sartre's thought as a monster 'which cannot stand the fresh air of reflection' and can only 'live its precarious life in some sort of twilight'[17]).

Marcel detects contradictory currents in Sartre's thought: that we are 'doomed' to be free makes freedom (in Marcel's words) 'our slavery much more than our victory', which makes freedom look like a lack, a defect. But in addition to this current there is another, according to which freedom consists in 'assuming responsibility or taking charge', which quite obviously cannot be taken to result 'from lack or from a disengagement with oneself'.[18] Before the

[14]Marcel 1951: 166.
[15]Marcel 1951: 183.
[16]Marcel 1953: 168.
[17]Marcel 1951: 169.
[18]Marcel 1951: 174.

clarifications of 'Existentialism Is a Humanism', both the 'optimistic' and the 'pessimistic' Sartre were read into *Being and Nothingness* – but their relation to one another provoked confusion.

Here as in subsequent works Marcel finds Sartre's analysis of being with others to be most forceful – particularly his descriptions of the gaze and of love. But the conclusion Sartre's descriptions evoke in Marcel is not that love is impossible per se, but rather that Sartre 'has nowhere succeeded … in conceiving it'.[19] Sartre writes that everything happens *as if* 'the *en soi* and the *pour soi* appeared in a state of disintegration in relation to an ideal synthesis. Not that the integration has ever taken place, but on the contrary precisely because it is always indicated and always impossible' (*BN* 643).

But how can this be? Marcel writes, 'Have we not reason to wonder whether the consciousness which receives this impression of a breaking up of the real is not led when it reflects upon its own state *to regard itself as degraded*, without being able, however, to think in concrete terms of the world before the Fall?' Marcel recognizes that Sartre rejects the world this Fall language invokes, but in doing so he 'condemn[s] himself to move in an infernal circle, a circle, moreover, wherein he has imprisoned himself of his own free will'. A merit of Sartre's work, therefore, is that he takes his metaphysics of refusal to its logical end.[20]

The seeds of Marcel's position vis-à-vis Sartre are all present in this early essay. Between its writing and the publication of the next text we shall consider Sartre gave the lecture 'Existentialism Is a Humanism', but Marcel does not explicitly refer to it. In 'Existence and Human Freedom' Marcel begins by saying that one cannot yet (in January of 1946) speak of 'Sartrean man' because, unlike 'Marxian man' or 'Nietzschean man', 'Sartrean man' was still in the making. His picture of 'Sartrean man' nevertheless drew on a wider range of sources than did Barth's or Tillich's – in this essay alone he refers to *Nausea*, *The Roads to Freedom* (although the third volume had not yet been published at this time), *No Exit* and *Being and Nothingness* (as well as Beauvoir's *She Came to Stay*). On the basis of these texts Marcel concludes that Sartre's

---

[19]Marcel 1951: 177.
[20]Marcel 1951: 183; emphasis in original.

philosophy results, 'whether deliberately or not, in the systematic vilification of man'.[21]

He insists that his attitude in writing this piece is not polemical.[22] Unlike his colleagues at the Sorbonne in 1943 (the year *Being and Nothingness* appeared), Marcel's opinion of Sartre's philosophy is that it is 'much too impressive, particularly to young people, not to be examined with the utmost seriousness and objectivity'.[23] Marcel asks his reader to see what is valid in Sartre's premises. What is the 'actual character of that initial experience of existence which Sartre has described with such vehemence and precision, particularly in *La Nausée*'? Marcel takes it as given that such experience is genuine, and moreover, that the identity of the hero is the author himself.[24]

The remainder of 'Existence and Human Freedom' is expository: Marcel analyses passages from *Nausea* which touch on the liquidity (the gooey, sticky, viscous parts) of existence, noting with participatory pride that once at his house he suggested Sartre should 'make analysis of the viscous', complimenting his 'remarkable' achievements in that vein and declaring himself 'happy and proud to have suggested it to him'.[25] Although he repeats some of his observations from 'Being and Nothingness', Marcel's objections to Sartre in 'Existence and Human Freedom' (because it is so wide ranging in the texts it considers and so lengthy in its quotations of Sartre) remain rather embryonic, anticipating the themes that will recur and be more fully developed in later treatments.

He discusses the 'fundamental absurdity' that Roquentin discovers as a 'revelation' or secular Enlightenment, noting that 'according to Sartre, what men commonly call wisdom or experience is most likely to be a deliberate way of lying to oneself and of concealing the fundamental absurdity which is existence itself.'[26] Marcel reads bad faith back into scenes in *Nausea*, in particular in the passages where Sartre describes his repugnance of the respectable delusions of the Bouville bourgeoisie:[27]

---

[21]Marcel 2002: 85.
[22]Marcel 2002: 47.
[23]Marcel 2002: 48.
[24]Although scholars debate just how literally one should interpret Sartre's statement, in *Words* he wrote that 'I was Roquentin' (*W* 156).
[25]Marcel 2002: 53.
[26]Marcel 2002: 56.
[27]Marcel 2002: 57.

They have dragged out their lives in drowsiness and half-sleep. They have scurried into marriage and they have conceived children by chance. They have met other men in *cafés* and at weddings and funerals. Now and then they have been caught in a whirlpool and have struggled to understand. But everything that went on around them began and ended out of their sight.

Marcel also reads Sartre in the tradition of Pascal, noting that, although Sartre and Pascal agree on the distinctiveness of human consciousness as presence to itself (alluding to the 'thinking reed', in Pascal's terms; the 'reflective consciousness', in Sartre's), in Pascal's case this is seen as a sign of 'ontological dignity'. In Sartre's thought, by contrast, 'presence is inferior to coincidence, because presence implies a separateness'.[28]

Marcel gives a clear exposition of the noncoincidence of the for-itself, drawing on two of Sartre's examples of bad faith (the waiter and the woman on a date) in order to conclude, with Sartre, that *we are what we are in the mode of not being it*. In Marcel's words, we are 'in transit', always on the way to or from being this or that being. But though Sartre's account is insightful, here again Marcel charges it with sophistry.[29] He presents a passage from *Being and Nothingness* in which Sartre discusses sadness:

> I 'am' sad. But is not this sadness myself in the sense that I 'am' what I am? Sadness is indeed the meaning of my mournful looks, of my hunched-up shoulders and of my bowed head. Yet, in the very act of assuming these postures, do I not know that I need not assume them? That, if a stranger came in suddenly, I would raise my head and change my expression; and what would be left of my sadness except the appointment I had made with it for a little later on, after my visitor has left? To be sad is to make oneself sad .... If I *make* myself sad I cannot *be* sad (in the sense in which a stone is heavy). The being of sadness escapes in and through the very act by which I assume it. The being-in-itself of sadness haunts my consciousness of being sad, but only as an unattainable ideal; it is an indication of my sadness but not its constituent modality. (*EN* 100–1; emphasis in original)

[28]Marcel 2002: 62.
[29]Marcel 2001b: 85.

Marcel uses two examples of bereavement to argue that Sartre's position is 'quite true' but 'only part of the truth'. Sartre is correct that there are cases where our sadness may be performed for reasons of social conformity, or concealed with the same motivation. But there are also sadnesses that infuse our consciousness in ways that Sartre's account fails to do justice. This example, Marcel concludes, shows that 'it is possible to start from a profoundly true and just observation and, by pushing it to its limit, to arrive at a conception of human life and sensibility which is not only false, but odiously offensive and degrading'.[30]

Despite its sophistry Marcel praises Sartre's work as 'masterly',[31] and says that its most remarkable contribution is 'his phenomenological study of the "other" as looking and of himself as exposed, pierced, bared, petrified by his Medusa-like stare'.[32]

For Sartre, being seen by another is being dispossessed, and this dispossession provokes the subjective reactions of fear, pride, and shame.

> Clearly for Sartre, the awareness of others is inseparable from the shock of the encounter with what he describes as a 'freedom', an alien freedom which is adverse and threatening to himself. To the question: In what way is it menacing? Sartre replies: 'because it tends to confine me within being-in-itself. In the eyes of the other I sit on this chair in exactly the same way as that inkpot stands on that table .... To be seen is to be at the mercy of a freedom which is not my own. The sense of shame is bound up with the sense of falling into the world.'[33]

But whether its form is the treatise or the theatre, Sartre carries the human condition 'to paroxism'.[34] *No Exit*, on Marcel's assessment, is governed by a 'Luciferian principle'[35] – again manifesting the Sartrean sophistry of starting with something 'quite true' – that humans can be hellish to each other – and claiming it is the whole truth.

[30]Marcel 2002: 67.
[31]Marcel 2002: 71.
[32]Marcel 2002: 71.
[33]Marcel 2002: 72.
[34]Marcel 2002: 73.
[35]*Horizon*, July 1945, reprinted in *L'Heure théâtrale* (Paris: Plon, 1959), p. 199.

What Sartre's account lacks is any glimpse of love, grace or positive freedom.

> I cannot be 'condemned' to freedom unless freedom is a
> deprivation, a loss. And indeed, for Sartre freedom is, like
> consciousness, a deprivation, a defect; it is only by a kind of
> paralogism that he later represents this defect as the positive
> condition of the emergence of a world and thus bestows upon it
> a creative value.[36]

It is worth citing this discussion at length, including Marcel's citation of a passage he takes to be 'one of the most significant and
explicit' in all of Sartre's work:

> freedom in its foundation coincides with the nothingness which
> is at the heart of man. Human reality is free because it is *not
> enough*. It is free because it is perpetually wrenched away from
> itself and because it has been separated by a nothingness from
> what it is and from what it will be…. Man is free because he is
> not himself but presence to himself. The being which is what it
> is can not be free. Freedom is precisely the nothingness [p. 463]
> which is *made-to-be* at the heart of man and which forces human-
> reality to *make itself* instead of *to be*. As we have seen, for human
> reality, to be is to *choose oneself*; nothing comes to it either from
> the outside or from within which it can *receive or accept*.[37]

Marcel writes that 'in the whole history of human thought', he does
not think that 'grace, even in its most secularised forms, has ever
been denied with such audacity or such impudence'.[38] Sartre's fatal
error, according Marcel, is that he equates freedom with choice.[39]
This is the root of his erroneous interpretation of being with others.
Along the way he makes minor errors, such as his exaggerated concept of negation, but ultimately, by equating freedom with choice,
Sartre renders *receiving* incompatible with freedom.[40]

[36]Marcel 2002: 78.
[37]*BN* 462–3; emphasis in original.
[38]Marcel 2002: 79.
[39]Marcel 2002: 80.
[40]Marcel 2002: 82.

Though it is sophistical, Marcel nevertheless emphasizes that Sartre's account is full of 'quite true' things. For Sartre,

> Man's life is an attempt, continually renewed and inevitably doomed to failure, at the divinisation of himself. Not that this is not without truth. It is true that man seems to be irresistibly urged to confer upon himself the attributes of divinity, and the progress of technics lends a disquieting semblance of truth to the tempter's promise: *eritis sicit dii*.[41]

But Marcel urges his reader not to be satisfied with the 'quite true' nor to let the 'rationalist acid' of Sartre's philosophy 'corrode the contemporary mind'.[42]

'Testimony and Existentialism'

In later writings Marcel's reply to Sartre gains a tighter focus. 'Testimony and Existentialism', written a month after 'Existence and Human Freedom', is shorter and devotes less space to exegesis. Instead, Marcel voices his main objection, namely that Sartre's account of being with others presents only the objectifying gaze of the 'onlooker' – something 'quite true' – and denies that human experience can involve the loving gaze of a 'witness'.

'Hardly a day goes by', he writes, 'without my being asked what is existentialism':

> (Usually it is a society lady who asks for this information, but tomorrow it may be my charwoman or the ticket-collector on the Underground.) It is perhaps hardly surprising that my answers tend to be evasive: I should like to say, 'It is too difficult', or 'It would take too long to explain'; but I realise that such answers are disappointing and should not be given too often. What I propose to do now is not so much to define existentialism as to try to throw some light on what seems to me its essence by bringing out its key notions – that is, the notions which give the clue to it from my standpoint, which, I need hardly add, is

---

[41]Marcel 2002: 84.
[42]Marcel 2002: 84.

very different from that of Sartre. Sartre has himself admitted
that there is a Christian version of existentialism which is not
to be confused with his own; though, for my part, I think it is
insufficient and even incorrect to stress its Christian character,
because I believe that many people are liable to adhere to it who
do not regard themselves as Christians."[43]

In particular, Sartre's denial of the possibility of nonconflictual
human relations (and particularly a way of being seen by the other
which Marcel calls 'testimony') comes under fire. Some 'modern
philosophers', Marcel writes,

> try to impale us on the horns of a false dilemma by saying to
> us: 'either you are only an onlooker, in that case you are not
> involved in reality; or you are an active and free being. You have
> nothing but the choice between these two ways, indeed you *are*
> nothing but the choice, or rather this way which chooses itself'.[44]

This false dilemma can distract us from 'the essential point of our
lives', Marcel says, namely, that we are witnesses to the being of
others and that this is an 'expression of our mode of belonging to
the world'.[45]

Marcel refers his reader to two passages in *Being and Nothingness*
before developing his own argument further, as evidence that Sartre
is unable to grasp the meaning of the word 'we' or the reality it
refers to, namely, that human beings are capable of opening themselves up to, and receiving from, others – without enslavement. The
passages he cites concern generosity:

> Gift is a primitive form of destruction … Generosity is, above all, a
> destructive function. The frenzy of giving which comes over certain
> people at certain times is, above all, a frenzy of destruction; but
> this frenzy of destruction, which assumes the guise of generosity,
> is, in reality, nothing other than a frenzy of possession.… To give is
> a form of destructive enjoyment, of destructive appropriation. But
> the gift also casts a spell over the one who receives … To give is to

[43]Marcel 2002: 91.
[44]Marcel 2002: 97; emphasis in original.
[45]Marcel 2002: 97.

enslave. It is to appropriate by destroying and to use the destruction to enslave another.[46]

Marcel acknowledges that 'a pathology of giving' does exist, wherein the giver gives to the extent of committing 'moral suicide', abdicating and annulling the self completely for the sake of the other. Marcel does not wish to defend this indefensible form but rather a self-giving that he describes as devotion. The conditions that make such self-giving possible depend on the meeting of certain conditions in the giver and the recipient. In true generosity, for the giver the object acquires the quality of being-for-another, for a *particular* person. For the recipient, if the gift truly is a gift, it is not just one possession among others but exists in the dimension of testimony – it is a testament to friendship or love. But its existence in this dimension is conditional: it must be recognized as existing in this way; it is an appeal which leaves the giver vulnerable.

Marcel gives the example of a small child bringing 'three bedraggled dandelions'. The child expects your admiration of them, waiting expectantly for your 'recognition of the value of its gift'. One can deny this value – Marcel does not deny the negating power of human freedom. But 'if you lose it, or put it down carelessly, or do not stop talking to express your delight, you are guilty of a sin against love'.[47]

For Sartre the gift is an attempt to appropriate the being of another; for Marcel, receiving a gift results in an 'accretion of being' in the receiver.[48] Although he does not explicitly say so in this work, Marcel's disagreement with Sartre on the possibility of intersubjective relationships (whether human or divine) rests on an underlying disagreement about the nature of freedom and its limits.[49] In the *Metaphysical Journal* Marcel wrote that 'the relation between God and myself is that of one freedom to another.... This relation is itself encapsulated in the act of faith .... [B]etween God and myself

[46]Cited in Marcel 2002: 99–100.
[47]Marcel 2002: 102.
[48]Marcel 2002: 102.
[49]In 'Truth and Freedom', for example, he writes that negatively, freedom is 'the absence of whatever resembles an alienation from oneself'; positively, an act is free when 'the motives of my action are within the limits of what I can legitimately consider as the structural traits of my self' (1965: 232).

there must be a relation of the same type as that which succeeds in binding lovers'.[50] The relationship that 'binds' lovers, for Marcel, does not enslave freedom, but liberates it.

The Mystery of Being

We see this further in *The Mystery of Being*, the Gifford lectures Marcel published in two volumes in 1949 and 1950. Marcel recognizes that he is not a systematic thinker (indeed, he has philosophical reasons not to be one), but he accepted the invitation to offer a systematic account of his philosophy as a 'call' that required his response.

In the lectures, Marcel affirms the importance of the *situation*, defining it as 'something in which I find myself involved ... not something which presses on the self merely from the outside, but something which colours its interior states'.[51] Although each human being has a unique situation, there are structural aspects of existence that many human beings share, such as the brokenness of the world. (The theme of brokenness runs through Marcel's works: for the world is 'on the one hand, riddled with problems and, on the other, determined to allow no room for mystery'.[52]) One structural aspect of the situation of his time, he thought, was a lack of intimacy: the world no longer understands the meaning of the words 'with' or 'togetherness', and human beings are bereaved of 'life's old intimate quality'.[53]

Sartre perpetuated this lack by persistently misrepresenting the relatedness of the human self to others. On Marcel's view, Sartre's ontological divide – the in-itself and for-itself – fails to appreciate that we participate in the world, that our being always-already related to the world and others is a *gift* that we should receive and recognize as a metaphysical reality.[54]

In volume 2 he defends this notion further by clarifying that his metaphysics has an 'anti-Cartesian character': it rejects the *I think*

---

[50]Marcel 1935: 58.
[51]Marcel 2001a: 8.
[52]Marcel 2002: 12.
[53]Marcel 2001a: 28.
[54]Marcel 2001a: 175 and 199.

for a starting point of *we are*. Sartre's famous line from *No Exit*, that the other is 'hell', is again cited as evidence of the impossibility of Sartre's position. He has no understanding of *philia* or *agape*, Marcel writes, but is stuck on the plane of an ambiguous and insatiable *eros*. The opposition of the in-itself and for-itself render intersubjectivity and participation in the world impossible. For the Sartrean subject it is impossible to 'be open to the other, to welcome him in the deepest sense of the word, and to become at the same time more accessible to oneself'.[55]

Where Sartre's ontology renders intersubjectivity impossible, Marcel wants to ground ontology on intersubjectivity. The enquiry into being, according to Marcel, cannot be conducted at the level of 'solipsistic reflection', but rather: 'I concern myself with being only in so far as I have a more or less distinct consciousness of the underlying unity which ties me to other beings of whose reality I already have a preliminary notion'.[56] The themes of alienation and participation would be taken up by another twentieth-century Catholic theologian, Karol Wojtyła (latterly Pope John Paul II).

Sartre and Wojtyła

Wojtyła's philosophical position has been called 'existential personalism'.[57] His engagement with Husserl and Scheler are well known (and acknowledged in his own works), as is his exposure to the Thomism of Gilson. He does not systematically engage with Sartre. Indeed, Sartre is rarely cited directly in Wojtyła's translated works. However, there are historical and theological reasons for considering him worthy of inclusion in the present volume. For as Rocco Buttiglione has noted, the influence of existentialism in Poland was significant both in its own right and as a correction to Marxism. Since Buttiglione has already offered a 'dialogue' between Wojtyła and Sartre, comparing their respective personalism and existentialism, this section outlines the historical context of Wojtyła's reception of and references to Sartre, arguing that the Sartre Wojtyła received was mediated by Marxist discussions of alienation.

---

[55]Marcel 2001b: 10.
[56]Marcel 2001b: 17.
[57]Woznicki 1980.

The Poland in which Wojtyła pursued his studies was not conducive to an open critical confrontation of Marx: 'One cannot, in fact, find in Wojtyła's work any direct reference to Marx'.[58] Those who know Wojtyła's works will know that this lack of direct citations is certainly not to be equated with a lack of engagement.[59] In the case of Sartre, I argue, Wojtyła's engagement has been underestimated. I have already intimated that there are historical and theological hypotheses that explain this lacuna. Let us turn to the history first.

Polish intellectual life during the years 1939–56 (before the so-called thaw) was far from flourishing. After the war, the Communist regime saw phenomenology as a threat to Marxist ideology – to such an extent that in the early 1950s Marxism was the only philosophy state universities could teach. It was 1939 when the young Wojtyła began his higher studies at Jagiellonian University in Cracow (where Copernicus also studied). He studied Polish letters, language and history, and wrote several plays. (Like Sartre and Marcel, the young Wojtyła was interested in human action in life and on stage.)

Wojtyła was a seminarian in the years 1942–46, during which time he first encountered Thomism. When he moved to the Pontifical University of St Thomas Aquinas in Rome, where he spent 1946–48, he met traditional and transcendental Thomists as well as the existentialist Thomism of Gilson. And in 1951 he was ordered by his archbishop to take a two-year sabbatical from pastoral work in order to write a habilitation thesis.[60] Wojtyła went on to write two dissertations: one on St John of the Cross and one on the compatibility of Christian ethics with Scheler's system.

Some scholars divide Wojtyła's subsequent works into the 'philosophical' and the 'theological',[61] classifying *Love and Responsibility* (first published in Polish in 1960) and *The Acting Person* (first published in Polish in 1969) in the former category, along with the scholarly articles written while he was professor at Lublin (of

---

[58]Buttiglione 1997: 270.

[59]In 'The Person: Subject and Community' Wojtyła comments on 'alienation' as the opposite and antithesis of participation, describing it as 'applied in Marxist philosophy' but 'independently one of the elements of modern anthropology' (Wojtyła 1979b: 306).

[60]On the possibility of a Christian ethics according to Scheler's system. See Kupczak 2000: 6.

[61]See Simpson 2001.

particular relevance for this discussion are 'The Person: Subject and Community' and 'Participation or Alienation?'). In the second category we find his book on the teachings of Vatican II, published in 1972 (published in English as *Sources of Renewal*), the thirteen encyclicals written during his papacy and several further addresses and writings delivered during the period after his professorship. We see engagement with Sartre in both authorships, although the manner in and extent to which Sartre is engaged can be seen as reflecting sensitivity to the double-injunction of *Humani Generis* – to understand and reply to Sartre without propagating his ideas.

In *Love and Responsibility* Wojtyła's describes the encounter with the other as the place in which the human person becomes aware of and fulfils herself. Whereas Sartre presents relations with others as inevitably oscillating between the mastery and slavery of the subject/object distinction, Wojtyła's answer to this problem is *love*. In *Love and Responsibility* Wojtyła writes against existentialism's 'false conception of freedom'. He writes that existentialist freedom of the will does not rest on 'truth in cognition': true freedom is displayed in morality through duty governed by love.[62]

On Wojtyła's understanding of persons, the person must be known through the prism of her efficient causality – in two senses: the causality she exercises on the world and the causality she exercises on herself in so affecting the world, through which she becomes good or evil as a person.[63] Wojtyła calls these two dimensions of human action 'transitive' and 'nontransitive': the transitive dimension affects the external world; the nontransitive 'remains in the subject', realizing the person's self. This is important because, Wojtyła writes, the human being has priority: as a subject of the act she *forms culture* through praxis.

But, as Woznicki has noted, Wojtyła rejects the praxeological priority of man exemplified by Marxist or (later) Sartrean conceptions of human praxis. In the former, the transitive character of humanity's productivity is overemphasized, such that work creates man, while in the latter, the nontransitive character is emphasized to the extent that the self-creation of an absolute, independent being leads to total isolation. Wojtyla, in attempting to balance these two aspects of human action, opposes Sartre's being-for-itself,

---

[62]Wojtyła 1981: 119–20.
[63]See Kupczak 2000.

suggesting that the nontransitive aspect of action consists in interiority, in 'in-one's-own-selfness'.[64] Understanding human existence in this way does not exclude the experience of the isolated self, but rather, interiority recognizes that it is not a complete self without going beyond itself in relation to others.

In the 1974 synod of bishops Wojtyła gave an address on the theme of 'Evangelization in the Modern World'. In the course of distinguishing between three theological meanings that can be given to the word 'world', the then-cardinal defined his third sense of the word as human flesh under *superbia*, the temptation of the Evil One. Here he developed his ideas of the 'anti-Gospel' and 'anti-evangelization', naming one general form this can take: the 'anthropocentrism' that places man in God's place, and the existentialism of Sartre.[65]

As Ramet notes, Wojtyła (speaking at the synod in 1974) knew that Sartrean existentialism shared common ground with Marxism, appreciated Merleau-Ponty's critique of Sartre (and his cohort of French Marxists) and 'subsumed Sartrean existentialism and Marxism under the generic label *atheistic anthropocentrism*'.[66] A year later we see a similar admixture in his lecture 'Participation or Alienation?'.[67] Here Wojtyła uses the term 'alienation' with a Sartrean inflection. The subject of the lecture was, characteristically, the *person* considered from his Thomist and phenomenological point of view. In particular, Wojtyła argues that 'the commandment of love' dictates that 'every human being must constantly regard as a duty the actual participation in humanity of other people, that is, the experiencing of the other as an "I", as a person'.[68] The person is not an isolated individual; rather, to truly be a person involves participation.

Wojtyła acknowledges that recognizing the personhood of others seems to come more naturally (or spontaneously) to some than to others. He sides with Scheler's analyses, which, Wojtyła claims,

---

[64]See Woznicki 1980: 48.
[65]Though there is no mention of Sartre in the Apostolic Exhortation that followed this assembly: see *Evangelii nuntiandi* (18 December 1975).
[66]Ramet 1990: 367; emphasis in original.
[67]The version published in *Person and Community* is based on a paper sent to the Fourth International Phenomenology Conference at Fribourg, Switzerland, 24–28 January 1975 (see Wojtyła 1993: 197). Some sources say it was also given at Emerson Hall at Harvard, 27 July 1976.
[68]Wojtyła 1977: 67.

furnish an argument that human beings have an inherent disposition to be open to others – *which* (he says in italics) '*Sartre seems to contradict*, whose analysis of consciousness leads to a consequent closing of the subject concerning the "others".'[69] In the conclusion of the same article, he writes that the concept of alienation is 'meeting with great success today' but that it is not 'a concept with a clear and thoroughly verified content'. He continues,

> According to Marxist philosophy, man is alienated by his own creations: the economic and political systems, property ownership, and labor. Marx had included religion in that concept, too. And so, a conclusion is drawn that it suffices to transform the world at the level of those creations, to change the economic and political system, undertake the struggle against religion – and the era of alienation will end, and there will come 'the kingdom of liberty', that is, a full self-realization for everyone and all together. However, some contemporary Marxists rightly draw attention to the fact that various forms of alienation are not overcome that way, and in fact, new ones arise, which in turn need to be overcome.[70]

Wojtyła cites Adam Schaff at the conclusion of this passage, whose 1961 work *Marxism vs. Existentialism* played a prominent role in bring existentialism into intellectual debate in Poland. In that work Schaff presented Sartre as an existentialist (not a phenomenologist), and the choice between 'existentialism and humanism' and 'marxism and humanism' as the kind of question Marxists could and should be asking.

Like Sartrean existentialism, Marxism saw God as a threat to human freedom, a Feuerbachean demon to be exorcised. Schaff offered the following description of the 'old Jehovah' and his relationship to existentialism:

> This miserable worm, with such means of knowledge at his command as the Ten Commandments, racks his brains as to

---

[69]Wojtyła 1977: 67 (here he includes a footnote referring to *Being and Nothingness*). NB the italics are in the original in the *Analecta Husserliana* version of this publication, but not always included in subsequent reprints.
[70]Wojtyła 1977: 72.

what to do in life's conflicting situations and lives in a state of discord and fear, only to earn condemnation at the end. And yet this miserable and helpless creature, worthy of both pity and contempt, is in the light of religion the sovereign individual, God's highest creation! Atheistic and religious Existentialism alike repeat the tale of the cruelty and maliciousness of the old Jehovah. They create their individual as supposedly sovereign in order to make him lonely. They condemn to helplessness and despair the wretched puppets who are the sport of malicious fate while wearing the hollow crown of 'sovereignty'.[71]

Other Marxist writers such as Novak criticized the inescapability of alienation in existentialism, equating existentialist alienation with original sin:

Alienation plays the same part in the existentialist metaphysics as Adam's fall from grace in Christian theology. It is the equivalent of original sin. Just as Jehovah expelled the erring pair from paradise and condemned their descendants to sin and suffering on earth forever after, so through the fatality of our existence as humans we are eternally and ineluctably withdrawn from others and enclosed within ourselves. There is no release or redemption from such estrangement.

Like the Marxist critics Sartre addressed in 'Existentialism Is a Humanism', Novak's complaint is that this alienation is irreversible and logically leads to quietism: 'Instead of indicating any exit from the state of alienation, existentialism makes it the permanent foundation of human life, reproducing and justifying it in metaphysical terms.'[72]

When Wojtyła asks in 'Participation or Alienation?' how we recognize, and what is really meant by, *alienation*, he is not rejecting Marx and Sartre outright: he admits that 'the concept of alienation seems to be necessary in philosophy of man', that 'it appears to suit the true state of human existence' and that it can usefully contribute

[71]Schaff, *Reflections on Man*, ed. Jesse Mann and R. Kreyche (Harcourt Brace, 1966), p. 305
[72]George Novak, *Marxism versus Existentialism*, Marxists.org, https://www.marxists.org/archive/novack/works/history/ch12.htm

to the 'analysis of human reality'. The diagnosis is accurate, but the etiology, and the proposed cure, is mistaken. For it is not by altering the external conditions of the world that alienation will be overcome but 'within the scope of the strictly inter-human relations'.

As Wojtyła defines it, participation is 'a positive relation to the humanity of other people' – to their concrete humanity, not their being human in general.[73] In order to conceive of this, however, we must begin with 'man' [sic] as a *person*.

> The problem of alienation cannot be considered in terms of man as an individual of the species or of his specific definition, but only from the point of view of man as a personal subject. I maintain that alienation is essentially a problem of the person and, in this sense, both humanistic and ethical.[74]

Alienation is thus not to be understood on Marx's terms. It is rather the opposite or antithesis of participation.[75] In participation, the person's transcendence is connected to participation: for we can only be realized and fulfilled, on Wojtyła's view, in 'we' and 'I–you' relationships. The early Sartre, through his denial of the possibility of participation, places the problem of alienation on its proper plane:

> The very core of the problem is always essentially 'human': *alienation is the negation of participation*. It cannot be linked to the world of human creations, production of structures, but refers to the place of the human being as a personal subject in this world.... Hence, the problem: participation or alienation remains the central problem of our age.[76]

[73]Wojtyła 1979b: 288.
[74]Wojtyła 1979b: 306.
[75]Wojtyła 1979b: 306 et passim.
[76]Wojtyła 1977: 72.

8

Sartre and Orthodox theology: Yannaras and Zizioulas

I loved Sartre.[1]
[He is] without doubt the most important theologian of the West's philosophical tradition.[2]

CHRISTOS YANNARAS

We have seen now that Sartre was an interlocutor for prominent twentieth-century Protestant and Catholic theologians. In this chapter we explore his influence on Orthodox thought. After a brief discussion of Vladimir Lossky this chapter turns to consider the role Sartre plays in the writings of Christos Yannaras and John Zizioulas.[3]

---

[1]Yannaras begins one of the chapters of his autobiographical work *Ta kath' eauton* with these words (*Ta kath' eauton* p. 104, cited in Louth 2015: 254).

[2]Yannaras 2015: 248.

[3]Needless to say there are other Orthodox theologians who have engaged with Sartre. Where Russian Orthodoxy is concerned, McLachlan (1992) has written an excellent study of freedom and the other in Sartre and Berdyaev, so Berdyaev will not be treated here. According to Yannaras, the first time that a Greek Orthodox theologian confronted the problems raised by existentialism was Nissiotis's 1956 doctoral dissertation, *Existentialism and the Christian Faith* (see Yannaras 2006: 281).

Vladimir Lossky

One of the best-known exponents of Orthodox apophatic theology in the West, Vladimir Lossky (1903–58) was raised in St Petersburg. His family was exiled from Russia after the revolution, and after a brief time in Prague he arrived in Paris in 1924. He enrolled at the Sorbonne, where he studied with Ferdinand Lot and Étienne Gilson. Twenty years later Lossky published *The Mystical Theology of the Eastern Church* (1944). Whether or not Lossky had read Sartre's 1943 work, Lossky's book would go on to shape later Orthodox responses to Sartrean problems – in particular, concerning what it means to be a person, to be in relation to other persons and for God to be, as Nietzsche famously declared, dead.

Lossky's work is famous for its advocacy of the apophatic tradition, and drew heavily on the works attributed to Dionysius the Areopagite. It opens with questions of definition that recur in discussions of mysticism: What is 'mystical theology'? Isn't all theology, by definition, mystical, insofar as it manifests divine mystery and the givens of revelation? Or are the two terms mutually exclusive, such that 'mysticism' is a domain inaccessible to knowledge in a way that theology is not? The latter conception can lead to Bergsonism, Lossky says, ossifying theology into 'static religion' and categorizing mysticism as 'dynamic'.

The Eastern tradition, Lossky argued, never neatly distinguished between mysticism and theology: for it personal experience and church dogma are inseparable.[4] Lossky argued that the West had lost the mysticism of the East – and with it several anthropological truths. For example, the Eastern Church regards choice as the mark not of freedom but of fallenness. Mere choice is a debasement of true liberty and a loss of the divine likeness: 'Our nature being overclouded with sin no longer knows its true good … and so the human person is always faced with the necessity of choice; it goes forward gropingly'.[5] The desire to choose autonomously, on Lossky's view, is not freedom but servitude. True freedom is revealed in Christ – who freely renounces his own will in order to live out the will of his Father.

---

[4]Lossky 1944: 5–6.
[5]The English translations here John E. Meyendorff's (Lossky 1976: 124 and 144).

On several doctrinal matters the Orthodox tradition Lossky defended is diametrically opposed to Jansenism: for the former, to deny the presence and reality of God is preternatural. Not sharing the Western doctrine of original sin, or the juxtaposition of grace and nature,[6] the Eastern Church (as Lossky presents it) held that every person retains an efficacious awareness of God, even after the Fall. 'Just because it is light,' writes Lossky, 'grace, the source of revelation, cannot remain within us unperceived. We are incapable of not being aware of God, if our nature is in proper spiritual health. Insensibility [to God] in the inner life is an abnormal condition.' Lossky adds that total unawareness of God 'would be nothing other than hell, the final destruction of the person'.[7]

Christos Yannaras

Christos Yannaras studied in Greece and Germany before coming to Paris. Lossky died in 1958, before Yannaras arrived, but his influence was still strong in the Paris School of Russian theology, and in Yannaras's intellectual development. Yannaras's philosophical formation is well documented. He has published two autobiographical volumes, *Katafygio ideon: Martyria* (Refuge of ideas: testimony) and *Ta kath' eauton* (About himself), which leave us in little doubt about the importance of Sartre in his thought. As we see in this chapter's epigraph, Yannaras 'loved Sartre'.[8] For this reason, we first consider his autobiographical writings before proceeding to analyze his engagement with Sartre in three works: *Person and Eros*, 'An Orthodox Comment on "The Death of God"' and *The Schism of Philosophy*.

Yannaras spent three solid years in Paris (and a further two intermittent ones), during which time he wrote a doctoral thesis entitled *Person and Eros*, which would eventually be published under the same title. During this period of research he read and engaged with the work of Sartre, whose works presented, in Yannaras's own words', 'probably the most crucial theological thought of the

[6]Lossky 1944: 121.
[7]Lossky 1976: 225 and 217.
[8]Both published in Athens by Ikaros, in 2000 (rev. edn) and 2005 (rev. edn) respectively.

century – theological as the negative of the picture – far more meta-physical than the western theologians'.[9]

Before moving to Paris Yannaras had studied in Germany, and his debt to Heidegger is widely acknowledged.[10] It is surprising that Sartre's role in his work has not drawn wider comment, given that he described himself as even more attracted to Sartre due to the latter's 'disarming honesty':

> Even Heidegger protected himself behind academic formality, even though he constructed his philosophical word poetically. Sartre dared to expose himself, to cry out.... He committed himself to desperate struggle, he went down to the streets, to demonstrations for social demands, he was thirsty for action. In almost every one of his lines I felt his claim for empirical certainty of an ontological character.... He would not be reconciled with rationalist replacements of the real and the experiential, opposed to the self-delusion of identifying the real with just the social phenomenology.[11]

In a later work Yannaras would write that Sartre was 'clearly more realistic' and 'acutely innovative' than Heidegger.[12] Over the course of his education, Yannaras writes, years went by before he came to the conclusion that the great Western theologians were 'incapable' of 'posing ontological questions':

> The explosive problematic of Heidegger and Sartre remained (and remains) incomprehensible for the West. So did the message that Nietzsche's 'madman' was putting across. What was certain was that the philosophers were in the vanguard; the theologians were following: Bultmann following Heidegger, Moltmann following Bloch.[13]

What the 'philosophers' had already realized was that, as Nietzsche's madman proclaimed, God was dead: the classical theistic concept

---

[9]Yannaras 2005: 62–4 and 72.
[10]See, e.g. Louth 2015: 254ff.
[11]Yannaras 2005: 104.
[12]Yannaras 2015: 255.
[13]Christos Yannaras Τὰ καθ' ἑαυτόν, (Athens: Ikaros, 2005), p. 35, cited and translated in Grigoropoulou 2008: 55.

of God was bankrupt.[14] And yet theologians were still trying to cash in on it.

After his time in Paris, Yannaras accepted Heidegger's critique of ontotheology and Lossky's apophaticism. But it is Sartre Yannaras credits with taking the Western philosophical and theological tradition to its 'highest moment'. In *The Schism of Philosophy* Yannaras argues that despite Sartre's international renown, 'the most important aspect of his philosophical contribution … remains largely unknown', namely,

> that for the first time in the history of Western European philosophy the ontological problem rediscovers in Sartre the radical quality of the Greek *theological* debate. However paradoxical it may seem, Sartre's ontological views represent for Western philosophy its highest *theological* moment – Sartre is without doubt the most important *theologian* of the West's philosophical tradition. (248; emphasis in original)

Person and Eros

Yanarras's high estimation of Sartre's importance (and his clear distinction between the achievements of Heidegger and Sartre) is evident in the published version of his doctoral work, *Person and Eros*, where Sartre is the first thinker Yannaras cites by name (in §1 of chapter 1, on 'The Ecstatic Character of Personhood'). As his argument develops, Yannaras sets out 'the ontological problem' with reference to Sartre, defining his own account of the 'person' against the Sartrean subject. He writes that the person does not '"precede nature" in the way Sartre declares that "existence precedes essence." The person is not just a self-awareness which is self-determined before it can be determined by any universal concept, that is, by a nature or essence.'[15]

Sartre exemplifies the tragedy of personhood outside of the 'reciprocal erotic relation' that is humanity's appropriate relationship to God (and all else, through God):

[14]Yannaras 1971: 43.
[15]Yannaras 2007: 31.

In our personal relation to the world, beings as 'things' reveal the existence of a personal God, the personal Word of the Creator God, the Person of God the Word, yet inevitably also the distinct absence of the Person. Outside the realm of reciprocal erotic relation, God is absence. The Church's theology of experience could justify Sartre's expression by summarizing the tragic experiential search for God by Western man after the 'death of God', the God of ontic categories: 'the absence of God'.[16]

Absence is not non-existence, for absence, Yannaras goes on to say, is 'experience of the privation of a personal immediacy, which presupposes the reality or the possibility of the relation'. Yannaras writes that

this experiential sense of loss of personal immediacy, the pain of the personal absence of God, sometimes shows through in Sartre's writings, as in the works of other contemporary Westerners who refuse to exhaust the truth about God simply in intellectual constructs. Sometimes the sense of personal absence can even arrive at the immediacy of an erotic fact. Sartre says: 'Let him condemn me to hell a hundred, a thousand times, only let him exist!' Only a privation of love can be indifferent to any benefit, provided the pain of absence can be exchanged for the certainty and immediacy of personal presence.[17]

The passages cited in this section are taken from one of Sartre's literary works, *The Devil and the Good Lord*, which makes appealing to them for autobiography questionable. But in *What Is Literature?* Sartre wrote that 'God, if he existed, would be, as certain mystics have seen Him, in a situation in relationship to man.'[18] Although I have found no evidence that Yannaras read this text, his assessment of Sartre's account of God suggests an uncanny sensitivity to the latter's theological position.

Yannaras's comment on Sartre's absent God implicitly replies to the Jansenist tradition from which Sartre drew. The Jansenist God is famously hidden, and those who desire him may be damned to

---

[16]Yannaras 2007: 68.
[17]Yannaras 2007: 68–9.
[18]*WL* 14.

dissatisfaction. On the Orthodox view Yannaras outlines in order for the pain of the loss of God to be erotic pain, a previous knowledge *and sense* of God is implied. Yannaras affirms the 'erotic pain' of not being in God's presence (citing Chrysostom: 'For if one has mind and senses, one already experiences hell when one is cut off from the face of God.'[19]) but interprets human yearning, the pained *eros* itself, as a testament to the *presence* of its source.

In Chapter 2 of *Person and Eros*, too (entitled 'Absence'), the first thinker to be named in the main body of the text is Sartre, who is credited here with making 'an exhaustive analysis of the relation between personal absence and space'. Although Yannaras realizes that Sartre's intention is not identical to his own (namely, to demonstrate 'the experience of absence as felt nearness'[20]), Yannaras nevertheless devotes several pages to the Pierre example from *Being and Nothingness* because of the light it sheds 'on the real relationship of absence with personal immediacy'.[21]

In developing his account of the person Yannaras draws on Sartre in distinguishing between the ecstasy of the person and the distantiality of the atomic individual. Yannaras wants to defend the otherness of persons as something which is 'revealed only in the fact of loving communion and relation' – in ecstasy (*ekstasis*).[22] But this is downgraded (never entirely destroyed) into distantiality, in which otherness becomes divisive dissimilarity. 'Dissimilarity as distantiality is the existential reverse of otherness as relation and reveals the falling away of the person into an objectified individual.'[23] Sartre's analysis of shame and *le regard d'autrui* is cited as showing the way in which the gaze, the faculty 'which is the initial potentiality of the immediacy of relation' which should enable us to experience otherness, 'proves to be, with the falling away into atomic individuality, the supreme experience of objectification'. Yannaras cites Sartre at length in this section, including the claim that shame is an 'original Fall' and Sartre's reference to the Genesis account, 'that Adam and Eve knew they were naked' (*BN* 312).

---

[19]Chrysostom, Homily 5 on Romans 6, cited in Yannaras 2007: 69.
[20]Yannaras 2007: 108.
[21]Yannaras 2007: 108.
[22]Yannaras 2007: 243.
[23]Yannaras 2007: 243.

On Yannaras's reading, what both the Bible and Sartre's work attest to is a fall from *person* to *individual*. Before the Fall there was no nakedness or shame. 'Love has no knowledge of the sense of nakedness, because it has no knowledge of the distantiality of objectification.'[24] Juxtaposing 'true eros' and the 'eros of Atomic existence' (à la Sartre), Yannaras writes that true eros glimpses 'personal otherness, the beauty of the prelapsarian integrity of the person' in the body. It is unaware of distantiality. But the eros of atomic existence divides the self: 'it sets the other apart in the distantiality of nakedness and defends itself against the demands of the other with shame'.[25]

Yannaras's description of shame reads like paraphrase of *Being and Nothingness*, with the slight modification that what Yannaras claims for 'the atomic individual', Sartre claims for all humankind. On Yannaras's definition, shame

> is the defense of atomic individuality against its objectification, the claim of its freedom to remain subjective within the limit of an objectified nature.... Atomic freedom is the knowledge and the defense of subjective self-completeness, which is why the distantiality of atomic individuality is defined by the freedom of the 'other' that undermines the autonomy and sovereignty of my own subjectivity. Thus every other atomic individuality is revealed as a threat to my own atomic freedom.[26]

But the fact of existential loneliness itself, Yannaras claims, presupposes a person to whom we can relate in otherness. *Only a person* can release us from the distances that characterize human relationships: 'Only a person who has not fallen into the distantiality of atomic individuality, but continues to send out to me an ecstatic summons to personal universal relation, only such a person can preserve my ecstatic reference as a failure of relation and experience of existential loneliness.'[27]

On this basis, Yannaras argues, Sartre's *theological* claims are entirely justified – insofar as they concern a divine *subject*. If being a

[24]Yannaras 2007: 244.
[25]Yannaras 2007: 245.
[26]Yannaras 2007: 245.
[27]Yannaras 2007: 246.

subject presupposes the autonomy of the atomic individual, that is, the desire to 'see without being seen', then the existence of God does indeed, as Sartre argued, preclude human freedom. The problem with the Western metaphysical tradition, and the foundation of Western atheism, is 'ignorance of, or disregard for, the truth of the person.'[28]

Just before Yannaras's section on soteriology we meet Sartre again: for who better than Sartre to tell us of our need of salvation? But Sartre's famous line from *No Exit* – *l'enfer c'est les autres* ('Hell is other people') – does not get the last word. Rather, we read that before Sartre, Dostoevsky's Father Zosima had already defined hell in a similar, but fuller, way that summarized the Orthodox teaching: 'Hell is the torment of not loving.'[29]

'An Orthodox Comment on the Death of God'

In *Person and Eros* Yannaras cites *Being and Nothingness* and 'Existentialism Is a Humanism' as well as *No Exit* and *The Devil and the Good Lord*. In this work he cites *Words* as well.[30] This short text (ten pages) discusses Nietzsche, Heidegger and Sartre. Yannaras's 'comment' is best summarized in his own words, that 'the absence of God is the drama of a personal loss'.

> The death of God crisis is taken to stem from 'the experience of isolation, from a sincere recognition that no amount of law making can safeguard the nature of 'personal' relationships. This awareness leads to despair, since men never give up the attempt to establish some kind of human relationship.... The prophetic insight of Nietzsche and Sartre can reveal the casual and counterfeit character of reality and thus lay bare the tragic quality of their deception. But that which is real and authentic, as ontological realities and not as metaphysical categories, only theology can reveal.[31]

[28]Yannaras 2007: 248.
[29]Dostoevsky, *The Brothers Karamazov*, A.6.3 (from the teachings and homilies of Zosima) cited in Yannaras 2007: 267.
[30]'An Orthodox Comment on the Death of God' was published first in *Sobornost*, Series 5 no. 4, Winter 1966.
[31]Yannaras 1971: 48 and 49.

The real message of the Gospel, according to Yannaras, is 'God with us': that there is a new human nature which brings those who believe together and restores them into true relationship.

The Schism of Philosophy

In *The Schism of Philosophy* Yannaras returns to Sartre's attempt to 'attribute an ontological content to the concept of freedom'.[32] After acknowledging Sartre's indebtedness to Kierkegaard, Husserl and Heidegger, Yannaras writes that Sartre takes phenomenological investigation to its 'most radical consequences'. Sartre's distinction between reflective and pre-reflective consciousness opens up the possibility of prephenomenological analysis, pushing analysis 'into a phase *before* even the unavoidable referentiality of knowledge, bracketing knowledge, or regarding the power of cognition as a given'.[33]

This empty consciousness, Yannaras writes, is achieved by a kenotic emptying of content and referentiality, and we can attain this only by living an experience of nausea, which reveals to us 'the possibility of existence without a particular *mode* of existence'. It reveals *being-in-itself*, being that does not refer back to itself reflectively but which simply *is*. Apart from human beings, all such beings are like this: they are what they are, and cannot on their own be otherwise.

This incapacity to be otherwise is a linchpin in Yannaras's interpretation of Sartre. For on Yannaras's reading, *being-in-itself* does not include *otherness*: 'it is never posited as *different* from another *Being*. The principle of identity arises from this theory not as an antithetical reference to otherness but only as self-assertion.'[34] The principle of identity for Sartre's *being-for-itself* involves reference to nothing but itself, and as such, Yannaras argues,

this description of a *thing-in-itself* (*en-soi*) derives not from an intellectual analysis, nor from a phenomenological version

---

[32]Yannaras 2015: 233. In this work Yannaras draws primarily on *Being and Nothingness*, *Nausea* (2015: 245) and 'Existentialism Is a Humanism' (2015: 48).
[33]Yannaras 2015: 245; emphasis in original.
[34]Yannaras 2015: 245; emphasis in original.

of the objects of worldly reality, but from the ability of the human consciousness to annul its referentiality and by this self-annulment to give meaning to the nonnothingness of the *thing-in-itself*.[35]

Human consciousness, by contrast, is capable of reflexivity, of referring back to itself – and consequently it experiences itself not as a convergence of identity but as a *relation* to itself.

Yannaras goes on at length about the account Sartre gives of consciousness in the introduction to *Being and Nothingness*, his equation of consciousness with nothingness, his insistence that nothingness enters the world through the human and his definition of *being-for-itself* as freedom:

> We cannot say of ourselves that first we *are* and later we are free. We can only say that there is no difference between our *Being* and our *being-free*.... Freedom is condemnation and absurdity (*absurdité*), seeing that we do not choose freedom but are free because we are unable not to choose, and the not-choosing is in reality the choice of not-choosing. The foundation of freedom is its self-nullification, and on this given foundation we experience our obligatory freedom as a presupposition of the ego's existence.[36]

We are condemned to be free, to exist and to give our lives meaning through our historical action in the world. It is our responsibility to give our lives meaning in the full knowledge that 'Man is that which he does.'

It is in the context of this discussion of Sartrean 'heroic despair' that we find the words quoted at the opening of this chapter, namely, that Sartre is 'without doubt the most important *theologian* of the West's philosophical tradition'.[37] For Sartre the problem of God is judged by 'the ontological content of freedom':

> either freedom *constitutes Being* as an event of communion and self-transcendence, and consequently as existential otherness (in

[35]Yannaras 2015: 246.
[36]Yannaras 2015: 247.
[37]Yannaras 2015: 248.

which case only the triadicity of God responds to the problem
of the hypostatic *principle of Being*), or freedom is the given
and uninterpreted *mode* of the existential otherness of the
subject, in which case its realization necessarily *nullifies* Being
as essence or nature (and then the existence of God is absolutely
contradictory).[38]

As Yannaras writes, Greek philosophy would have agreed with
Sartre on the shape of the dilemma: one can understand freedom
as *love* or *nothingness*. Sartre clearly rejects the possibility of the
former, and offers an ontological theory which 'rules out any illu-
sory escape from the absurdity and tragicness of freedom'. Sartre's
autonomous individual is constantly confronted by nothingness,
experiencing 'the void of the absence of God, the "original fall" of
coexistence in the world – this "hell" that is "other people"'. It is
'chiefly through Sartre', Yannaras writes, 'that the epistemological
theism of European theology has been shown to be a most consistent ontological nihilism': for if the existential principle of Being is
not the *person* as the *hypostasis* of Being, Yannaras argues, then the
very concept of God is incoherent and absurd – a useless intellectual
hypothesis.[39]

Yannaras distinguishes between two apophaticisms: 'of essence'
and 'of the person'. The former, he thinks, is well known in the
Western tradition, where there has been a dialectic between cataphatic and apophatic theology, with the latter checking the former
and leading to God by way of analogy. The latter apophaticism is
characteristic of the Greek East, and speaks of the personal as inex-
haustible when the person is encountered in the ecstatic experience
of self-transcendence in love.

Sartre is the legitimate heir of the apophaticism of essence. But
the apophaticism of the person is Yannaras's reply: there is a universe of persons who are irreducible to one another and whose
existence need not be characterized by distantiality and meaninglessness. *Persons* find their meaning relationally, through mutual
ecstatic encounter in love – a love grounded in the creative, self-
emptying love of God.

---

[38]Yannaras 2015: 249; emphasis in original.
[39]Yannaras 2015: 250.

John Zizioulas

John Zizioulas was born in Greece in 1931. He studied at the universities of Thessaloniki and Athens and spent a semester at the Ecumenical Institute at Bossy in 1954–55.[40] He then studied for a master's at Harvard University under Florovsky (in theology) and Tillich (in philosophy). Several scholars have noted Zizioulas's indebtedness to his Orthodox predecessors – including Yannaras.[41] This section discusses his engagement with Sartre in one text, *Being and Communion*, to argue that although Zizioulas does not systematically engage with Sartre's philosophy, he nevertheless uses it as a symbol of the tragic aspect of human personhood.

In *Being as Communion*, Zizioulas affirms divine–human communion as the starting point of all theology. When a human being is a member of the church, he takes on God's 'way of being', which is not an accomplishment but rather 'a way of *relationship* with the world. With other people, and with God, an event of *communion*' that cannot be achieved by an individual.[42] At the end of the work's introduction he writes that it was intended to 'offer their contribution to a "neopatristic synthesis" capable of leading the West and the East nearer to their common roots, in the context of the existential quest of modern man'.[43]

On Zizioulas's account, the ecclesial experience of the Church Fathers revealed to them that 'the being of God is a relational being'. Zizioulas makes clear that his understanding of communion does not reorder essence and existence. The Father as *cause* is a paradox, because the Father also 'exists as an event of communion'. There can be no 'Father' without 'Son', so this causal relation is not to be understood in the usual, linear, X → Y way.[44] God 'owes his existence to the Father', which shows that

> His being is the consequence of a free person; which means …
> that not only communion but also *freedom*, the free person,
> constitutes true being. True being comes only from the free

---

[40]See Louth 2015: 216 for further biographical information.
[41]Torrance 1996: 35 n.69; Rise 2016: 59.
[42]Zizioulas 1985: 15; emphasis in original.
[43]Zizioulas 1985: 26.
[44]Zizioulas 1985: 17.

person, from the person who loves freely – that is, who freely affirms his being, his identity, by means of an event of communion with other persons.[45]

Zizioulas sees this vision of the person as arising *only* within the mystery of the church. Humanism and sociology, therefore, struggle to affirm the importance of man. He singles out 'the existentialist philosophers' in particular for having shown '– with an intellectual honesty that makes them worthy of the name philosopher – that, humanly speaking, the person as an absolute ontological freedom remains a quest without fulfilment'.[46]

Zizioulas's aim to address the 'existential quest of modern man' is restated at the outset of chapter 1 (on personhood and being), where he situates his discussion of the person in the context of attempts by 'contemporary humanism' to 'detach the concept of the person from theology and unit[e] it with the idea of an autonomous morality or with an existential philosophy which is purely humanistic'.[47] Although Sartre is not mentioned by name here, he is mentioned later in the book when Zizioulas discusses the 'dilemma' of freedom.

On Zizioulas's view, Trinitarian theology offers a foundation that is unavailable to humanism since the Trinitarian God exists on account of a *person*, not a substance. The significance of this claim is not just academic, Zizioulas writes, but *existential*. For the 'ultimate challenge to the freedom of the person is the "necessity" of existence.' The 'freedom' of Western philosophy is equated with choice: one is free if one chooses between possibilities. But this freedom is already limited by the 'necessity' of the possibilities available to the human being in question, and Zizioulas writes, the 'ultimate and most binding of these "necessities" for man is his existence itself: how can a man be considered absolutely free when he cannot do other than accept his existence?'[48]

Readers of Sartre will know what a recurrent theme this is in his plays and novels. Zizioulas gives the literary example of Kirilov, from Dostoevsky's novel *The Possessed*, as indicative of the tragic

---

[45]Zizioulas 1985: 18; emphasis in original.
[46]Zizioulas 1985: 18.
[47]Zizioulas 1985: 27.
[48]Zizioulas 1985: 42.

side of the person's quest: he wants to transcend the 'necessity' of existence – he wants to see his life not as a 'given fact but as the product of his free consent and self-affirmation'.[49] The tragedy of this quest is that it comes into conflict with the createdness of humanity, for human beings as creatures cannot escape the 'necessity' of existence. If suicide is the only way out (as Kirilov expresses) then freedom leads to nihilism.

Zizioulas holds this 'existential alarm, the fear of nihilism' responsible for relativizing the concept of the person, writing that

> indeed every claim to absolute freedom is always countered by the argument that its realization would lead to chaos. The concept of 'law', as much as in its ethical as in its juridical sense, always presupposes some limitation to personal freedom in the name of 'order' and 'harmony', the need for symbiosis with others. Thus 'the other' becomes a threat to the person, its 'hell' and its 'fall', to recall the words of Sartre.[50]

Sartre shows, par excellence, how powerless humanism is to affirm personhood.

In contrast to the radical freedom of Kirilov or Sartre, Zizioulas goes on to argue that the only true exercise of freedom ('in an ontological manner') is *love*.

> The expression 'God is love' (1 John 4:16) signifies that God 'subsists' as Trinity, that is, as a person and not as substance. Love is not an emanation or 'property' of the substance of God – this detail is significant in the light of what I have said so far – but is *constitutive* of His substance, i.e. it is that which makes God what He is, the one God. Thus love ceases to be a qualifying – i.e. secondary – property of being and becomes *the supreme ontological predicate*. Love as God's mode of existence 'hypostatizes God, *constitutes* his being. Therefore, as a result of love, the ontology of God is not subject to the necessity of the substance. Love is identified with ontological freedom.[51]

[49]Zizioulas 1985: 42.
[50]Zizioulas 1985: 43.
[51]Zizioulas 1985: 46; emphasis in original.

Unlike the 'tragic person of humanism', which does not see beyond the biological hypostasis, the eucharistic hypostasis 'does not draw its being from what it is now but is rooted ontologically in the future'.[52]

Zizioulas therefore presents a dilemma (to which Yannaras referred, above): the person must choose between freedom as love or freedom as negation. To choose negation is to express person-hood (for only persons can seek negative freedom), but this choice entails death: 'Death for a person means ceasing to love and to be loved, ceasing to be unique and unrepeatable, whereas life for the person means the survival of the uniqueness of its hypostasis [personification], which is affirmed and maintained by love.'[53] On Zizioulas's account being a person is a mystery in which 'otherness and communion are not in contradiction but coincide'. This communion does not dissolve diversity 'into one vast ocean of being' but rather affirms otherness 'in and through love'. 'In the context of personhood,' Zizioulas writes, '*otherness* is incompatible with *division*.'[54]

To whom should Zizioulas turn for an example of the divisive and destructive character of the 'individualized and individualizing Adam'? Sartre's passage on the other as my 'original sin' is cited in support of Zizioulas's conclusion that 'a human being left to himself cannot be a person.'[55]

Conclusion

In Yannaras we see that the apophaticism of the person is used to answer the nihilism of Sartre and the alleged emptiness of the Western concept of God. In Zizioulas, the problem of freedom

---

[52]Zizioulas 1985: 64.
[53]Zizioulas 1985: 49.
[54]Zizioulas 1985: 106, 107; emphasis in original.
[55]Zizioulas 1985: 107. Zizioulas appeals to Sartre on this topic in popular writings, too: 'Communion and otherness – how can these two be reconciled? Are they not mutually exclusive and incompatible with each other? Is it not true that by definition the other is my enemy and my "original sin," to recall the words of Jean-Paul Sartre?' (see http://incommunion.org/2004/12/11/communion-and-otherness/).

and creatureliness is addressed at great length, and the eucharistic hypostasis of the Fathers is contrasted with the 'tragic person of humanism' – to show that the 'existential quest' of modern man can indeed meet fulfilment through salvation: 'the realization of personhood in man'.[56]

[56]Zizioulas 1985: 50.

9

Sartre and Liberation theology: James H. Cone

When man denies his freedom and the freedom of others, he denies God.[1]

JAMES H. CONE

The second half of the twentieth century saw the emergence of several theologies of liberation. From various parts of the world, oppressed peoples – whether their oppression was rooted in sex, labour or race – voiced their dissatisfaction with a Christianity that spoke to the rights and wrongs of the 'soul' and ignored the concrete injustices affecting (and sometimes arising from) their bodies. Feminist, black and South American liberation theologians all preached a Gospel of liberation not merely from the ties that bound their inner selves but also from the oppressive structures of unjust societies.

Sartre's account of the body-for-others in *Being and Nothingness*, as we saw in Chapter 4, included a phenomenological analysis of the experience of being reduced to an object. Physical appearance is presented as an 'objective characteristic' which 'defines me in my being-for-others' in a way I cannot refuse to assume: a black person cannot NOT be seen as black. This is part of her facticity.

As we saw in Chapter 1, where anti-black racism, colonialism and anticolonial counterviolence were concerned, Sartre spoke and wrote against oppression and provided the oppressed with a

---

[1]Cone 1997: 137.

platform from which to speak on their own terms. Although his political judgement was not irreproachable (with the benefit of hindsight), Sartre stood against oppression without attempting to speak for the oppressed, which has inspired anti-black racism campaigners to this day,[2] and as we shall see here, played a role in the development of black liberation theology.

Before 'liberation theology' was made famous by its South American[3] and feminist exponents, Sartre's message of freedom was informing the developing minds of Martin Luther King Jr. and Cone. In his 1958 essay 'Pilgrimage to Nonviolence', King recounts his early dissatisfaction with Protestant liberalism and neo-orthodoxy: for liberalism focused disproportionately on the human capacity for good, and neo-orthodoxy on the human capacity for evil. The existentialists caught his attention and 'stimulated [his] thinking' because existentialism 'grasped certain basic truths about man and his condition'.[4] But it is Cone who would give Sartre a prominent role in a systematic theology of liberation.

Black liberation theology

In the late 1960s, Cone was frustrated that his seminary and PhD studies had not included discussions of racism and segregation. His professors refused to see racism as a *theological* problem, so Cone set his mind to articulating why it was.[5] Cone was studying in the height of the civil rights movement, but the problems his American theology professors addressed were, on his view, European problems. After completing his doctorate at Northwestern University, he published *Black Theology and Black Power* in 1969 – a book which launched a movement and reshaped American theological discourse.[6]

Cone's book drew heavily on the theology of Barth. But it also drew on Sartre, offering an existentialist justification for the

[2]E.g. Gordon 1995.
[3]Gustavo Gutierrez's *A Theology of Liberation* was first published in Spanish in 1971.
[4]See 'Pilgrimage to Nonviolence', p. 3, available online at The King Center, http://www.thekingcenter.org/archive/document/pilgrimage-nonviolence.
[5]Cone 1986: 37.
[6]Bradley 2010: 36.

autonomy of black consciousness combined with hope in the transcendent truth that black people are fully human and made in the image of God. God sees them that way, whether white people do or not.

Cone perceived a 'desperate need for a *black theology*, a theology whose sole purpose is to apply the freeing power of the gospel to black people under white oppression'.[7] And in *Black Theology and Black Power* and his 1970 work, *A Black Theology of Liberation*, he draws extensively on Sartre in articulating his concept of liberation.

Black Theology and Black Power

It is evident in the 1969 work that Cone had read Fanon[8] and several existentialists: he applies the notion of the absurdity to American black experience in a heartrending way. He notes that most existentialists do not say simply that 'man' or 'the world' is absurd; rather, the absurdity arises when the human being confronts the world, looking for meaning.

> The same is true in regard to my analysis of the black man in a white society. It is not that the black man is absurd or that the white society as such is absurd. Absurdity arises as the black man seeks to understand his place in the white world. The black man does not view himself as absurd; he views himself as human. But as he meets the white world and its values, he is confronted with an almighty No and is defined as a thing. This produces the absurdity.[9]

The crucial question for the black man, Cone writes, is 'how should I respond to a world that defines me as a nonperson?' The black man knows that he is a person. But when he attempts to relate to the world as such, the world 'demands that he respond as a thing'. So what should he do, Cone asks? 'Should he respond as he knows himself to be, or as the world defines him?'[10]

---

[7]Cone 1997: 31; emphasis in original.
[8]Cone 1997: 24.
[9]Cone 1997: 11.
[10]Cone 1997: 11.

Black people need to be liberated, but Cone is insistent that they cannot be 'given' freedom or be helped to get it. In order to be free, Cone argues, they must determine their own existence rather than be defined by others:

> And in this sense Sartre is right: 'Man is freedom'; or, better yet, man 'is condemned to be free'. A man is free when he accepts the responsibility for his own acts and knows that they involve not merely himself but all men. No one can 'give' or 'help get' freedom in that sense.[11]

Cone also follows Sartre in arguing that when liberation occurs it is not only the oppressed who are liberated but also the oppressor – it is not only for blacks' sake that liberation should be pursued, but for whites' too. Thirty years ago, he writes,

> it was quite acceptable to lynch a black man by hanging him from a tree; but today whites destroy him by crowding him into the ghetto and letting filth and despair put the final touches on death. Whites are thus enslaved to their own egos. Therefore, when blacks assert their freedom in self-determination, whites too are liberated. They must now confront the black man as a person.[12]

Cone repeatedly reminds his reader that we should not forget what the existentialists call 'the burden of freedom'. Authentic freedom, he insists, is not the individualism of laissez-faire, it is not the 'right of the businessman to pursue without restraint the profit motive or the pleasure principle which is extolled by Western capitalistic democracies'. Rather, *authentic* freedom is grounded in 'the agonizing responsibility of choosing between perplexing alternatives regarding his existence'.[13] Such freedom, however, can neither be taken for granted nor assumed to guarantee an 'easy or happy way of life':

> That is why Sartre says man 'is condemned to freedom'. Freedom is not a trivial birthday remembrance but, in the words of

[11]Cone 1997: 28
[12]Cone 1997: 41.
[13]Cone 1997: 41–2.

Dostoevsky's Grand Inquisitor, 'a terrible gift'. It is not merely an opportunity but a temptation. Whether or not we agree with the existentialists' tendency to make man totally autonomous, they are right in their emphasis on the burden of freedom.[14]

Cone's 'whether or not we agree' clause concerning the autonomy of existential freedom clearly indicates some reservation (or at least, the anticipation of reservations among some of his readers). So Cone goes on to discuss the 'burden of freedom' with reference to the New Testament, which, he says, describes the burden in terms of freedom from the law. To be free in Christ, he writes, 'means that man is stripped of the law as a guarantee of salvation and is placed in a free, mature love-relationship with God and man, which is man's destiny and in which Christ is the pioneer'. To be free in Christ means being 'a slave for Christ in order to do his will'. But because Christ is against the world, to be free in Christ is to be against the world.

Having defined his notion of freedom in this way, Cone makes three assertions about Black Power:

1) '*The work of Christ is essentially a liberating work*, directed toward and by the oppressed. Black Power embraces that very task.'

2) '*Christ in liberating the wretched of the earth also liberates those responsible for the wretchedness*. The oppressor is also freed of his peculiar demons. Black Power in shouting Yes to black humanness and No to white oppression is exorcizing demons on both sides of the conflict.'

3) '*Mature freedom is burdensome and risky, producing anxiety and conflict for free men and for the brittle structures they challenge*. The call for Black Power is precisely the call to shoulder the burden of liberty in Christ, risking everything to live not as slaves but as free men.'[15]

To state the obvious, Cone writes not from the comfort of a Parisian café, where 'slavery' is a component of a Hegelian dialectic or a Bérullian anthropology to be debated or dismissed on conceptual

[14]Cone 1997: 42.
[15]Cone 1997: 42–3; emphasis added.

grounds, but from a context in which his ancestors *were slaves*. He calls on their songs of freedom, reminding his listeners of generations of collective longing, and their conviction that freedom was, to speak in phenomenological terms, not merely an *internal* matter:

> The black slave knew that to fight for freedom is to do the work of God. For him, death was preferable to life if the latter must be in slavery. Consequently, he sang: 'Oh, freedom! Oh freedom! Oh freedom o-ver me! An' be-fo' I'd be a slave, I'd be buried in my grave, and go home to my Lord an' be free'.

In this and other spirituals, he writes, there is 'no suggestion … that Christianity is merely private, isolated and unrelated to the conditions of this life'.[16] Rather, 'Christianity has to do with fighting with God against the evils of this life. One does not sit and wait on God to do all the fighting, but joins him in the fight against slavery. Therefore, they sang, comparing themselves with Joshua, "Joshua Fit de Battle of Jericho."'[17] These slaves, in their songs, implicitly and explicitly challenged their oppressors: Look, white man! Look what your Gospel preaches. Why don't we live it?

Cone argues that Christianity and earthly freedom were inseparable for the black man, which led to the birth of the independent black churches and free black preachers: 'The black church was born in protest', he writes, and 'in this sense, it is the precursor of Black Power'.

> Unlike the white church, its reality stemmed from the eschatological recognition that freedom and equality are at the essence of humanity, and thus segregation and slavery are diametrically opposed to Christianity. Freedom and equality made up the central theme of the black church; and protest and action were the early marks of its uniqueness, as the black man fought for freedom. White missionaries sought to extol the virtues of the next world, but blacks were more concerned about their freedom in this world.

---

[16]'Other Spirituals which revealed the slave's determination to relate Christianity to a life of freedom in this world are: "I'm Going to Lay Down My Life for My Lord," "Lord, I Want to Be a Christian in My Heart," "I'm A-going to Do All I Can for My Lord," and "I Want to Live so God Can Use Me"' (Cone 1997: 94).
[17]Cone 1997: 94.

Ironically it was the black man's deep concern for freedom and equality which led him to accept Christianity. He saw that the white master's religion was the best way to freedom.[18]

The task of black theology, therefore, is to '*to analyze the black man's condition in the light of God's revelation in Jesus Christ with the purpose of creating a new understanding of black dignity among black people, and providing the necessary soul in that people, to destroy white racism.*'[19] But in doing so the task of black theology is to restore all of humanity to a freedom that more truly corresponds to their destiny as bearers of God's image. Cone argues that biblical freedom means not allowing another to define your existence. The meaning of the *imago dei* is that God has created human beings in such a way that their 'destiny is inseparable from [their] relation to their creator' – *all* men bear this image. Consequently, 'when man denies his freedom and the freedom of others, he denies God. To be for God by responding creatively to the *imago Dei* means that man cannot allow others to make him an It.' This fact, Cone argues, makes black rebellion 'human and religious'.[20]

A Black Theology of Liberation

A year later, in 1970, *A Black Theology of Liberation* appeared, in which Cone offers a further, systematic development of his black theology. His theology is again rooted in the contention that 'Christianity is essentially a religion of liberation', and that the task of its theologians is 'to do theology in the light of the concreteness of human oppression as expressed in color' so that they may 'interpret for the oppressed the meaning of God's liberation in their community'.[21]

Acknowledging the seriousness of the charge that Christianity is a false friend of the oppressed, Cone admits to seeing why the temptation to ditch God is great. Of course it is appealing to 'refuse to be associated with Christian murderers':

[18]Cone 1997: 94.
[19]Cone 1997: 117; emphasis in original.
[20]Cone 1997: 137–8.
[21]Cone 1990: v.

Some existentialist writers – Camus and Sartre – have taken this course, and many black revolutionaries find this procedure appealing. Reacting to the ungodly behavior of white churches and the timid, Uncle Tom approach of black churches, many black militants have no time for God and the deadly prattle about loving your enemies and turning the other cheek. Christianity, they argue, participates in the enslavement of black Americans.

But the answer is not to reject talk of God, Cone writes, but rather to free it from the 'ungodly influences of white religion'.[22] Such an emancipation must take place concretely. In its emphasis on the concrete, Cone writes, black theology resembles existentialism, and particularly 'its conviction that "existence precedes essence" (to use Sartre's phrase)':[23]

> This means that the concrete human being must be the point of departure of any phenomenological analysis of human existence. According to Sartre, there is no essence or universal humanity independent of persons in the concreteness of their involvement in the world. All persons define their own essence by participating in the world, making decisions that involve themselves and others.

Cone notes that Sartre's emphasis on concreteness and the overwhelming responsibility of freedom has 'led him to deny the reality of God', that his view of freedom necessarily excludes the existence of God or human nature as concepts that deprive human beings of freedom. Although black theology does not see the need to deny God's existence, Cone writes that he is 'glad for the presence' of Sartre (and Camus) because they 'remind theologians' of something theology had forgotten: 'that the God-problem must never be permitted to detract from the concern for real human beings. The sole purpose of God in black theology is to illuminate the black condition so that blacks can see that their liberation is the manifestation of God's activity'.[24]

[22]Cone 1990: 57.
[23]Cone 1990: 84.
[24]Cone 1990: 84–5.

Many theologians will regret the limited usefulness Cone assigns God here: defining the 'sole purpose' of God as such (even if for rhetorical purposes) has the potential to alienate many otherwise sympathetic readers. But again Cone draws on Sartre – in this case, the literary character Mathieu from *The Age of Reason* – to argue that *black* liberation brings liberation for oppressor and oppressed. He writes that 'the truly free' identify with the humiliated because

> they know that their own being is involved in the degradation of their brothers and sisters. They cannot stand to see them stripped of their humanity. This is so not because of pity or sympathy, but because their own existence is being limited by another's slavery. They do not need to ask whether their fellow human being is at fault. All they know is that there is a fight going on, and they must choose sides, without any assurance of who is right in the 'Christian' sense of future victory.[25]

In the *Age of Reason*, Brunet attempts to persuade the novel's protagonist, Mathieu, to join the communist party. But Sartre describes Mathieu's realization of the difficulty of freedom, as the conversation unfolds – because it involves the renunciation of false freedoms:

> 'At this moment, at this very moment, there are men firing point-blank at one another in the suburbs of Madrid, there are Austrian Jews agonizing in concentration camps, there are Chinese burning under the ruins of Nanking, and here I am, in perfect health, I feel quite free, in a quarter of an hour I shall take my hat and go for a walk in the Luxembourg'. He turned towards Brunet and looked at him with bitterness. 'I am one of the *irresponsibles*', he thought.

Cone uses Sartre's novel to demonstrate that freedom is *more* than the 'intellectual articulation of an existential attitude'. True freedom involves committing one's whole being to the cause of the oppressed. That, Cone writes, is why Brunet says,

> 'You're all the same, you intellectuals: everything is cracking and collapsing, the guns are on the point of going off, and you stand

[25]Cone 1990: 95.

there calmly claiming the right to be convinced. If only you could see yourselves with my eyes, you would understand that time presses'.[26]

But Brunet is wasting his time, Cone says: 'oppressors never see themselves as the oppressed see them', and if they have to be '*told* about the inhumanity around them, there is little hope for them' (emphasis in original). Mathieu knows that Brunet is right, that he should make a choice. But to make a free choice a person must make choices that are not dependent on oppressive systems:

> Mathieu is able to live an irresponsible life that some might call 'freedom' because he participates in a society that protects him. He is insensitive to the suffering of others, even that of his own mistress, Marcelle. If he cannot choose a freedom that involves his intimate friend, it is not likely that he will be able to choose a freedom that involves unknown sufferers. As Sartre says: 'The only way of helping the enslaved out there is to take sides with those who are here.'[27]

A few pages later Cone engages at length with 'Existentialism Is a Humanism', and in particular Sartre's discussion of anguish, forlornness and despair, because these three human experiences 'point to the suffering which is inseparable from being-in-the-world'. Cone relates each in turn to his own project, writing that we experience anguish because our actions 'involve all humanity'.

> 'Man is anguish', writes Sartre, in that we are creatures capable of involvement, realizing that it is not possible to accept responsibility for all and not have some anxiety about it. We are thrown into the world with a multiplicity of possibilities but with no guide for correctness in choice. But whatever choice we make, it is not simply a choice for us; it is a choice for all human beings. We assume the responsibility for humanity and declare what we consider to be humanly possible. Who can make such a choice without feeling at the same time a deep sense of

[26]Cited in Cone 1990: 95.
[27]Cone 1990: 96.

anxiety? This is the choice that blacks make. They are alone and yet not alone, and there is no way to evade the seriousness of their responsibility.[28]

Cone notes the atheistic nature of Sartre's 'forlornness' and its denial of values rooted in heaven, but nevertheless he considers Sartre's analysis of forlornness to be particularly appropriate for the oppressed:

> Oppression means that society has defined truth in terms of human slavery; and liberation means the denial of that truth. The God of society must be destroyed so that the oppressed can define existence in accordance with their liberation. In the moment of liberation, there are no universal truths; there is only the truth of liberation itself, which the oppressed themselves define in the struggle for freedom. To be forlorn is to accept the task of choosing humanity without any certainty beyond the existing moment.[29]

Moreover, Cone asserts, 'it is not possible to experience oppression without also experiencing despair' (where despair is defined in Sartre's words as being confined 'to reckoning only with what depends upon our will, or on the ensemble of probabilities which make our action possible'). Our earthly possibilities, after all, are limited.[30]

Cone clearly invokes Sartrean freedom as part of his rallying call for black liberation. But he also notes that Sartre does not have a monopoly on describing freedom as intimately related to suffering. This relationship, Cone argues, is also evident in the Biblical tradition, where Israel is called 'to share in Yahweh's liberation'. In the Israel of the Old Testament as in the existentialism of the Left Bank, Cone writes, freedom

---

[28]Cone 1990: 99.
[29]Cone 1990: 100.
[30]Again Cone 1990: 100–1 cites *EH*: 'I am left in the realm of possibility; but possibilities are to be reckoned with only to the point where my action comports with the ensemble of these possibilities and no further.'

is not a position of privilege but of terrible responsibility. To be Yahweh's people, Israel must be willing to fight against everything that is against this liberation. Therefore, the whole of its history is a description of the movement of this people in relation to God's liberating work. This involves suffering because liberation means a confrontation between evil and the will of the God who directs history.[31]

Whereas Barth, Tillich, Marcel, Wojtyła, Yannaras and Zizioulas discuss Sartre primarily as a hamartiological figure who demonstrates the tragic aspect of human personhood when its fulfilment is sought outside of God, Cone reads Sartre as a Socratic gadfly who will not let theologians rest in complacency, reminding them that the 'God-problem must never be permitted to detract from the concern for real human beings'.[32]

South American liberation theology

The same degree of engagement with Sartre is not evident in the writings of the South American liberation theologians. Although Gustavo Gutierrez does approvingly cite Sartre in *A Theology of Liberation*, Sartre's words are merely invoked in order to appeal to an even higher authority (on Gutierrez's view): Karl Marx.[33]

Even so, it is worth noting that some historians have traced liberation theology's roots to the early 1960s,[34] and in particular to Fanon's *The Wretched of the Earth*, which we have seen, also influenced Cone. Fanon's violent indictment of colonialism was preceded by Sartre's equally violent preface, in which he wrote that 'the Third World finds *itself* and speaks to *itself* through this voice':

---

[31]Cone 1990: 101.

[32]Cone 1990: 84–5.

[33]The line cited is that 'Marxism, as the formal framework of all contemporary philosophical thought, cannot be superseded', from Sartre's 'Marxism and the Philosophy of Existence', cited in Gutierrez 2001: 53. See Dussel et al. 1992 on liberation theology and varieties of Marxism.

[34]Although Gallagher 1990 shows that Sartrean liberation themes appear in South American literature: in the 1950s Llosa was inspired by the Sartrean idea that literature could shape revolution and change the world.

Europe is springing leaks everywhere. What then has happened? It simply is that in the past we made history and now it is being made of us. The ratio of forces has been inverted, decolonization has begun; all that our hired soldiers can do is to delay its completion.[35]

Feminist liberation theology

Where Sartre and feminist liberation theology are concerned, different challenges apply. Many readers have noted Sartre's apparent abhorrence for the body – and especially the female body. Although his portrayals of female objectification (and self-objectification, in the case of the woman on the date in *Being and Nothingness* or Estelle in *No Exit*) are perceptive, liberating women was not an explicit aim. Although some scholars, such as Barnes, dismiss Sartre's sexism in *Being and Nothingness* as incidental to a work that 'demands feminism as one of its natural consequences',[36] others, such as Le Doeuff,[37] argue that Sartre's philosophical categories and the manner in which he uses them are both problematic.

Feminist theologians such as Daly have found in Sartre a prime candidate for their catalogue of sexist patriarchs.[38] Although Charmé has argued that Sartre's 'patriarchal atheism' has more in common with feminist theology than first meets the eye, it seems to the present author that assessing Sartre's influence on feminist theology would require an analysis of Beauvoir's *The Second Sex* and wider questions concerning the directionality of influence between Sartre and Beauvoir – questions which would take us well beyond the scope of this book.[39]

---

[35]Fanon 1967: 9 and 23; emphasis in original.
[36]Barnes 1990: 346.
[37]Le Doeuff 2007: 48.
[38]In *Gyn/Ecology* Daly notes Sartre's disdain for viscous 'gook' (the description of which Marcel praised so highly) – and his association of it with the feminine (Daly 1978: 332ff).
[39]See Charmé 2010.

10

Sartre's theological future

God, if he existed, would be, as certain mystics have seen Him, in a situation in relationship to man.

JEAN-PAUL SARTRE (*WL* 14)

The stated aim of this book was to demonstrate that Sartre was influenced by and influenced theology in a manner that neither Sartre scholars nor theologians have adequately recognized. Part 1 surveyed Sartre's life and early intellectual formation, showing that prior to Sartre's discovery of phenomenology he read theological accounts of lived experience and interiority, reading mystics such as St John of the Cross and Teresa of Ávila as well as their interpreters Baruzi and Delacroix. We saw that Sartre's concept of freedom took root in intellectual soil where 'free will and determinism' had several theological aliases, for example, 'freedom and sin' or 'freedom and grace'. And we saw that his concept of freedom drew on a theological anthropology of nothingness that is indebted to Augustine and his French interpreters – both philosophical (in the works of Descartes, Jansen, Port-Royal, Malebranche and Pascal) and literary (in the works of La Rochefoucauld, Pascal, Racine, Molière and Corneille as well as Mauriac, Bernanos and Claudel).

Part 2 turned to *Being and Nothingness*, considering the 'pessimistic' and the 'optimistic' Sartre that would provoke reactions from the theologians in Part 3. After considering Sartre's anthropology of nothingness and the consequences of nothingness for the lived experience of consciousness – the impossibility of identity, anxiety, bad faith, the body and being with others – this part presented

Sartre's concept of freedom and his exposition of existentialism's 'optimism' in the popular lecture 'Existentialism Is a Humanism'.

Part 3 then presented detailed accounts of seven theologians' engagement with Sartre, covering prominent figures in twentieth-century Protestant, Catholic, Orthodox and Liberation theology. We saw that Sartre features in the systematic theologies of Barth and Tillich as well as in the anthropology of Marcel and Wojtyła's discussion of participation and alienation. We saw that Yannaras and Zizioulas both deploy Sartre in their discussions of person-hood, and that James H. Cone drew heavily on Sartre in developing his black liberation theology.

Having covered this ground we are now in a position to ask a final question in closing: will Sartre have a theological future?

Chapter 9 noted that the majority of the theologians considered in Part 3 engaged with Sartre primarily in the context of their doc-trines of sin – which is to say, in their discussions of how human beings fall short of being all they were created to be. Marcel's charge of sophism – that Sartre convincingly disguises partial truths for the whole truth – is a charge that several of the later theologians also made, each in his own way. In Barth's *das Nichtige*, Tillich's halfway demythologization of sin, Wojtyła's account of alienation and Yannaras's and Zizioulas's depictions of the 'tragic' aspect of human personhood when its fulfilment is sought outside of God, we are presented with one half of a theological picture, because, for these theologians, 'deliverance and salvation' are not an unfulfilled promise in a controversial footnote but a reality that can be lived here and now. Cone, by contrast, reads Sartre as a Socratic gadfly, goading theologians not to forget that the 'God-problem must never be permitted to detract from the concern for real human beings'.[1]

Part of the reason these theologians found Sartre fascinat-ing, I contend, is because his 'consistent atheist position' offers a phenomenology of sin from a graceless position. Sartre provides theologians today with a rich resource – particularly for the phe-nomenology of religion,[2] hamartiology and relational ontology.[3] Before drawing the book to a close, therefore, I would like to allay one possible objection, namely that Sartre's philosophy was 'of its

---

[1]Cone 1990: 84–5.
[2]Kirkpatrick 2016.
[3]Kirkpatrick forthcoming.

time, for its time'. That Sartre's phenomenological ontology was deemed worthy of the responses we considered in Part 3 may just be a testament to these theologians' desire to seem culturally current with a major trend of the mid-twentieth century. But given their varied methodological stances it seems more likely to the present author that Sartre's phenomenology – though not the whole truth – offers an insightful analysis of aspects of human existence (and our own behaviour) that we would often rather ignore, for example,

- the propensity to look on others with objectifying gazes that reduce them to a single dimension of their personhood (for example, sex, race, wealth, poverty, education or social role);
- the desire to control others, especially how we are perceived by them;
- the fear that love is an illusion and participation (or true intersubjectivity) is impossible; and
- the recognition that we are responsible for ourselves, the way we look at others and how we shape the world.

To dismiss these Sartrean preoccupations is to deny both their present relevance and their provenance. Whether one wishes to support the claim theologically in the name of sin or sociologically in the name of injustice, it is clear that human beings today engage in objectifying behaviours which demean both victims and perpetrators. Although the objectifications of 2017 are not identical to those of 1943, the structure of human experience still involves the possibility of reducing or being reduced to the status of an object. The desire for power and the esteem of others is no less pertinent – indeed, in the age of social media questions of self-objectification, and of where to draw the line between *seeming* and *being*, are difficult to avoid. And the possibility of love – of the other or the self – is being interrogated from numerous disciplinary perspectives, for love could be reducible to evolutionary psychology, patriarchal oppression or a 'survival' of a religion that is, as Bernanos said, in decay.

Sartre's preoccupations are not 'of their time'. We saw in Parts 1 and 2 that Sartre received a theological inheritance of 'nothingness', of *sin*, which led to various pessimisms about the human ability to know itself or others. I hope that, in light of this provenance, my theological readers will no longer be content to read Sartre as a straw atheist, or indeed as a carbon copy of Heidegger. Sartre's atheism is fascinating for theologians because it is a theologically informed atheism haunted by questions of divine love, freedom and grace. The God he rejects is not only the God of the philosophers but also the God of the mystics. This and his philosophy of the imagination, in particular, may provide theologians with insight into the theological, and *a*theological, imaginations.

For philosophers, knowing the provenance of *Being and Nothingness*'s *néant* and its consequences will illuminate its conceptual divergences from the German phenomenological tradition. But it may also provide an opportunity to follow the advice Harry Frankfurt offers in *Necessity, Volition, and Love*. Frankfurt argues that 'philosophers need to pay more attention to issues belonging to the domain that is partially occupied by certain types of religious thought – issues to do with what people care about, with their commitments to ideals, and with the protean role in our lives of the various modes of love'.[4] If we are to consider these things, 'religious thought' suggests that we should consider not only their successes but also their failures – lives in which the *absence* of care, commitment and love cast long shadows.

[4]Frankfurt 1999: x.

WORKS CITED

Anderson, Thomas C. (2010) 'Atheistic and Christian Existentialism: A Comparison of Sartre and Marcel', in Adrian Mirvish and Adrian van den Hoven (eds), *New Perspectives in Sartre*. Newcastle: Cambridge Scholars Publishing.

André, Y. M. ([1886] 1970) *La Vie du R. P. Malebranche*. Geneva: Slatkin Reprints.

Aristotle (1979) *Metaphysics*, trans. Hugh Tredennick, Loeb Classical Library. Cambridge, MA: Harvard University Press.

Aron, Raymond (1990) *Memoirs: Fifty Years of Political Reflection*, trans. George Holoch. New York: Holmes and Meier.

Aronson, Ron (1996) 'Introduction' to *Hope Now: The 1980 Interviews*, by Jean-Paul Sartre and Benny Lévy, trans. Adrian van den Hoven. Chicago: University of Chicago Press.

Aumann, Jordan OP (1985) *Christian Spirituality in the Catholic Tradition*. London: Sheed & Ward.

Ayer, A. J. (1945) 'Novelist-Philosophers, V: Jean-Paul Sartre', *Horizon* 12: 12–26.

Bachmann, Jakob (1964) *La Notion du temps dans la pensée de Pierre de Bérulle*, Winterthur: Éditions P. G. Keller.

Badiou, Alain, with Nicolas Truong ([2009] 2012) *In Praise of Love*, trans. Peter Bush. London: Serpent's Tail.

Baldick, Robert (2006) *The Life of J.-K. Huysmans*, ed. Brendan King. Sawtry: Dedalus Books.

Barnes, Hazel (1990) 'Sartre and Sexism', *Philosophy and Literature* 14 (2): 340–7.

Barrès, Maurice (1902) *Scènes et doctrines du nationalisme* (Paris: Emile-Paul).

Barrett, Lee C. (2013) *Eros and Self-Emptying: The Intersections of Augustine and Kierkegaard*. Grand Rapids, MI: Eerdmans.

Barth, Karl (1958–60) *Church Dogmatics*, vol. 3. Trans. J. W. Edwards, O. Bussey, Harold Knight. Edinburgh: T&T Clark. (References in the text follow the convention of abbreviating this work as 'CD' followed by the volume, part and page number.)

Barth, Karl (1933) *Epistle to the Romans*, trans. Edwyn C. Hoskyns. 6th edn. Oxford: Oxford University Press.

Baruzi, Jean (1924) *Saint Jean de la Croix et le problème de l'éxperience mystique*. Paris: Alcan.

Bayer, Oswald (2009) 'Tillich as Systematic Theologian', in Russell Re Manning (ed.), *The Cambridge Companion to Paul Tillich*. Cambridge: Cambridge University Press.

Beauvoir, Simone de (2006) *Diary of a Philosophy Student, vol. 1: 1926–27*. Urbana, IL: University of Illinois Press.

Beauvoir, Simone de (2001) *Memoirs of a Dutiful Daughter*, trans. James Kirkup. London: Penguin.

Beauvoir, Simone de ([1960] 1989) *La Force de l'âge*. Paris: Gallimard.

Beauvoir, Simone de ([[1981] 1984) *Adieux: A Farewell to Sartre*, trans. Patrick O'Brian. New York: Pantheon.

Beauvoir, Simone de (1977) *Force of Circumstance: Hard Times*. New York: Harper & Row.

Beauvoir, Simone de ([1960] 1965) *The Prime of Life*, trans. Peter Green. London: Penguin.

Beauvoir, Simone de (ed.) (1993) *Quiet Moments in a War: The Letters of Jean-Paul Sartre to Simone de Beauvoir 1940–1963*, trans. Lee Fahnestock and Norman Macafee. London: Hamish Hamilton.

Bellemare, Rosaire (1959) *Le Sens de la créature dans la doctrine de Bérule*. Paris: Desclée de Brouwer.

Bergson, Henri ([1946] 1992) *The Creative Mind*, trans. Mabelle L. Andison. New York: The Citadel Press (translation of *La Pensée et le mouvant*).

Bernanos, Georges ([1936] 1937) *The Diary of a Country Priest*, trans. Pamela Morris. London: Catholic Book Club.

Bérulle, Pierre de (1944) *Opuscules divers de piété*, ed. Gaston Rotureau. Paris: Aubier.

Boulé, Jean-Pierre (2005) *Sartre, Self-Formation, and Masculinities*. Oxford: Berghahn.

Bradley, Anthony B. (2010) *Liberating Black Theology: The Bible and the Black Experience in America*. Wheaton, IL: Crossway.

Brunschvicg, Léon (1931) 'La Notion de la philosophie chrétienne', *Bulletin de la Société française de Philosophie* (31): 37–93.

Buggiglione, Rocco (1997) *Karol Wojtyła: The Thought of the Man Who Became Pope John Paul II*. Grand Rapids, MI: Eerdmans.

Cain, Seymour (1995) *Gabriel Marcel's Theory of Religious Experience*. New York: Peter Lang.

Calder, Andrew (2002) *Molière: The Theory and Practice of Comedy*. London: A&C Black.

Casseville, C. (1993) *Mauriac et la critique sartrienne*. In *Nouveaux Cahiers François Mauriac*, no. 1. Paris: Grasset.

Catalano, Joseph (2009) 'The Body and the Book: Reading Being and Nothingness,' in Katherine J. Morris (ed.), *Sartre on the Body*. London: Palgrave Macmillan.

Caws, Peter (1979) *Sartre*. London: Routledge.

Chabot, Alexis (2016) 'Cruel Atheism', *Sartre Studies International* 22 (1): 58–68.

Charmé, Stuart Z. (2010) 'Sartre and the Links between Patriarchal Atheism and Feminist Theology', in Julien S. Murphy (ed.) *Feminist Interpretations of Jean-Paul Sartre*. University Park: Penn State University Press.

Chaubet, François (1998) 'Les Décades de Pontigny (1910–1939)', *Vingtième siècle, revue d'histoire* 57 (Jan.–Mar.): 36–44.

Chervel, André (1993) *Histoire de l'agrégation: Contribution à l'histoire de la culture scolaire*. Paris: Editions Kimé.

Cicero (1927) *Tusculan Disputations*, trans. J. E. King. Cambridge, MA: Loeb Classical Library.

Claudel, Paul (1969) *Journal II*. Paris: Gallimard.

Claudel, Paul (1967) *Vers d'exil*, vol. 7, *Oeuvre poétique*. Paris: Pléiade.

Cognet, Louis (1949) *La spiritualité française au XVIIe siècle*. Paris: La Colombe.

Cohen-Solal, Annie (1987) *Sartre: A Life*. New York: Pantheon.

Cone, James ([1969] 1997) *Black Theology and Black Power*. Maryknoll, NY: Orbis Books.

Cone, James ([1970] 1990) *A Black Theology of Liberation*. 20th anniversary edn. Maryknoll, NY: Orbis Books.

Cone, James (1986) *My Soul Looks Black*. Maryknoll, NY: Orbis Books.

Contat, Michel, and Michel Rybalka (1974) *The Writings of Jean-Paul Sartre*, 2 vols., Evanston, IL: Northwestern University Press. Volume number is indicated in brackets.

Coplestone, Frederick (1954) *Metaphysical Journal* by Gabriel Marcel, trans. Bernard Wall. *Philosophy* 29 (109): 170–1.

Cotkin, George (2003) *Existential America*. Baltimore: Johns Hopkins University Press.

Cox, Gary (2009) *Sartre and Fiction*. London: Continuum.

Daly, Mary (1978) *Gyn/Ecology: The Metaethics of Radical Feminism*. Boston: Beacon Press.

Daniel-Rops, ed. (1941) *Mystiques de France: Textes choisis et commentés*. Paris: Éditions Corréa.

Delacroix, Henri ([1908] 1938) *Les Grand mystiques chrétiennes*. Paris: Alcan.

Deranty, Jean-Philippe (2015) 'Existentialist Aesthetics', *The Stanford Encyclopedia of Philosophy* (spring 2015 edn), Edward N. Zalta (ed.), <http://plato.stanford.edu/archives/spr2015/entries/aesthetics-existentialist/>.

Descartes, René (1988) *Selected Philosophical Writings*, trans. John Cottingham, Robert Stoothoff and Dugald Murdoch, with an introduction by John Cottingham. Cambridge: Cambridge University Press.

Descartes, René (1981) *Méditations métaphysiques*, avec présentation et introduction par Jean-Paul Marty. Paris: Hachette.

Descartes, René (1969) *The Philosophical Works of Descartes*, ed. and trans. by Elizabeth Haldane and G. R. T. Ross. Cambridge: Cambridge University Press, 2 vols.

Donneau, Olivier (2010) 'Christianisme, bourgeoisie, modernité: Sartre accumulateur critique de matériaux historiques', *Études sartriennes* 14: 55–70.

Doyle, William (2001) *Jansenism: Catholic Resistance to Authority from the Reformation to the French Revolution*. New York: St. Martin's Press.

Dreisbach, Donald (1980) 'Essence, Existence, and the Fall: Paul Tillich's Analysis of Existence', *Harvard Theological Review* 73 (3/4): 521–38.

Dupré, Louis, and Don. E. Saliers (eds) with John Meyendorff (1989) *Christian Spirituality: Post-Reformation and Modern*. London: SCM Press.

Dussel, Enrique, Irene B. Hodgson and José Pedrozo (1992) 'Liberation Theology and Marxism', *Rethinking Marxism* 5 (3): 50–74.

Economist (2003) 'Hands across a Century: Review of *Sartre: The Philosopher of the Twentieth Century* by Bernard-Henri Levy', August 28, http://www.economist.com/node/2020767.

Elkaïm-Sartre, Arlette (2004) 'Historical Introduction' to Jean-Paul Sartre, *The Imaginary*. London: Routledge.

Esslin, Martin (1970) 'Sartre's Nativity Play', *ADAM International Review*, Nos. 343–5.

Les Études philosophiques (1929) 'Le Travail philosophique', 3e Année, No. 2/3, Paris: Presses universitaires de France: 138–41.

Fanon, Frantz ([1961] 1967) *The Wretched of the Earth*. London: Penguin.

Fénelon, François (1880) *De l'Existence de Dieu; Lettres sur religion, etc.*, avec introduction par le Cardinal de Bausset. Paris: Garnier Frères.

Foreaux, Francis (2010) *Dictionnaire de culture générale*. Paris: Pearson Education France.

Frankfurt, Harry (1999) *Necessity, Volition, and Love*. New York: Cambridge University Press.

Friedman, Michael (2010) 'Descartes and Galileo', in Janet Broughton and John Carriero (eds), *A Companion to Descartes*. Oxford: Wiley.

Fullbrook, Edward, and Kate Fullbrook (2008) *Sex and Philosophy: Jean-Paul Sartre and Simone de Beauvoir*. London: Continuum.

Fulton, Ann (1999) *Apostles of Sartre: Existentialism in America, 1945–1963*. Evanston, IL: Northwestern University Press.

Gaines, James F. (2002) *The Molière Encyclopedia*. Westport, CT: Greenwood Press.

Gallagher, Michael (1990) 'Liberation in Latin American Fiction', *Studies* 79 (315): 281–8.

Gardner, Sebastian (2009) *Sartre's* Being and Nothingness: *A Reader's Guide*. London: Continuum.

Gerassi, John (2009) *Talking with Sartre: Conversations and Debates*. New Haven, CT: Yale University Press.

Geroulanos, Stefanos (2010) *An Atheism That Is Not Humanist Emerges in French Thought*. Stanford: Stanford University Press.

Gillespie, John (2014) 'Sartre and God: A Spiritual Odyssey, Part 2', *Sartre Studies International* 20 (1): 45–56.

Gillespie, John (2013) 'Sartre and God: A Spiritual Odyssey, Part 1', *Sartre Studies International* 19 (1): 71–90.

Gilson, Etienne (1939) *Christianity and Philosophy*, trans. Ralph MacDonald. New York: Sheed & Ward. (*Christianisme et Philosophie*, Paris: Vrin, 1936.)

Gilson, Etienne (1913) *La doctrine cartésienne de la liberté et la théologie*, PhD diss., Faculté des Lettres, Université de Paris.

Gines, Kathryn T. (2012) 'Reflections on the Legacy and Future of the Continental Tradition with Regard to the Critical Philosophy of Race', *Southern Journal of Philosophy* 50 (2): 329–44.

Goldmann, Lucien (1964) *The Hidden God: A Study of the Tragic Vision in the* Pensées *of Pascal and the Tragedies of Racine*, trans. Philip Thody, London: Routledge.

Gordon, Lewis (1995) *Bad Faith and Antiblack Racism*. Amherst, NY: Humanity Books.

Grigorapoulou, Evaggelia (2008) *The Early Development of the Thought of Christos Yannaras*, PhD diss., Durham University. http://etheses.dur.ac.uk/1976/.

Gutierrez, Gustavo (2001) *A Theology of Liberation: History, Politics, Salvation*. London: SCM.

Hayman, Ronald (1992) *Sartre: A Biography*. New York: Carroll & Graf.

Heinemann, F. H. (1953) 'German Philosophy', *Philosophy* 28: 355–8.

Hopkins, Jasper (1994) 'Theological Language and the Nature of Man in Jean-Paul Sartre's Philosophy', in *Philosophical Criticism: Essays and Reviews*, Minneapolis: Arthur J. Banning Press.

Howells, Christina (1988) *Sartre: The Necessity of Freedom*. Cambridge: Cambridge University Press.

Howells, Christina (1981) 'Sartre and Negative Theology', *Modern Language Review* 76: 549–55.

Huysmans, J. K. (2004) *Against the Grain*, trans. John Howard. Project Gutenberg.

Izumi-Shearer, Shigeko (1976) 'Le corps ambigu chez Jean-Paul Sartre', *Études de langue et de littérature françaises* 28: 96–115.

Jopling, David, (1986) 'Kant and Sartre on Self-Knowledge', *Man and World* 19 (1): 73–93.

Kirkpatrick, Kate (forthcoming) *Between Being and Nothingness: Sin in Jean-Paul Sartre*. Oxford: Oxford University Press.

Kirkpatrick, Kate (2016) 'Analytic Theology and the Phenomenology of Faith', *Journal of Analytic Theology* 4: 222–33.

Kirkpatrick, Kate (2015) 'Sartre: An Augustinian Atheist?', *Sartre Studies International* 21 (1): 1–20.

Kirkpatrick, Kate (2013) 'Jean-Paul Sartre: Mystical Atheist or Mystical Antipathist?' *European Journal for Philosophy of Religion*, 5 (2): 159–68.

Kolakowski, Leszek (1998) *God Owes Us Nothing: A Brief Remark on Pascal's Religion and on the Spirit of Jansenism*. Chicago: University of Chicago Press.

Kupczak, Jaroslaw (2000) *Destined for Liberty: The Human Person in the Philosophy of Karol Wojtyła*. Washington, DC: Catholic University of America Press.

La Rochefoucauld, François de (1664) *Réflexions ou sentences et maximes morales*. Electronic edition by Ebooks libres et gratuits, http://www.ebooksgratuits.com/pdf/la_rochefoucauld_maximes.pdf.

Lavelle, Louis (1948) *Bérulle et Malebranche*. Paris: Association Fénelon.

Le Doeuff, Michèle ([1989] 2007) *Hipparchia's Choice: An Essay Concerning Women, Philosophy, etc.*, trans. Trista Selous. New York: Columbia University Press.

Le Doeuff, Michèle ([1980] 2002) *The Philosophical Imaginary*, trans. Colin Gordon. London: Continuum.

Leak, Andrew (2006) *Jean-Paul Sartre*. London: Reaktion.

Leduc-Lafayette, Denise (1996) 'Vouloir ne vouloir pas', in *Fénelon: Philosophie et Spiritualité*, ed. Denise Leduc-Lafayette. Geneva: Librairie Droz.

Levinas, Emmanuel ([1930] 1963) *La Théorie de l'intuition dans la phénoménologie de Husserl*. Paris: Vrin.

Levy, Bernard-Henri (2003) *Sartre: The Philosopher of the Twentieth Century*, trans. Andrew Brown. London: Polity.

Lewis, Philip E. (1994) 'Jansenist Tragedy', in Denis Hollier and R. Howard Bloch (eds), *A New History of French Literature*. Cambridge, MA: Harvard University Press.

Light, Stephen (1987) *Shuzo Kuki and Jean-Paul Sartre*. Urbana, IL: Southern Illinois University Press.

Lossky, Vladimir (1976) *The Mystical Theology of the Eastern Church*, trans. John E. Meyendorff. Crestwood, NY: St Vladimir's Seminary.

Lossky, Vladimir (1944) *Essai sur la théologie mystique de l'église d'orient*. Paris: Aubier.

Louandre, Charles (1847) 'L'Histoire du Jansénisme', *Revue des Deux Mondes* 19: 713–27.

Louette, Jean-François (1998) '*Huis clos* et ses cibles (Claudel, Vichy)', *Cahiers de l'Association internationale des études françaises* 50 (1): 311–30.

Louth, Andrew (2015) *Modern Orthodox Thinkers: From the Philokalia to the Present*. Downers Grove, IL: IVP.

Louth, Andrew (2012) 'Apophatic and Cataphatic Theology', in Amy Hollywood and Patricia Beckman (eds) *The Cambridge Companion to Christian Mysticism*. Cambridge: Cambridge University Press.

Maistre, Joseph de (1838) *Considérations sur la France*. Brussels: Rusand.

Manser, Anthony (1983), 'Unfair to Waiters?', *Philosophy* 58 (223): 102–6.

Marcel, Gabriel (2002) *The Philosophy of Existentialism*. New York: Citadel Press.

Marcel, Gabriel (2001a) *The Mystery of Being, Volume I: Reflection and Mystery*. South Bend, IN: St Augustine's Press.

Marcel, Gabriel (2001b) *The Mystery of Being, Volume II: Faith and Reality*. South Bend, IN: St Augustine's Press.

Marcel, Gabriel (1975) 'La Liberté en 1971', *Les Études philosophiques* 1 (Jan.–Mar.): 7–17.

Marcel, Gabriel (1965) 'Truth and Freedom', *Philosophy Today* 9 (4): 227.

Marcel, Gabriel (1958) *La Dimension Florestan*. Paris: Plon.

Marcel, Gabriel (1951) *Homo Viator: Introduction to a Metaphysic of Hope*. London: Victor Gollancz.

Marion, Jean-Luc (1991) *God without Being*, trans. Thomas A. Carlson; foreword by David Tracy. Chicago: University of Chicago Press.

McKelway, Alexander (1964) *The Systematic Theology of Paul Tillich*. London: Lutterworth Press.

McLachlan, James Morse (1992) *The Desire to Be God: Freedom and the Other in Sartre and Berdyaev*. New York: Peter Lang.

McLean, Stuart D. (1981) *Humanity in the Thought of Karl Barth*. Edinburgh: T. & T. Clark.

Melzer, Sara E. (1986) *Discourses of the Fall: A Study of Pascal's* Pensées, Berkeley: University of California Press.

Menn, Stephen (2002) *Descartes and Augustine*. Cambridge: Cambridge University Press.

Mesnard, Jean (1992) 'Jansenism et littérature', in *La Culture de XVIIe siècle: enquêtes et synthèses*. Paris: PUF.

Meszaros, Julia (2016) *Selfless Love and Human Flourishing in Paul Tillich and Iris Murdoch*. Oxford: Oxford University Press.

Mikkelsen, Hans Vium (2010) *Reconciled Humanity: Karl Barth in Dialogue*. Grand Rapids, MI: Eerdmans.

Moran, Dermot (2011) 'Sartre's Treatment of the Body in *Being and Nothingness*: The "Double-Sensation",' in Jean-Pierre Boulé and Benedict O'Donohoe (eds), *Jean-Paul Sartre: Mind and Body, Word and Deed*. Newcastle: Cambridge Scholars Publishing.

Moriarty, Michael (2006) *Fallen Nature, Fallen Selves: Early Modern French Thought II*. Oxford: Oxford University Press.

Morris, Katherine J. (2008) *Sartre*. Oxford: Blackwell.

Mueller, Marieke (2014) 'Flaubert's Destiny: Freedom and Alienation in *L'Idiot de la famille*', *Sartre Studies International* 20 (2): 17–31.

O'Connell, David (1994) 'Bourgeois Sin', in Denis Hollier and R. Howard Bloch (eds), *A New History of French Literature*. Cambridge, MA: Harvard University Press.

O'Doherty, E. F. (1954) 'Sartre and Existentialism', *University Review* 1 (1): 45–57.

Olson, Robert G. ([1962] 2012) *An Introduction to Existentialism*. New York: Dover.

Parrella, Frederick J. (2009) 'Tillich's Theology of the Concrete Spirit', in Russell Re Manning (ed.), *The Cambridge Companion to Paul Tillich*. Cambridge: Cambridge University Press.

Perrin, Maurius (1980) *Avec Sartre au stalag 12D*. Paris: Jean-Pierre Delarge.

Philonenko, Alexis (1981) 'Liberté et mauvaise foi chez Sartre', *Revue de Métaphysique et de Morale* 86 (2): 145–63.

Pius XII (1950) *Humani Generis*. Vatican City: Libreria Editrice Vaticana.

Plantinga, Alvin (1958) 'An Existentialist's Ethics', *Review of Metaphysics* 12 (2): 235–56.

Plantinga, Alvin, and Nicholss Wolterstorff (eds) (1983) *Faith and Rationality: Reason and Belief in God*. Notre Dame, IN: University of Notre Dame Press.

Protevi, John (2006) *A Dictionary of Continental Philosophy*. New Haven, CT: Yale University Press.

Racine, Jean (1963) *Phaedra and Other Plays*, trans. John Cairncross. London: Penguin.

Ramet, Sabrina P. (1990) *Catholicism and Politics in Communist Societies*. Durham, NC: Duke University Press.

Ramsey, Paul (1962) *Nine Modern Moralists*. Englewood Cliffs, NJ: Prentice Hall.

Reijnen, Anne Marie (2009) 'Tillich's Christology'. in Russell Re Manning (ed.), *The Cambridge Companion to Paul Tillich*. Cambridge: Cambridge University Press.

Richmond, Sarah (2013) 'Nothingness and Negation', in Steven Churchill and Jack Reynolds (eds) *Jean-Paul Sartre: Key Concepts*, Durham, NC: Acumen.

Richmond, Sarah (2007) 'Sartre and Bergson: A Disagreement about Nothingness', *International Journal of Philosophical Studies* 15: 77–95.

Richmond, Sarah (2004) 'Introduction' to Jean-Paul Sartre, *The Transcendence of the Ego*, trans. Andrew Brown. London: Routledge, 2011.

Rise, Svein (2016) *Key Theological Thinkers: From Modern To Postmodern*. Abingdon: Routledge.

Salvan, Jacques (1967) *The Scandalous Ghost*. Detroit: Wayne State University Press.

Sartre, Jean-Paul (1981) *Oeuvres romanesques*. Paris: Gallimard.

Sartre, Jean-Paul (1978) *Sartre by Himself*. New York: Urizen. (This book of interviews was produced from the 1972 interviews filmed for the documentary *Sartre par lui-même*.)

Sartre, Jean-Paul (1976a) *Situations X: Politique et Autobiographie*. Paris: Gallimard.

Sartre, Jean-Paul (1946) 'Portraits of Paris' *Vogue*, June, 152–62.

Sartre, Jean-Paul (1945) 'The New Writing in France: The Resistance "Taught That Literature Is No Fancy Activity Independent of Politics"' *Vogue*, July, 85.

Sartre, Jean-Paul (1944) 'Paris Alive: The Republic of Silence', *Atlantic Monthly*, December, 39–40.

Sartre, Jean-Paul (1939) 'Monsieur François Mauriac et la liberté', *La Nouvelle revue française*, 1 February, 112–232.

Schilpp, Paul (1982) 'Interview with Jean-Paul Sartre,' in *The Philosophy of Jean-Paul Sartre*, La Salle, IL: Open Court.

Schrift, Alan D. (2008) 'The Effects of the *Agrégation de Philosophie* on Twentieth-Century French Philosophy', *Journal of the History of Philosophy* 46 (3): 449–73.

Schüßler, Werner (2009) 'Tillich's Life and Works', in Russell Re Manning (ed.), *The Cambridge Companion to Paul Tillich*. Cambridge: Cambridge University Press.

Selinger, Suzanne (1998) *Charlotte von Kirschbaum and Karl Barth*. University Park: Pennsylvania State University Press.

Sellier, Philippe (2000) *Port-Royal et la littérature*, vol. II: Le siècle de saint Augustin, La Rochefoucauld, Mme de Lafayette, Sacy, Racine. Paris: Champion.

Sicard, Michel (1990) 'Carnet Midy: Notice', in Jean- Paul Sartre, *Écrits de jeunesse*, ed. M. Contat and M. Rybalka. Paris: Gallimard.

Simon, Pierre-Henri (1957) *Le Littérature du péché et de la grâce*. Paris: Arthème Fayard.

Simpson, Peter (2001) *On Karol Wojtyła*. Belmont, CA: Wadsworth.

Stawarska, Beata (2013) 'Sartre and Husserl's *Ideen*: Phenomenology and Imagination', in Steven Churchill and Jack Reynolds (eds), *Jean-Paul Sartre: Key Concepts*. Durham, NC: Acumen.

Thomas, John Heywood (2000) *Tillich*. London: Continuum.

Thompson, William M. (1989) 'Introduction' to Pierre de Bérulle, *Bérulle and the French School: Selected Writings*, ed. William M. Thompson; trans. Lowell M. Glendon. New York: Paulist Press.

Thweatt, Vivien (1980) *La Rochefoucauld and the Seventeenth-Century Concept of the Self*. Geneva: Librarie Droz.

Tillich, Paul (1964a) *Systematic Theology*, vol. 3. London: Nisbet.

Tillich, Paul (1964b) 'The Theological Significance of Existentialism and Psychoanalysis', in *Theology of Culture*, ed. Robert C. Kimball. Oxford: Oxford University Press.

Tillich, Paul (1957) *Systematic Theology*, vol. 2. London: Nisbet.

Tillich, Paul (1956) 'The Nature and Significance of Existentialist Thought', *Journal of Philosophy* 53 (23): 739–48.

Tillich, Paul (1953) *Systematic Theology*, vol. 1, London: Nisbet.

Tillich, Paul (1952) *The Courage to Be*. New Haven, CT: Yale University Press.

Tillich, Paul (1948) *The Shaking of the Foundations*. New York: Charles Scribner's Sons.

Tillich, Paul (1939) 'The Conception of Man in Existential Philosophy', *Journal of Religion* 19 (3): 201–15.

TIME (1946) 'Existentialism', 28 January, 28–9.

Torrance, Alan (1996) *Persons in Communion: Trinitarian Description and Human Participation*. London: Bloomsbury.

Troisfontaines, Roger (1953) *De l'Existence à l'être*. Paris: Vrin.

Van Den Abbeele, Georges (1994) 'Moralists and the Legacy of Cartesianism', in Denis Hollier and R. Howard Bloch (eds), *A New History of French Literature*. Cambridge, MA: Harvard University Press.

Voltaire ([1728] 1819) *L'Anti-Pascal*, in *Œuvres complètes de Voltaire*, vol. 29. Paris: Antoine-Augustin Renouard.

Vuilleumier, Jean (2005) *L'Enjeu: Essai*. Paris: L'Age d'homme.

Wahl, Jean (1945) 'Existentialism: A Preface', *New Republic*, October.

Wang, Stephen (2009) *Aquinas and Sartre: On Freedom, Personal Identity, and the Possibility of Happiness*. Washington DC: Catholic University of America Press.

Warnock, Mary (1965) *The Philosophy of Sartre*. London: Hutchinson University Library.

Webber, Jonathan (2004) 'Philosophical Introduction' to Jean-Paul Sartre, *The Imaginary*, trans. Jonathan Webber. London: Routledge.

Wojtyła, Karol (1993) *Person and Community: Selected Essays*. New York: Lang.

Wojtyła, Karol (1981 English [1960]) *Love and Responsibility*, trans. H. T. Willetts. London: Fount.

Wojtyła, Karol (1979a [1969]) *The Acting Person*, trans. Anna-Teresa Tymieniecka. *Analecta Husserliana* X. Dordrecht: D. Reidel Publishing Co.

Wojtyła, Karol (1979b [1976]) 'The Person: Subject and Community', *Review of Metaphysics* 33 (2): 273–308.

Wojtyła, Karol (1977) 'Participation or Alienation?' *Analecta Husserliana* 6: 61–73.

Woznicki, Andrew N. (1980) *A Christian Humanism: Karol Wojtyła's Existential Personalism*. New Britain, CT: Mariel Publications.

Yannaris, Christos ([1980–81] 2015) *The Schism of Philosophy: The Hellenic Perspective and Its Western Reversal*, trans. Norman Russell. Brookline, MA: Holy Cross Orthodox Press.

Yannaris, Christos ([1987] 2007) *Person and Eros*, trans. Norman Russell. Brookline, MA: Holy Cross Orthodox Press.

Yannaris, Christos ([1992] 2006) *Orthodoxy and the West*, trans. Peter Chalmers and Norman Russell. Brookline, MA: Holy Cross Orthodox Press.

Yannaris, Christos ([1966] 1971) 'An Orthodox Comment on the "Death of God", in A. M. Allchin (ed.) *Orthodoxy and the Death of God: Essays in Contemporary Theology*. London: Fellowship of St. Alban and St. Sergius.

Young, Stark (1946) 'Weaknesses', *New Republic*, 9 December, 764.

Zizioulas, John D. (1985) *Being as Communion: Studies in Personhood and the Church*. London: Darton, Longman, and Todd.

INDEX